EXCELLENCE IN
ADVERTISING

EXCELLENCE IN
ADVERTISING

RETAIL REPORTING CORPORATION • NEW YORK

Retail Reporting Corporation
302 Fifth Avenue
New York, NY 10001

Distributors outside of the United States and Canada
Hearst Books International
105 Madison Avenue
New York, NY 10016

Library of Congress Cataloging in Publication Data:
Main Entry under the title: Excellence in Advertising

Printed and Bound in Hong Kong
ISBN 0-934590-43-5

Designed by Judy Shepard

CONTENTS

INTRODUCTION

This is a book about retail advertising. And about those who create it. It has been compiled to showcase the best in the field.

In the winter of 1991 on a cold and windy Chicago evening, the Retail Advertising & Marketing Association presented their 39th annual RAC Awards. These awards have always been coveted by those in the retail industry — not only for the prestige of winning . . . but because the judges of RAC Awards are peers of the "contestants."

The public's fascination with the field of advertising has made it fair game for criticism (or praise) by those who have no business with our business. Unlike other professions, advertising has become so familiar and so much a part of the American idiom . . . that anyone who wishes to — can fancy himself or herself as a "critic."

Facing the challenge of establishing professional standards on which retail advertising could — and should, be properly judged, the Retail Advertising Marketing Association has set up the machinery for the most critical evaluation of judging good advertising: a prestigious panel of practicioners from the retail advertising arena. Tough judges. Tough standards.

This book celebrates those who have earned recognition for creating the best in retail advertising in 1990. This book salutes excellence. It honors the creative and the clever . . . the daring and the innovative . . . the sale makers and the image builders. And most importantly, it honors advertising that has worked and has proven successful.

Because the subject of this book is broad and complex, the awards have been separated into eight different categories: multi-media, direct mail, magazine, newspaper, radio, television, outdoor/point-of-sale, in-store. Two traditional features of the RAC Awards Competition are, the Heineman Trophy for "Best of Show," and the annual election of an outstanding individual, to the Retail Advertising Hall of Fame. Both were announced at the 1991 RAC Awards Banquet.

You will see the work of those who have won the top awards as well as those whose excellence have earned them honors as finalists in each competition. This book features the best of the best — an extraordinary compilation of advertising creations. Flashes of brilliance from little known retailers around the country, the continent, the world.

Few (if any) of the winning advertising have been created by a single individual. Art directors, copywriters, creative directors along with printers and agencies have each contributed their own range of talents to produce an ultimate original product. This book takes note of these team players . . . and lists well-earned credits for each winning entry.

In bringing the best of retail advertising together in one exciting volume, we have endeavored to provide a lively, vital reference book. But more than that . . . more than just a chronicle of the best of retail advertising . . . it is our hope that this book will be a source of inspiration for those who would like to pursue excellence and achieve honors in the years to come.

CREATIVITY
A FOREWORD BY PETER GLEN

Creativity is the continuous improvement of the soul.

Creativity is evidence of the child still alive in every individual. When you quit playing, you are dead.

Creativity is about you. If you live creatively, you design your life instead of just surviving it. The practice of creativity enables you to live your life in your own way.

Creativity is the courage to express your mind and heart exactly as they are. You must not care about consequences or the opinions of others. Trust your own convictions, knowing that delivering your heart and mind can make things change.

Creativity translates ideas into action. Ideas are not enough, nor are intentions, nor are any of the tribes of might-have-been.

Creativity does not stop to make excuses. Using what it's got, instead of lamenting what it's not, it continues the adventure.

Creativity takes place now, not in the past, not in the future. The past is over. Study it, salute it, then move on. The future comes!

Creativity does not happen *to* you. *You* must begin it and there is no previous path or certain destination. You must go with no assurance — loving the questions and not expecting answers. Whatever your destination, creativity is the strongest way.

Creativity is the exercise that makes your spirit strong.

Creativity originates while all other actions recreate, co-ordinate, or imitate.

Creativity is the extra ten percent that makes *all* of the difference.

Creativity is good rehearsal, visualizing the outcome of a project or a feeling or design soon enough and clearly enough to improve the plan before action.

Creativity is control. It changes chaos into order, calms a catalog of fears, and brings the future gladly.

Creativity is a grace that has been given to everyone. If you do not use it you abuse the gift, diminish your hopes of happiness, and cancel your chances to grow.

Creativity can lead you to yourself.

Creativity is your best gift — yourself, unselfish — therefore a gift of love.

Creativity is the seed of hope and faith and love. These are not easy acts, nor are they automatic. But hope and faith and love can be grown, even from ashes.

Creativity can overcome calamity and arm against the pain of common days. Creativity can charge an ordinary day with radiance and give wings to your routine.

Creativity can never be defeated. It is your spirit, and therefore, inextinguishable.

Creativity is God in action.

The Best of Show Targets the Earth

The Heineman Trophy winner for Best of Show for RAC '91 goes to Target for "Kids for Saving Earth." It's neither an advertising campaign, nor a marketing program; it's a genuine from-the-heart-of-the-heartland program created to empower the inheritors of our Earth, children.

Target channeled its resources to enhance a movement initially undertaken by children. They brought this important issue to the attention of world leaders and average citizens alike. A philosopher said . . . "The child sees everything which has to be experienced and learned as a doorway. So does the adult. But what to the child is an entrance is to the adult only a passage." It took children to point to the doorway to saving the Earth. The people at Target were young enough to see it in the same way.

A Salute to W. B. Doner

We pause to honor an advertising pioneer who has passed from the scene, but will never be forgotten. W.B. "Brod" Doner set standards that continue to inspire all of us.

His lifetime of achievements are a matter of advertising history. And like much of history, larger and more remarkable than fiction. Starting his working life with a chance to enter the family business — a chandelier company — Brod chose the advertising business and joined a local Detroit firm.

After 18 months he and several others were fired. Unable to find another job in mid-depression, Doner did what any right-thinking ad person would do — he started his own business. So, in March 1937, the agency we know and love as W.B. Doner opened its doors, with two employees.

The agency has grown to more than 575 employees in nine offices. Its clients range from pickles to yogurt, from hospitals to supermarkets. And it regularly walks off with boxes full of RAC awards.

In his 53 years at the helm of W.B. Doner, Brod accomplished what most people considered impossible; he established a major advertising agency based in Detroit without an automobile account.

By basing human, often humorous advertising on solid marketing strategies, the agency has created successful advertising for its clients. "I believe it takes the right combination of the head, the heart and the funnybone to solve advertising problems," said Brod Doner.

Some things never change. Brod Doner's advice, like his strong influence on the careers and philosophies of those who worked with and for him over the past 53 years, will always be revered.

We not only remembered Brod Doner during the 39th annual RAC — we salute him.

And, from our hearts, we thank him.

The Retail Marketing Compaign of the Year

Advertising Age Imports IKEA

In 1990 what does a retailer have to do to create a sensation in one of the most heavily pressured retail merchandise categories, in the northeast where business is the toughest to come by — to literally stall traffic in all directions and virtually sell out to the bare walls in a few days?

Open a new furniture store in the New York Metropolitan area.

Sounds easy. And it is for IKEA. Easy that is when everything else is right on target. The merchandise, the marketing strategy, the advertising, the location, the store, the prices and a very carefully positioned appeal that is poised to take advantage of changing demographics, new consumer expectations and emerging lifestyles.

The first annual *Advertising Age* Retail Marketing Campaign of the Year Award goes to IKEA, for writing and living the outstanding retail marketing story of 1990. This award recognizes not only current success at the cash register, but a solid, established and soundly positioned path to future growth.

IKEA is rewriting what a furniture store is.

A Welcome to Maggie Gross

The 1991 Retail Advertising Hall of Fame inductee is Maggie Gross, Senior Vice President, Advertising and Marketing, The GAP, San Francisco.

There are two distinct periods in the life of the GAP. One is "Pre-Maggie" and Two, "Post-Maggie." "Pre" is the land of "Fall into the Gap" and a sea of commodity goods, at promotional prices. The GAP-land we know today is something quite different.

"Individuals of Style," possibly the most talked about print campaign of the '80s was Maggie's creation. In this inspired merger of art and commerce, hot fashion photographers — like Herb Ritts, Annie Leibovitz, Mathew Rolston and Steven Meisel — were commissioned to shoot famous and not-so-famous urban people in GAP goods. The result: GAP's image was immortalized — the hippest looks at surprising prices. The campaign won a lot of awards, including one from the Council of Fashion Designers. A real honor.

This past fall, in a stunning move, GAP abruptly shifted their advertising focus away from "Individuals of Style" to a new one that simply treated individual items as stars. Simple. Stunning. Bold. Surprising to the uninitiated — and absolutely right on target. As that popular philosopher, Kenny Rogers says, "You got to know when to hold, know when to . . . ," well you know.

The outpouring of votes that elected Maggie Gross to the Retail Advertising Hall of Fame was impressive. And her victory was not for the "Individuals of Style" campaign alone. Maggie has a long history of highly successful breakthrough creative work in support of strong and goal-satisfying positioning programs. Clearly implicit in Maggie's election, is a vote of confidence that Maggie will continue to lead rather than follow. And that she will continue to be a bold and greatly admired innovator in the world of retail advertising and marketing. Maggie, congratulations. You are our RAC '91, Retail Advertising Hall of Famer.

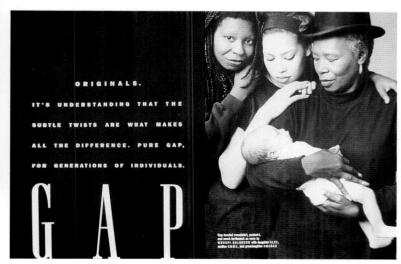

THE PANEL OF RAC
JUDGES

Judy Biasetti
Creative Director
Retail Advertising
Sears, Chicago

Kathleen Holliday
Sr Group Advertising Mgr
JCPenney, Dallas

Jeanne Chinnard
Sr VP/Mgng Director
Creative Services
Ayer, New York

Nan Cooper
VP/Creative Director
Macy's NW, New York

Betty Bryant
Marketing Director
Woodfield Mall
Schaumburg, IL

Anne O'Malley
Creative Director
Spiegel
Oakbrook, IL

Claudia Laupmanis
VP-Retail Development
Amercian Express, Chicago

John Jay
Executive VP-Sales Promotion
Bloomingdale's, New York

David Murphy
Retail Ad Director
Chicago Tribune, Chicago

George Love
President
George W. Love Associates
Chicago

Don Simmons
Account Executive
Newspapers First
Chicago

Jeff Green
VP-Retail
NAB, Chicago

AWARDS CHAIRMAN
Tom Holliday
Executive VP
RAMA, Chicago

Direct Mail

Special Merit Award

DAYTON'S HUDSON'S
MARSHALL FIELD'S
Minneapolis, MN
"Men's Advanced, Fall '90"
"Men's Advanced - Spring '90
A Show of Hands"
"Heaven/Earth Spring '90 Oval
Room"

Traffic Builder Mailer

"A Show Of Hands, A Chorus Of
Voices - Oval Room, Fall '90"

Traffic Builder Catalog
Department Store
Over 500 mm

Stew Widdess-Marketing Sales
Promotion Director; Jack
Mugan-Advertising Director;
Connie Soteropulos-Executive Art
Director; Eric Erickson-Copy
Chief; Cheryl Watson-Art Director;
Vicky Rossi-Writer
Amy Quinlivan-Art Director
Amie Valentine-Writer
Bill Thorburn, Debra Herdman-
Art Directors

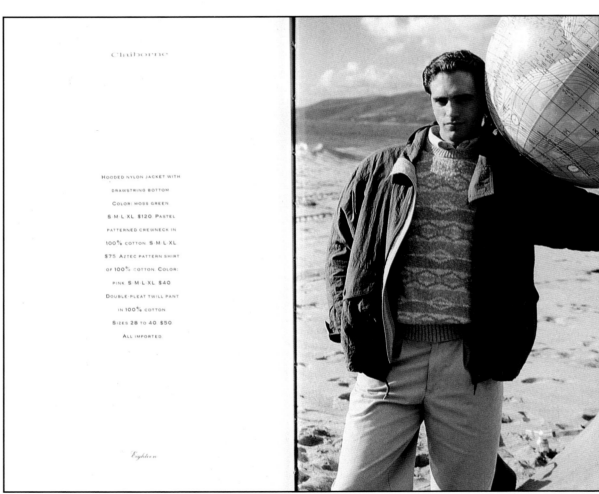

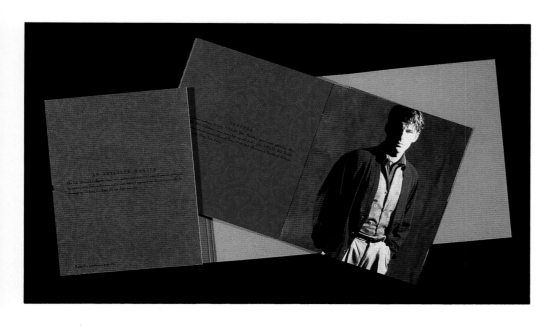

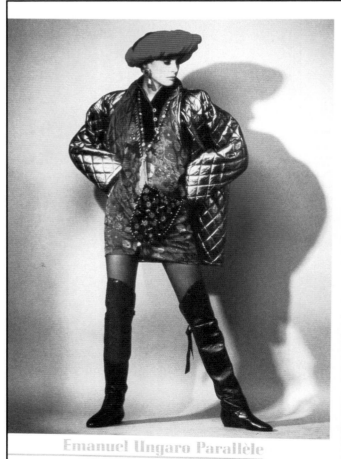

Emanuel Ungaro Parallèle

Gianfranco Ferre

Ralph Lauren

Calvin Klein

Winner

I. MAGNIN
San Francisco, CA
"Designer"

Traffic Builder Catalog
Apparel Specialty Store
250-500 mm

Wilmer Weiss-Sr
VP/Communications; Anita
Porter-Copy Chief; Dan
Holland-Art Director; Dana
Leone-Production Manager
PRODUCTION: DIVERSIFIED
GRAPHICS: Guzman-Photographer

Give her
our best
Neiman Marcus

Finalist

NEIMAN MARCUS
Dallas, TX
"NM Edits Series"

Campaign
Apparel Specialty Store
Over 500 mm

Bernie Feiwus-Sr VP Sales
Promotion; Daria Retian-VP
Creative Communication Services;
Karen Muncy-Copy Chief

GIVE HER OUR BEST.
NM for Mother's Day.

On the cover:
Fernando Sanchez silk chiffon
robe, with shirred yoke,
436.00. Stretch lace off-the-
shoulder surplice top, 74.00.
Satin-back crepe pants,
208.00. Intimate Apparel.

Forget kitchenware
and calculators.
They're perfectly
respectable gifts for
other occasions, but
they aren't personal
enough for Mother's
Day. This is a time
to indulge her
with something
extravagant — or
extravagantly
sentimental. Treat her

to something
luxurious that she
would never buy for
herself. Surprise her
with something rare
or imaginative or
wonderfully witty. Of
course, we're famous
for precisely that kind
of gift. For a Mother's
Day she'll never
forget, come to
Neiman Marcus.

Silk georgette blouse, in
marigold, by Blassington,
200.00. Sport Shop.

NM exclusive 14-karat gold-
plated shell jewelry by Iris
Feinberg. Necklace, 250.00.
Bracelet, 200.00. Earrings,
75.00. Accessories.

Baccarat crystal parrots, in
amber, lavender, ink green,
and light blue. Each, 90.00.
The Galleries.

Created exclusively for Neiman Marcus, Volage is a truly individual
fragrance inspired by the free-spirited Art Deco era. The collection,
40.00 to 185.00. Cosmetics.

Guerlain "Meteorite" compact with pastel powders that create a
translucent glow. Compact, 125.00. Loose powder, 35.00. Deluxe
makeup brush, 90.00. Basic brush, 19.50. Cosmetics.

The fragrances of Christian Dior: classic Miss Dior (1947), romantic
Diorissimo (1956) and provocative Dioressence (1980). Each collection,
24.00 to 64.00. Cosmetics.

Elizabeth Taylor's Passion, 25.00 to 175.00. Bag with travel sizes of eau
de toilette spray, body lotion and cream, bath/shower gel, loyal talc, and
dusting powder, 37.00. Cosmetics.

Adagio color-block silk
lingerie, with French lace trim.
Teddy, 178.00. Bra, 68.00.
Panty, 38.00.
Intimate Apparel.

Seek out something
fun, something
fragrant, something
delicately sensual.

Finalist

BLOOMINGDALE'S
New York, NY
"Painted Desert"

Campaign
Department Store
Over 500 mm

Gordon Cooke-Executive VP/Sale
Promotion; Wendy Levine-Media
Director; John C. Jay-Sr
VP/Art Director; Francey
Smith-VP/Direct Mail; Brian
Leitch-Copy Chief; Ronni
Ascagni-Art Director; Steven
White-Photographer; Jill
Glover-Stylist

coming to **you.**

south coast plaza.

Winner

BARNEYS NEW YORK
New York, NY
"Barneys Calendar"

Campaign
Apparel Specialty Store
50-100 mm

Neil Kraft-VP
Advertising/Marketing; Glenn
O'Brien-Copy Chief; Douglas
Lloyd-Art Director
AGENCY: BNY ADVERTISING: Sara
Hardie-Production Manager

Direct Response Catalog
Apparel Specialty Store
50-100 mm

Neil Kraft-VP
Advertising/Marketing; Glenn
O'Brien-Copy Chief; Douglas
Lloyd-Art Director
AGENCY: BNY ADVERTISING: Sara
Hardie-Production Manager

may we **help** you?

you bet.

please, darling.

constantly.

i'll help myself.

Winner

EDDIE BAUER
Redmond, WA
"Eddie Bauer: A Legend
for Four Generations"

Direct Response Catalog
Apparel Specialty Store
Over 500 mm

Davia Kimmey-VP/Sales
Promotion; Marsha
Savery-Advertising Director;
Robert Prevost-Copy Chief; Lori
McFadden-Art Director; Drennan
Lindsay-Designer

IDITAROD
The Last Great Race

The challenge of the Iditarod is not new to Eddie Bauer. We sponsored our first sled dog team in 1975, and today we are proud to be the outfitters for the team of DeeDee Jonrowe from Willow, Alaska. A veteran of seven Iditarods, and fourth place finisher last year, she is considered a strong contender for the 1990 title.

As a "tune-up" for that grueling 1,049-mile race in March, DeeDee is set to defend her title in the 475-mile John Beargrease Dog Marathon, this January in Minnesota. She won the 1989 Beargrease in record time, besting the previous winning time by more than five hours!

Finisher's patch

The Iditarod, called "the last great race on earth," is a 1,049-mile-long race from Anchorage to Nome that runs through two jagged mountain ranges, and over desolate tundra and windswept coastline.

In March, temperatures are far below zero, winds can obliterate visibility, blowing snow can cover the trail, and the entire race takes place in darkness.

The Iditarod was organized to commemorate the life-saving trip made by intrepid dog mushers in 1925 to deliver serum to diphtheria-stricken Nome. Today, mushers of all ages compete to be the first dogsled into Nome.

Crucial to the race is the dog team, whose training can determine the outcome of the race. When the mushers leave the starting gate, their lives will depend on their dog team until they cross the finish line.

Three-time winner Susan Butcher says a good lead dog can find the trail even when it's covered with snow. Once, when she'd slipped off the sled, the dogs raced back to get her.

Even if you never intend to race in the Iditarod, you want winter clothes that could. We've assembled

Eddie Bauer will supply protective clothing for DeeDee Jonrowe (above); her sled dogs and her support team as they prepare for and race the 1990 Iditarod and beyond.

here our premier winter products for women in honor of this unique-in-the-world race.

LEFT We named this parka "Premier" because it ranks #1 in weather protection and style. Beginning with more Premium Bauer Goose Down than any of our women's parkas, the Premier's comfort range extends all the way to –30° F. The shell is constructed of wind- and water-repellent Super Microft™, a synthetic fabric with a soft, cottony texture. The hood ruff of natural Canadian coyote fur naturally resists icing. Dry clean; ruff removes for cleaning. Imported. Length size M, 32½". Colors: Ivory; not shown, Black or Crimson. Sizes S-XL. #5592K Premier Polar Parka $395.00

RIGHT Designed exclusively by us in honor of the Iditarod, this unusual sweater is hand knit of finest 100% Shetland wool. The design features a team of huskies setting out through a snowfield backed by mountain peaks. (See full sweater pattern on page 38.) Dry clean. Made in USA. Sizes S-XL. #8096K Iditarod Sweater $85.00

Inspired by the ski pants of yesterday, we've designed these wool/nylon blend stretch pants for comfort and warmth in any winter activity. Cut full in the leg, they have four flattering front pleats, then taper at the ankles to fit easily into your boots with a stirrup foot. Fabric is 66% nylon/32% wool/2% Lycra®. Brass-zippered side pockets. Belt loops. Dry clean. Made in USA. Color: Black. Sizes 6-16 even. #8108K Pleated Stretch Pants $125.00

A magnificent headband of downy Canadian coyote fur. Lined with woven 50% cotton/50% polyester. Width is 5". Professionally fur clean. Color: Silver. One size. #1098K Fur Headband $90.00

Timberland® Lightweight Pac Boots were designed for the conditions of the Iditarod Race. For details, turn to page 38. Color: Tan buck. Sizes Medium (B) 5-10 (half sizes order next size up). #3209K Lightweight Pac Boots $115.00

For sizing information, see the order form.

Leather Ski Gloves, page 39

LEFT Our 100% cotton ...er-Stitch Turtleneck ...h an impressive 1.5 lbs. ...M. Machine wash. ...rted. Colors: Natural or ...n. Sizes S-L. ...1K Shaker-Stitch ...leneck $45.00

...Our Brushed Twill Field ...f boasts an emblem patch ...n your flight wings on. ...sic double tucks at each ...of the back yoke; button ...s. Made in USA of machine ...able cotton. Color: ...ral. Sizes S-XL. ...99K Brushed Twill Field ... $55.00

...ght Pin is 24K gold-plated ...two tie-tack-style backs. ...6K Flight Pin, 3" $30.00

...ushed cotton twills are mil... ...style eased by soft pleats ...a full cut. Back darts con... ...the fit. Side pockets; one ...pocket. Machine wash. ...in USA. Color: Khaki. ...6-16 even. ...7K Pleated Brushed Twill ... $55.00

...ur modern adventure gets ...he ground with shearling- ...Pilot Boots. Top-grain ...er uppers with wool lin... ...EVA midsoles and ...am® lug outsoles. Color: ...n. Sizes Medium (B) 5-10. ...nen's boots, see page 36. ...61K Pilot Boots $95.00

Pin, above

World War II Campaign Medal and Victory Medal awarded to WASPs in 1981

LEFT Our Flight Jacket enters the supersonic age with insolation of Premium Bauer Goose Down. Soft-as-butter lambskin and a luxurious sheared lamb collar give warmth down to +15° F.

Authentic double-stitched epaulets, snap-flap pockets and ribbed wool trim. Brass collar snaps and underarm grommets. Satin lining. Professionally leather clean. Imported. Color: Brown. Sizes S-L. #8064K Leather/Down Flight Jacket $425.00

Beryl Markham prized one and so will you. The pilot's cap of supple goatskin with pigsuede lining. Adjustable neck strap; snapped loops for securing goggles (not included). Color: Brown. Sizes S-L. #8998K Goatskin Cap $75.00

FACING PAGE Ray-Ban® sunglasses developed in the 1930s for the Army Air Corps. Gray glass lenses absorb 100% UV and over 85% infrared light. Frames are plated with 24K gold or black chrome. Large Metal I lens is 58mm across; Large Metal II lens is 62mm. #66-20K Large Metal I $52.00 #6644K Large Metal II $56.00

For sizing information, see the order form.

Order toll-free at home
1-800-356-8889

9

Winner

SPIEGEL
Oak Brook, IL
"For You From Spiegel"

Direct Response Catalog
Direct Marketer
1-10 mm

Ann O'Malley-Creative Director;
Pat Walsh-Art Director; Paula
Benson-Sr Copywriter; G. Paul
Haynes, Danny Sit, Bob
Jacobs-Photographers

...to a place far away, where the phone doesn't ring and time stands still. Where you begin to remember that nature is the rule and not the exception. That life was meant to be lived, not rushed through. Outside. Alone. Together. A feeling that could only happen here...

Winner

FAO SCHWARZ
New York, NY
"The Ultimate Toy
Catalogue 1990"

Direct Response Catalog
Other Specialty Store
50-100 mm

Brooke Adkins-Marketing
Director; Larry Jennings-Creative
Director; Maurice Grun-Copy Chief;
Mitch Rubenstein-Catalogue
Manager; Charles
Nesbit-Photographer

THE FURS OF NEIMAN MARCUS

SPORTS COVERAGE

DONNA KARAN

WARMING TREND

FENDI

6

Winner

NEIMAN MARCUS
Dallas, TX
"Neiman Marcus Fur Book"

Traffic Builder Catalog
Apparel Specialty Store
Over 500 mm

Bernie Feiwus-Sr VP Sales
Promotion; Daria Retian-VP
Creative Communication Services;
Karen Muncy-Copy Chief

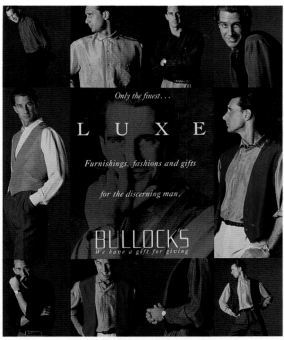

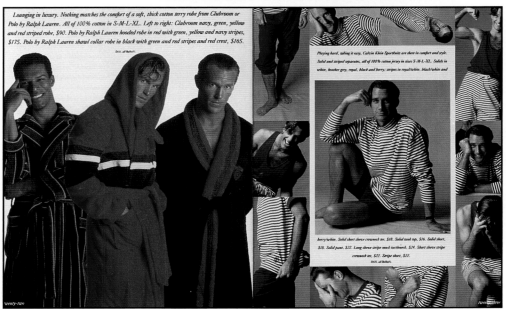

Finalist

MACY'S SOUTH/BULLOCK'S
Atlanta, GA
"Mens Xmas Giftbook Luxe"

Traffic Builder Catalog
Department Store
Over 500 mm

Helane Blumfield-Creative
Director; Joseph Garbarino-Sr
VP/Sales Promotion Director

Finalist

MACY'S SOUTH/BULLOCKS
Atlanta, GA
"A Distance Beyond
Autumn/Scotland"

Traffic Builder Catalog
Department Store
Over 500 mm

Helane Blumfield-Creative
Director; Joseph Garbarino-Sr
VP/Sales Promotion Director

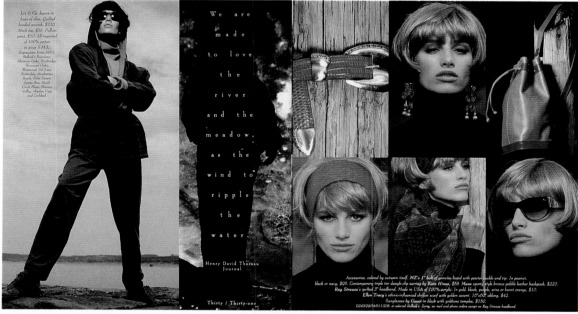

Winner

NORDSTROM
Seattle, WA
"It's Our World the Whole Thing"

Traffic Builder Catalog
Apparel Specialty Store
Over 500 mm

Cindy Demme-Sales Promotion
Director; Linda Toschi
Finn-Advertising Director; Randy
Mecham-Copy Chief; Cheryl Fujii
Zahniser-Corporate Art Director

ITALIAN TOUCHES FROM IACOVELLI: 7A. The fashionable 'tie boot' in navy/green leather/nubuck,
49.95 B. The leather-lined 'speedlace' boot with nubby sole, in brown/blue or navy nubuck, 49.95. Both,
Italian sizes 23–30 (American 7–12). In Children's Shoes.

NORSPORT 'WASHABLE BLT': **33A.** Our own washable leather active shoe for boys and girls. Pink, white or navy, 4–12m.w; 24.95. (Wide widths not available at all stores.) B. Sugar & Spice 27-inch laces. Pink grosgrain with white-dotted rosette or red grosgrain with white-dotted bow; 5.50. Also available, **C.** Lilac ribbon with pink/blue corkscrew; 5.95. **In Children's Shoes.**

Is it getting smaller, or are we getting bigger?

HOT TOTS: **34A.** Celestial print tie-top; 30.00. B. Matching skirt; 27.00. C. Matching leggings; 19.00. All, made of domestic cotton, 4–6x. In Plum Avenue.

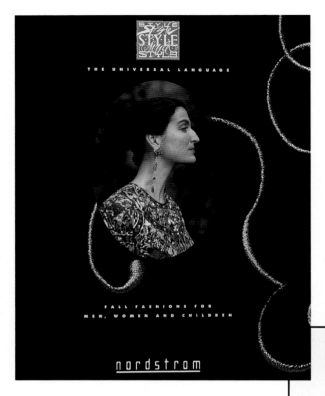

Finalist

NORDSTROM
Seattle, WA
"Northern California"

Traffic Builder Catalog
Department Store
Over 500 mm

AGENCY: ARKADIA GROUP

Finalist

NORDSTROM
Seattle, WA
"BP-To Thine Own Style
Be True"

Traffic Builder Catalog
Apparel Specialty Store
Over 500 mm

Cindy Demme-Sales Promotion
Director; Linda Toschi
Finn-Advertising Director; Randy
Mecham-Copy Chief; Cheryl Fujii
Zahniser-Corporate Art Director

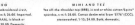

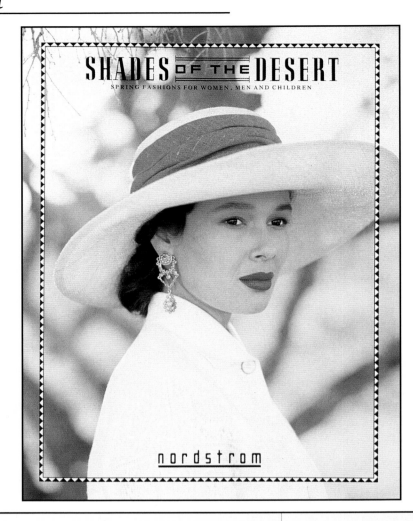

Finalist

NORDSTROM
Seattle, WA
"Shades of the Desert"

Traffic Builder Catalog
Apparel Specialty Store
Over 500 mm

Cindy Demme-Sales Promotion
Director; Linda Toschi
Finn-Advertising Director; Randy
Mecham-Copy Chief; Cheryl Fujii
Zahniser-Corporate Art Director

MOROCCO

ROAD TO

On the road again. 39A. The ultimate 'jean jacket' in soft, supple suede. From Timberland, in spring loden, s-m-l-xl; 360.00. B. Coordinating long sleeve denim shirt of indigo cotton, s-m-l-xl; 65.00. Imported. C. Coordinating batik-print walking shorts. Imported cotton, in tobacco, 30-40; 57.50. In Men's Sportswear.

Traveling in style. 40A. Unik nubuck leather jacket of satiny buffed cowskin, in brown, xs-s-m-l; 370.00. In Point of View.

A call to adventure: spirited sportswear that's just perfect for getting away from it all.

SHADES OF THE DESERT

Spring fashions for women, men and children

nordstrom

Winner

NAN DUSKIN
Philadelphia, PA
"Nan Duskin Fall"

Traffic Builder Catalog
Apparel Specialty Store
10-50 mm

AGENCY: SMATT FLORENCE:
Karin Smatt-Creative/Art Director

Winner

COLUMBUS CITY CENTER
Columbus, OH
"Holiday '89"

Traffic Builder Catalog
Shopping Center

Connie Hollenberg-Marketing
Sales Promotion Director
AGENCY: W. T. QUINN: Orlando
Vivas-Creative Director; Anne
Picone-Production Manager;
Joseph Picayo-Photographer

EXPECTING . . .
THE BEST

*Holiday elegance for expectant
mothers. Sparkle in only the
best that holiday dressing has
to offer . . . for discriminating
women who are . . . Expecting
. . . The Best. 221-9145.*

SAN FRANCISCO
MUSIC BOX COMPANY

*Celebrate the season with
music! We have the perfect
gift with the perfect tune.
Free giftwrapping. 221-4410.*

Finalist

WOODWARD & LOTHROP
Washington, DC
"I Know What I Like"

Traffic Builder Catalog
Department Store
Over 500 mm

Joel Nichols-Marketing Sales
Promotion Director; Mary
Wilson-Creative Director
AGENCY: HOWARD RAPP
ENTERPRISES: Marne Zafar-Art
Director; Andrea Lawson-Account
Executive

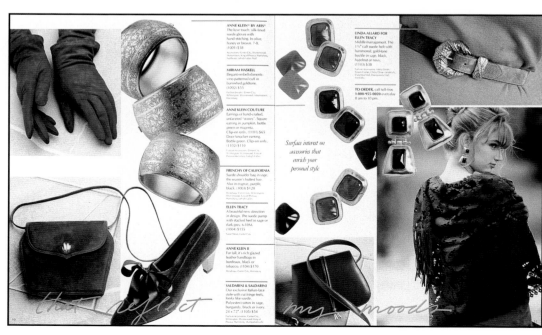

to the ENDS of the EARTH

Harrods
KNIGHTSBRIDGE

Finalist

HARRODS
London, England
"Harrods, To The
Ends of The Earth"

Traffic Builder Catalog
Department Store
Over 500 mm

Mark Springett-Marketing Sales
Promotion Director; Meg
Gilmore-Advertising Director;
Caroline Rawlence-Copy Chief

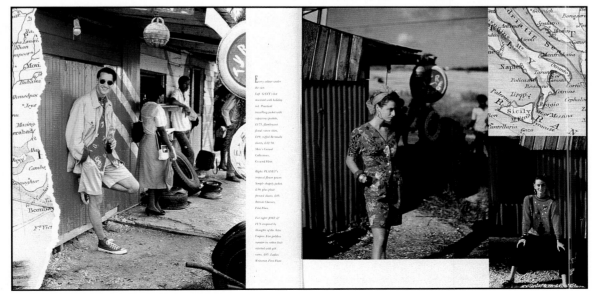

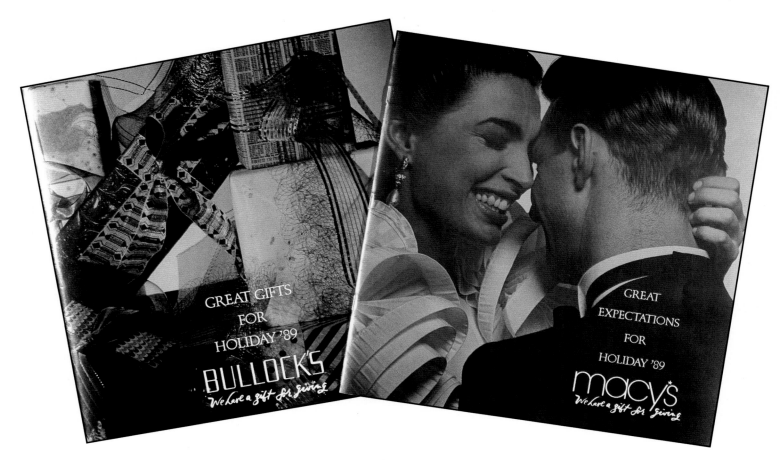

Finalist

MACY'S SOUTH/BULLOCK'S
Atlanta, GA
"Great Gifts Holiday '89"

Traffic Builder Catalog
Department Store
Over 500 mm

AGENCY: ARKADIA GROUP

Finalist

BLOOMINGDALE'S
New York, NY
"Max Fur Booklet"

Traffic Builder Catalog
Department Store
Over 500 mm

Gordon Cooke-Executive VP/Sale
Promotion; Wendy Levine-Media
Director; John C. Jay-Sr
VP/Art Director; Francey
Smith-VP/Direct Mail; Brian
Leitch-Copy Chief; Michael
Poe-Designer; Michel
Comte-Photographer; Jill
Glover-Stylist

Finalist

LENOX SQUARE
Atlanta, GA
"Holiday Gift Guide"

Traffic Builder Catalog
Shopping Center

Brenda Gilpatick-Marketing Sales
Promotion Director
AGENCY: HERSHEY
COMMUNICATIONS: Garry
Burrell-Creative Director; Judy
Alper-Copy Chief; Shelley
Willig-Account Executive; Herb
Burdette-Production Manager;
Mark Chaillie-Vice President

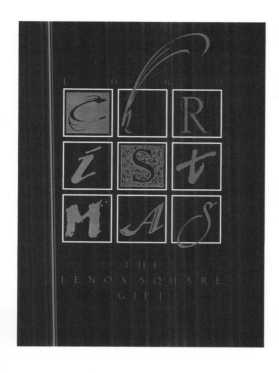

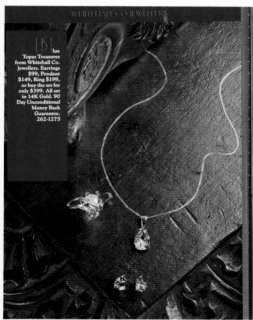

Finalist

BLOOMINGDALE'S
New York, NY
"Infinite Style"

Traffic Builder Catalog
Department Store
Over 500 mm

Gordon Cooke-Executive VP/Sale
Promotion; Wendy Levine-Media
Director; John C. Jay-Sr
VP/Art Director; Francey
Smith-VP/Direct Mail; Brian
Leitch-Copy Chief; James
Streacker-Art Director; Shawn
Peacock-Copywriter; Kurt
Marcus-Photographer

Finalist

SOUTH COAST PLAZA
Costa Mesa, CA
"SCP Magazine"

Traffic Builder Catalog
Shopping Center

Maura Eggan-Marketing Sales
Promotion Director
AGENCY: HERSHEY
COMMUNICATIONS: Garry
Burrell-Creative Director; Judy
Alper-Copy Chief; Ron
Brady-Account Executive; Herb
Burdette-Production Manager

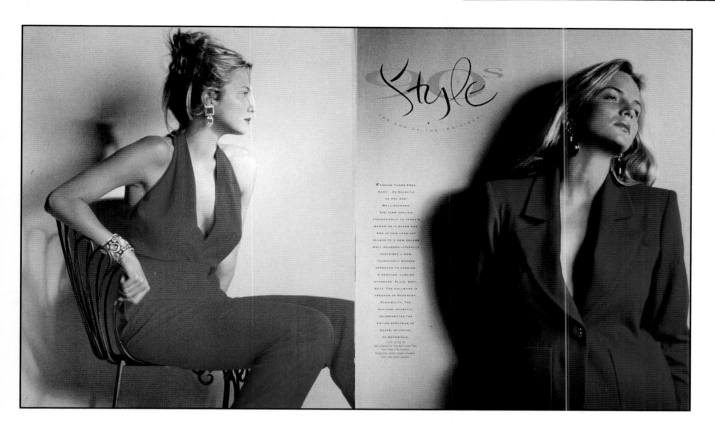

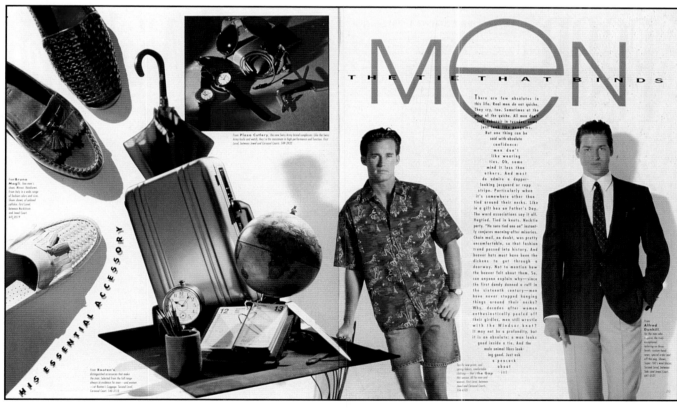

Finalist

FASHION MALL AT
PLANTATION
Plantation, FL
"Fall"

Traffic Builder Catalog
Shopping Center

Patty Dornfield-Marketing
Director
AGENCY: SAFFER/USA
ADVERTISING: Claudia
Hammer-Art Director; Sandra
Soczyk-Copy Chief; Amy
Zimmerman-Account Executive;
Bill Sviatko-Production Manager

WHITE CAPS ON THE LAKE

SUMMER MENSWEAR, 1990

RIDGEDALE

Winner

RIDGEDALE SHOPPING
CENTER
Minnetonka, MN
"White Caps on the Lake"

Traffic Builder Mailer
Shopping Center

Joan Schlegel-Manager-
Sales/Marketing
AGENCY: WEDEMEYER
ADVERTISING/DESIGNS: Cheryl
Wedemeyer-Creative/Art Director;
Chris Kittleson-Copy Chief; Pat
Sizer-Production Manager
PRODUCTION: PARALLEL: Tom
Berthiaume-Photographer

BLOOMINGDALE'S

Winner

BLOOMINGDALE'S
New York, NY
"A New Cool"

Traffic Builder Mailer
Department Store
Over 500 mm

Gordon Cooke-Executive VP/Sale
Promotion; Wendy Levine-Media
Director; John C. Jay-Sr
VP/Art Director; Jill Glover-Stylist

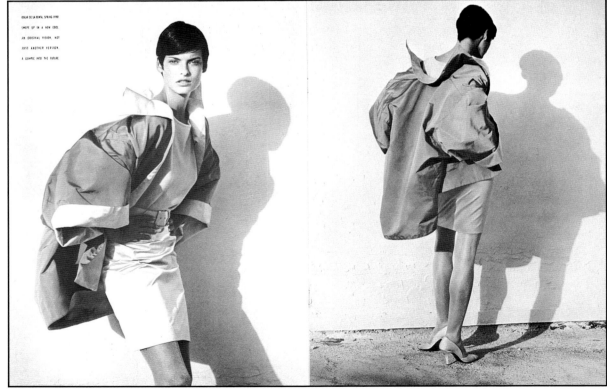

CHRISTIAN LACROIX, SPRING 1990.
A COOL FOR OUR TIME. A
NOT-SO-SERIOUS STATEMENT.
AFTER ALL, THERE'S A PLACE IN
THE WORLD FOR FRIVOLITY.

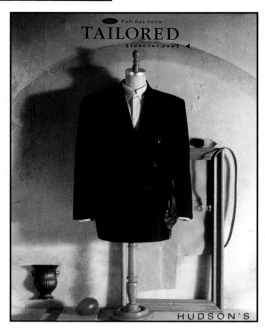

Finalist

DAYTON'S HUDSON'S
MARSHALL FIELD'S
Minneapolis, MN
"Tailored Just For You"

Traffic Builder Mailer
Department Store
Over 500 mm

Stew Widdess-Marketing Sales
Promotion Director; Jack
Mugan-Advertising Director;
Connie Soteropulos-Executive Art
Director; Eric Erickson-Copy
Chief; Lisa Henkemeyer-Art
Director; Dyer Davis-Writer

Finalist

DAYTON'S HUDSON'S
MARSHALL FIELDS
Minneapolis, MN
"Petite Perspectives Fall '90"

Traffic Builder Mailer
Department Store
Over 500 mm

Stew Widdess-Marketing Sales
Promotion Director; Jack
Mugan-Advertising Director;
Connie Soteropulos-Executive Art
Director; Eric Erickson-Copy
Chief; Elizabeth Baldwin-Art
Director; Lisa Christensen-Writer

THE HARRY ROSEN
REPORT ON MEN'S WEAR

SPRING·SUMMER·1990

Winner

HARRY ROSEN
Toronto, ON
"The Harry Rosen Report On
Men's Wear Spring/Summer
1990"

Traffic Builder Mailer
Apparel Specialty Store
100-250 mm

Mary Pompili-Marketing Sales
Promotion/Advertising Director
AGENCY: RBA ADVERTISING: Reid
Bell-Creative/Art Director; Martin
Keen-Copy Chief

Midweight pure wool suit, $650, cotton dress shirt, $65, and printed silk tie, $37.50, all by Sedgewick.

Summer Dressing Should be a Breeze

Due to popular demand and no small amount of common sense, the last few seasons have seen a dramatic move to fabrics that will very comfortably see you through all four seasons of the year.

Except for those few days when the humidex approaches meltdown, a pure wool Rosen suit in a 9-ounce cloth will look and feel just as appropriate in July as it does in February.

Making the assumption that you have a couple of these in your closet, let's begin to build the perfect summer wardrobe.

Unfortunately commerce does not cease simply because downtown becomes an oven, so you'll still require a business suit or two that is strictly summer in weight and appearance.

Begin with a dark blue in a 7-ounce, superfine wool. It's a dressy suit that you'll need for warm-weather social occasions as well. Add to this a mid- to dark grey and a mid-blue in any of the classic patterns. (If you have the last two in the year 'round cloth referred to earlier and you feel you don't need these alternatives in a lighter weight, you're covered.)

Classic tan — or this season, most definitely olive — are the obvious places to head next. All the Rosen collections offer them in lightweight fabrics from all wool to wool/silk and wool/polyester blends. (Don't shudder. In abundance polyester knows no equal in ugliness, but just a touch of it can hold a garment's crispness through the muggiest of weather.)

Then there's the unstructured suit. The suit with 'the guts removed'. If you're able to forego a knife-like crease in your trousers and sleeves that hang straight as an arrow, then you'll love the breezy, rather rumpled good looks of cotton and linen fabrics.

And consider if you will the light weight, wool crepes to be found amongst the Rosen collections. In lighter tones of olive and grey, in fine houndstooths, tie weaves and pic-patterns, they are the embodiment of continental cool.

So there you have, in one combination or another, what should add up to a five-suit summer wardrobe.

For evenings or Sunday afternoons at the club, a lightweight navy blazer and white slacks are matchless.

You might add a jacket in a silk and linen fabric that has ingeniously managed the look of texture while achieving a leather-like feel. Or, those of a more youthful state-of-mind might try what we call a 'relaxed' jacket. A nifty look for Saturday's with a polo shirt and jeans. (See page 16.)

And that should do it. With the obvious addition of the proper shirts, a linen or cotton silk tie or two and, if the urge arises, a lightweight raincoat, you're set.

With a properly thought-out summer wardrobe from Harry's, when it's hot, you're not.

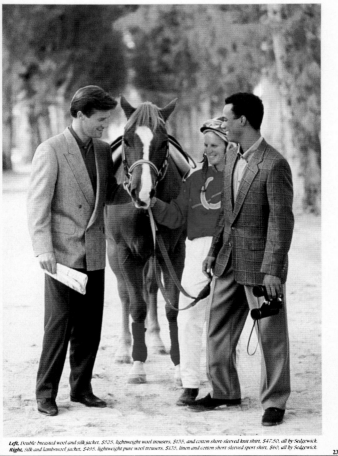

Left, *Double breasted wool and silk jacket, $525, lightweight wool trousers, $135, and cotton short sleeved knit shirt, $47.50, all by Sedgewick.*
Right, *Silk and lambswool jacket, $495, lightweight pure wool trousers, $135, linen and cotton short sleeved sport shirt, $60, all by Sedgewick.*

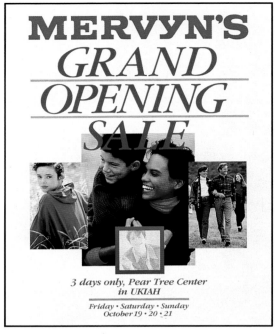

Winner

MERVYN'S
Hayward, CA
"Grand Opening"

Traffic Builder Mailer
Department Store
Over 500 mm

Sue Sprunk-VP/Marketing Sales
Promotion; Patricia
Holt-Advertising Director; David
Bennington-Creative Manager;
Chuck McCalla-Copy Editor; Debi
Harrison-Art Director; Terri
Torquato-Art Director/Photo;
Michael Collins-Copywriter; Jon
Fisset

Finalist

JCPENNEY
Dallas, TX
"Fernand Aubry Fall"

Traffic Builder Mailer
Department Store
Over 500 mm

AGENCY: AYER SOUTHWEST: Don Sedei-Creative/Art Director; Brice Campbell-Account Executive; Barbara Brown-Production Manager; Jim Hradecky-Management Director Creative Service; Shep Kellam-Copy Chief
PRODUCTION: WILLIAMSON
PRINTING: Debra Turbeville, Richard Reens, Joyce Ravid, Chris Hawker-Photographers

CREATIVITY

Thomas Edison is reputed to have said, "Genius is 99% work and 1% inspiration." Creativity, unlike Athena, does not spring from the head fully formed, fully wise and fully armed for battle. Rather it results from a thorough, careful study of the problem and then it is channeled to produce a desired shift in consumer behavior, awareness or perception.

Man can not live on data alone.

Creative people intuitively understand that while man can not live on data alone he can not live without it either. Data is the raw material for solutions in the same manner that paint is the raw material for art. A creative mind turns data into a new solution.

Divergent thinking.

The creative person is a divergent thinker. Divergent thinking involves the use of the policeman and the kid in each of us. The policeman is a yes or no person . . . Does it make sense? Is it logical? The policeman is comfortable with black and white but has a hard time with gray.

The kid asks: Wow! Where can I go with this? What can I do with this concept? If it were true what would happen? The policeman has a window in his mind. It is called experience and only if the idea fits the shape of the window of experience is it accepted. It is the policeman in us that makes possible the many daily decisions we make.

It is the kid in us that enables us to accept the narrow confines of the window of prior experience and to create a differently shaped window. It is the policeman that enables us to focus the view thru the new window to the problem at hand.

What is creativity?

What then is creativity? Creativity is the ability to look at things differently. Creative thinking is the ability to find solutions to problems by changing your point of view when normal channels fail to give you answers.

Everyone is creative!

I believe that everyone is creative. Ideas can and do come from everyone. If this is true, why is creativity such a limited commodity in so many retail organizations? It is, I feel, because most retail managements promote a win/lose situation rather than a win/win one. Managements encourage ideas to develop the "best" idea. By definition some are losers. A truly creative environment is one of teamwork where there are no losers but only participants in the creative process.

No one every bats 1000. Retail managements recognize this in the merchandising area by creating a markdown budget for creative merchandising errors. These same managements do not exhibit the same tolerance for creative "errors." Consequently, creativity in retailing managements rarely has a chance to flourish.

There are no impossible dreams — only limited dreamers.

Far too often in today's retail environment one hears "it can't be done. It is not our policy. If it were possible we would already be doing it. We tried it once but it didn't work. Why don't you do it the same as last year? Here, copy this other store's ad." Creative people know that there are no impossible dreams, only limited dreamers.

The kids in the creative people I have had the good fortune to have worked with over the years were dreamers. What could be was more important than what is. The policeman in them shaped those dreams into what can be and resulted in consistently creative solutions to retail opportunities. This is how creativity has worked for me. Give it a chance to flourish and it will work for you.

— Paul LeBlang

Magazine

Winner

EDDIE BAUER
Redmond, WA
"Eddie Bauer
National Advertising"

Campaign
Apparel Specialty Store
Over 500 mm

David Kimmey-VP/Sales
Promotion; Marsha
Savery-Advertising Director;
Robert Prevost-Copy Chief; Lori
McFadden-Art Director
AGENCY: EVANS/CAFT; Mike
Mogelgaard-Creative Director;
Michelle Kellett-Art Director;
David Horsfall-Copy Chief; Paula
Heath-Accout Executive

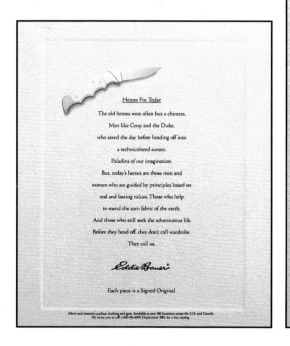

Wherever there's a love of the outdoors you'll find Eddie Bauer.

Exclusive outdoor clothing and gear for men and women,

available at over 180 locations nationwide. We invite you

to call 1-800-356-8889, Department BBJ for a free catalog.

Eddie Bauer ®

Each Piece is a Signed Original

White-tailed deer, Grand Lake Sebois, Maine.

Trail to Horseshoe Mesa, Grand Canyon, Arizona.

Our guarantee: Every item we sell will give you complete satisfaction or you may return it for a full refund.

Nature is unrepentant. It bestows its gifts, but always asks a price. The lingering desert sun belies the freezing night that creeps up on the arroyo. Here things are sharp, elemental and we take note. Not for us the fitful winds of fashion, but rather the essentials to see you through the passing seasons. Even if your only trip outside is a walk down the lane, we prepare you. Nature doesn't care if you get chilled to the bone. But we do.

Eddie Bauer

Each Piece is a Signed Original

Patented the down parka, 1936. Outfitted the American conquest of Mt. Everest, 1963. Team sponsor in the Alaska Iditarod, 1990.
Available at over 180 locations nationwide. Or call 1-800-356-8889 Department AAQ for a free catalog.

Snow and Ross's Geese, Tule Lake, California.

Our guarantee: Every item we sell will give you complete satisfaction or you may return it for a full refund.

There is harmony in the flight of the wild geese. The dissonance of many wings becomes a single chord. They rise in fluid waves, every individual movement part of a greater pattern. And so it is, with us. Each piece of clothing or gear stands alone, but must ring true to the overall design. Seams are built to last. Form follows function. Imagination takes flight, only when it serves the whole. That is our nature. All the better to feather your nest.

Eddie Bauer

Each Piece is a Signed Original

Men's and women's outdoor clothing and gear. Available at over 180 locations across the U.S. and Canada.
We invite you to call 1-800-356-8889 Department AAP for a free catalog.

Winner
BARNEYS NEW YORK
New York, NY
"Dallas and Beyond; Great
Style Is Never Out Of Place;
Duty vs Fun"

Campaign
Apparel Specialty Store
50-100 mm

Neil Kraft-VP
Advertising/Marketing; Glenn
O'Brien-Copy Chief; Douglas
Lloyd-Art Director
AGENCY: BNY ADVERTISING:
Sara Hardie-Production Manager
PRODUCTION: GRAPHIC ART
SERVICE: William Claxton

The world's best paints.
And wallcoverings to match.

ASK SHERWIN-WILLIAMS FOR IMPERIAL WALLCOVERINGS.

We wouldn't put our 124-year reputation in paint on the line with anything but the best wallcoverings. That's why you'll find hundreds of Imperial's newest patterns in every one of our stores. From the elegance of the new Ellen Tracy designer collection to the freshness of Imperial's southwestern looks. No retailer sells more wallcovering than Sherwin-Williams. So get rolling. At your local Sherwin-Williams store.

© 1990. The Sherwin-Williams Company

Winner

SAKS FIFTH AVENUE
New York, NY
"Very Saks Fifth Avenue 1990"

Campaign
Apparel Specialty Store
Over 500 mm

William Berta-Marketing Sales
Promotion Director; Bette
Chabot-Advertising Director;
Rebecca Wong Young-Creative
Director; Susan Alai-Copy Chief;
Gary Lowe-Art Director; Ross
Bonanno-Production Director;
Suzanne Pandjiris-Styling
Manager; Robert Farber, Nana
Watanabe, Roy
Volkmann-Photographers

VERY SAKS FIFTH AVENUE

UNDER COVER OF DARKNESS, LEATHER GOES OUT STRONG, SLEEK, RICH, AND ALTOGETHER DYNAMIC. FROM MAXIMA, THE BLACK DOUBLE-BREASTED BLAZER, SIZES 4 TO 12, $698 (95704); BLACK SLIM SKIRT, SIZES 4 TO 14, $280 (95705); AND BROWN CLUTCH COAT, SIZES XS, S, M, L, $897 (95706). ALL OF LAMBSKIN LEATHER. TO ORDER, CALL 1-800-345-1454. TO FAX YOUR ORDER, CALL 1-914-337-5900. TO RECEIVE A COMPLIMENTARY COPY OF OUR LATEST FOLIO CATALOGUE, CALL 1-800-222-7257. WE ACCEPT ALL MAJOR CREDIT CARDS.

VERY SAKS FIFTH AVENUE

A CLUTCH OF LITTLE BLACK DRESSES, ALL THAT'S REQUIRED FOR SETTING THE NIGHT ON FIRE. FROM FOR SIZES 4 TO 12, $261 (95706); NICOLE MILLER RAYON MOSS CREPE SHEATH WITH LATEX DOLMAN 4 TO 14 EXCEPT WHERE INDICATED. TO ORDER BY PHONE, CALL 1-800-345-1454. BY FAX, 1-914-337-5900. THE EVENING WEAR COLLECTIONS AT SAKS FIFTH AVENUE. EXPO'S PUCKERED RAYON VELVET AND POLYESTER SATIN FORM-FITTING DRESS NECK, $260 (95706); A.J. BARI RAYON VELVET DRESS, $170 (95707); AND GOLD POLYESTER SATIN EVENING TRENCH, $330 (95706). ALL FOR SIZES TO RECEIVE A COMPLIMENTARY COPY OF OUR LATEST FOLIO CATALOGUE, CALL 1-800-222-7257. WE ACCEPT ALL MAJOR CREDIT CARDS.

Green means go.

Darrell Green, Washington Redskins. Three-time NFL's fastest man.

Winner

ZUBAZ
Roseville, MN
"Green means Go,
Dolphin Found in Zubaz,
Snake Charmer"

Campaign
Vendor
10-50 mm

Dan Stock-Vice President; Bob
Truax-President
AGENCY: PETERSON PEARSON
MILLA: Dave
Peterson-Creative/Art Director;
Joe Milla-Copy Chief; Tim
Pearson-Account Executive; Barb
Knoche-Production Manager
PRODUCTION: ARNDT
PHOTOGRAPHY: Jim
Arndt-Photographer; Craig
Gjerness-Producer

Dolphin found inside zebra.

Miami Dolphin Dan Marino in Zubaz zebra print pants.

Snake charmer.

Supermodel Claudia Schiffer in Zubaz snake print pants.

CLASSIC
COMFORT

Go for a spin
in a classic Van Heusen.
Fancy striped shirt, $30.
Crew neck sweater
in solid color
textured cotton, $48.
VAN HEUSEN®

JCPenney Fashion comes to life

Available at most large JCPenney stores. Prices higher in Alaska, Hawaii and Puerto Rico. © 1990, JCPenney Co., Inc.

Winner

JCPENNEY
Dallas, TX
"Men's Division"

Section
Department Store
Over 500 mm

AGENCY: AYER SOUTHWEST: Don Sedei-Creative/Art Director; Shep Kellam-Copy Chief; Scott Sund-Account Executive; Barbara Brown-Production Manager; Jim Hradecky-Management
PRODUCTION: BRADLEY: Richard Reens-Photographer

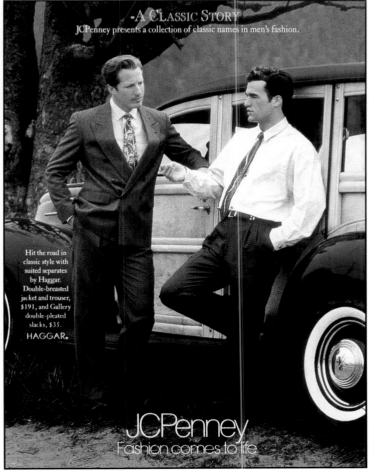

The craftsmanship of Rolex,

Winner

BAILEY BANKS & BIDDLE
Irving, TX
"Party Scene"

Single Ad
Other Specialty Store
250-500 mm

AGENCY: BOZELL: Ed
Pitkoff-Creative Director; Greg
Evans-Art Director; Donna
Manyin-Accout Executive; Judy
Riley-Production Manager

the quality of Baccarat,   the brilliance of diamonds share a great heritage.

Bailey Banks & Biddle has epitomized quality and craftsmanship since our founding, when we pioneered the sterling silver standard in America. Because of this passion for superior artistry, we feature extraordinary diamonds. Spectacular watches. And elegant giftware.

Our commitment to excellence extends to our work for the U.S. government. We've designed or furnished many of our country's medals and insignia, including the Medal of Honor, the Navy Cross and the Distinguished Service Medal.

And just as important are the treasures we've provided for your life. The diamond ring for your wedding. The Baccarat vase on your anniversary. The Rolex watch for your birthday.

For a century and a half, we've been dedicated to quality and craftsmanship.

SHARE THE HERITAGE.

BAILEY BANKS & BIDDLE

JEWELERS SINCE 1832

Atlanta · Boston · Chicago · Cleveland · Denver · Detroit · Ft. Lauderdale · Honolulu · Los Angeles · Memphis · Miami · Nashville
New Orleans · Philadelphia · Phoenix · Pittsburgh · San Francisco · Seattle · Short Hills · Tampa · Washington, D.C. · West Palm Beach

Winner

BRITCHES
Herndon, VA
"Santa's Suit"

Single Ad
Apparel Specialty Store
50-100 mm

Susan Wallert Rushford-Marketing Sales Promotion Director; Donna Reid Nogay-Advertising Director; Kim Gallagher-Copy Chief; Janet Daniel-Art Director; Emily Russell-Assistant Art Director
AGENCY: EXTENSION 229: Suzanne K. Egan-Account Executive; Laura Ciccone-Production Manager
PRODUCTION: STEPHENSON: Michael Pohuski-Photographer

There Are Coats That Look Best Wrinkled.

A man's suit coat, however, is not one of them. Nor, for that matter, his accompanying trousers.

At Britches, we've ironed out the wrinkles in men's business attire. By treating select pure wools with a patented fabric finish, we can make suits that, for all practical purposes, remain crisp and pressed all day long. Of the lightweight worsted wool that travels well, year-round.

We've cut our collection of solids and stripes for our most classic soft-shoulder model, our Barrett II.

A collection that, from $335 to $345, we've tailored to suit most everybody.

Clothing for Life®

BRITCHES *of GEORGETOWNE* *Fine Clothiers Since 1967*®

Washington, D.C., Maryland, Virginia, Dallas, Atlanta, Richmond, Baltimore, Chicago.

Winner

BRITCHES
Herndon, VA
"The Barrett II"

Single Ad
Apparel Specialty Store
50-100 mm

Susan Wallert Rushford-Marketing Sales Promotion Director; Donna Reid Nogay-Advertising Director; Kim Gallagher-Copy Chief; Emily Russell-Assistant Art Director
AGENCY: EXTENSION 229: Suzanne K. Egan-Account Executive; Laura Ciccone-Production Manager
PRODUCTION: PRINTED SPECIALTIES: Jayne Langdon's Animals Animals

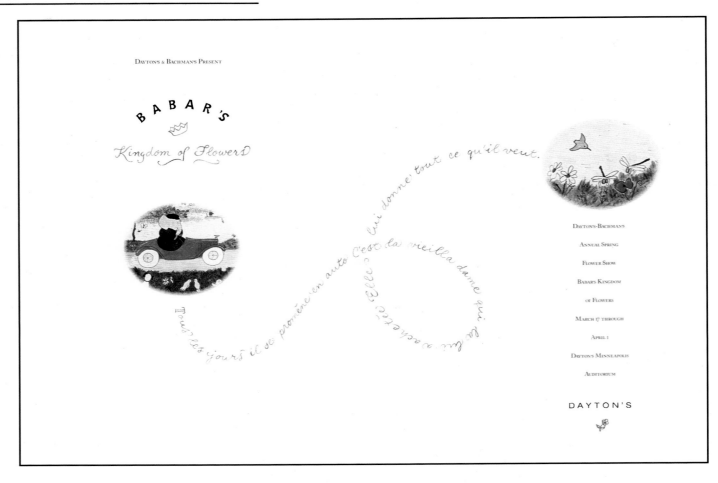

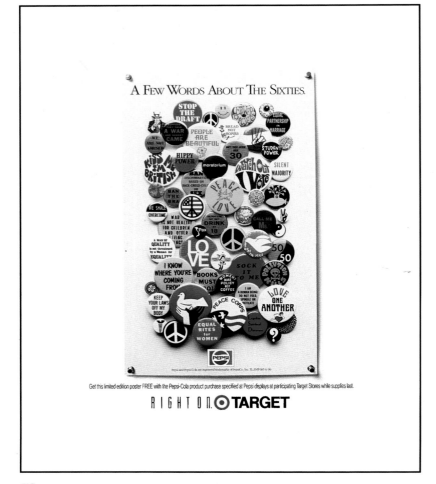

Winner

TRIMINGHAM'S
Hamilton, Bermuda
"Enchanted Beauty"

Single Ad
Department Store
10-50 mm

Connie Weeks-Advertising
Director; Karla Lacey-Creative
Director; Mary Van deWeg-Copy
Chief; Judith McKirdy-Art
Director; Stephen
Raynor-Photography

CREATIVITY

The hot advice, today, is to create dramatic advertising that will "cut through the clutter." This book is full of great examples of advertising that fulfills that challenge. Look. Study. Learn. That's the purpose of the Retail Advertising Conference and the RAC Awards to spotlight the best and to challenge each one of us to stretch, to reach to become better at our craft. Some folks have trouble accepting that challenge. Instead they make excuses. Sometimes folks say to me, "It's easy to produce breakthrough advertising with a Bloomingdale's budget and a Sak's staff, but my total advertising budget is only $75,000 (or my budget is $500,000 but I have to cover stores in four media markets). I could never afford those beautiful Nordstrom double trucks."

My answer is always the same. "Stop feeling sorry for yourself." That sounds tough, but please think about it for a minute. Some retailers, obviously, have more money than others, but much of their advertising adds to the clutter rather than cutting through. For all their billions of dollars and their 65 million newspaper circulation, Toys R Us runs small space ads every week; the size most small stores can afford. Even in 5"x10" ads their current "check it out" campaign is cutting through the clutter.

Let's talk about that campaign for a minute. It's not a creative breakthrough. It wasn't photographed in Nairobi with 104 camels and a cast of thousands. It won't win any awards (except in sales). Why do I say it's cutting through the clutter? Because it represents a very solid merchandising/marketing strategy, crisply executed to tell the customer exactly what she wants to hear, today. It's no secret. The best stores are proving it every day. The customer doesn't care much about our markdowns. She is caring less every day about our additional percentage off. She is looking for the items *she wants* at proven value price points. I see it every week as I travel stores. This is what the winners are advertising and it's working.

So advertising should start with a merchandising/marketing strategy that is *customer* driven. I have never learned how to produce newsworthy advertising without newsworthy merchandising. If there is a lesson in all of this, that's lesson #1.

Now let's talk about creative. Solid execution of fresh creative ideas is the easiest way to cut through the clutter. It is a fact. An ad that is noticed will not be read. That's not a new truth from the mountain top. Sek Seklemian was preaching this 50 years ago. "You must burn down City Hall to get attention." He used to quote Bernice Fitzgibbons who always reminded her writers of an old Irish proverb:

If you want to be noticed,
you have to make a disturbance.

That's lesson #2.

Why don't more stores make this happen? If it's not a question of budgets, what then? I think it comes down to one of two things. In some stores, I'm sorry to admit, the folks in charge of the advertising are not trying to reach for breakthough advertising. But what I hear most is, "management won't approve." Well, if you don't feel the killer need for breakthrough advertising to cut through the clutter, you probably can't be helped. But if it's a management problem, real or perceived, stay tuned.

Now, I have been on all sides of this thing. I have been a copywriter. I have been an advertising manager. I have been a sales promotion VP. I have been a merchandiser. And I have been a CEO. Like the elephant the blind men examined, this question looks different from every side. But one thing remains constant . . . The idea that will "Burn Down City Hall" *positively* and *profitably* for the store has to have more than raw shock power, more than off-the-wall, more than mere cute.

Creative for creative sake will not sell to your buyers or your CEO *or* your customers. The solid creative idea must grow out of a store strength, or must support the merchandise or address something of special interest to the customer. Don't complain if your management rejects advertising ideas that are no more than quirky or cute. Quirky and cute don't sell. Good advertising sells. And that's our job to sell the store, to sell merchandise.

The next time you develop the great breakthrough idea, take the time to re-examine that inspiration. How can you sharpen it to build on store strength, to strengthen a merchandise offering, to reach out and grab the customer. When you are sure it's perfect, comp it up and sell it all the way to the top. Finally, if it is really that good and "they" won't let you do it, start looking for another job. There are always some perceptive managements looking for great creative talent.

So, we have looked at the merchandising side and we have looked at the creative side. Both are important if you are going to cut through the clutter out there. We can't do great ads without strong merchandising. We can't do great ads without great ideas.

We need the great ideas. But great ideas don't come from big volume, nor necessarily, from big budgets. Big volume comes from great ideas.

— Fred. Newell

Newspaper

FOR THE LOYAL FANS OF RALPH LAUREN. Sleek as a high-performance sports car, his racy, hooded duffle coat in soft black leather, over a black wool skinny-ribbed turtleneck sweater and narrow black wool cavalry twill 'Hutton' trousers. From the Fall collection in The Shop for Ralph Lauren on Boulevard Four, New York. And selected stores. For the pinnacle of professional shopping assistance, simply call June Selig in "At Your Service" at (212) 705-3135, or call Hope Golden in "Hope's Corner" at (212) 705-3375.. They can help with a wide variety of Fall fashion needs.

Special Merit Award

BLOOMINGDALE'S
New York, NY
"Sport Story"

Campaign
Department Store
Over 500 mm

Gordon Cooke-Executive VP/Sale
Promotion; Wendy Levine-Media
Director; John C. Jay-Sr
VP/Art Director; Brian Leitch-Copy
Chief; Jill Glover-Stylist

Special Merit Award

Bloomingdale's
New York, NY
"Broadway '90"

Department Store
Over 500 mm

Gordon Cooke-Executive VP/Sale
Promotion; Wendy Levine-Media
Director; John C. Jay-Sr
VP/Art Director; Brian Leitch-Copy
Chief; Ronni Ascagni- Art Director;
Ruven Afonador-Photographer; Jill
Glover-Stylist; Robert
Valentine-Graphics

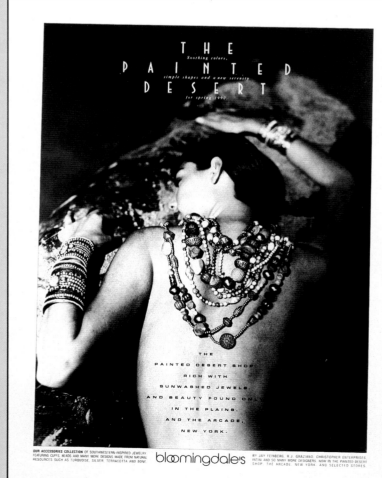

Special Merit Award

BLOOMINGDALE'S
New York, NY
"Time To Be Dad"

Campaign
Department Store
Over 500 mm

Gordon Cooke-Executive VP/Sale Promotion; Wendy Levine-Media Director; John C. Jay-Sr VP/Art Director; Brian Leitch-Copy Chief; James Streacker-Art Director; Shawn Peacock-Copywriter; Geof Kern-Photographer; Stephen Romano-Stylist

"Painted Desert"

Campaign
Department Store
Over 500 mm

Gordon Cooke-Executive VP/Sale Promotion; Wendy Levine-Media Director; John C. Jay -Sr VP/Art Director; Brian Leitch-Copy Chief; Ronni Ascagni-Art Director; Steven White-Photographer; Jill Glover-Stylist

Special Merit Award

BLOOMINGDALE'S
New York, NY
"Coat Sale Ads"

Campaign
Department Store
Over 500 mm

Gordon Cooke-Executive VP/Sale
Promotion; Wendy Levine-Media
Director; John C. Jay-Sr
VP/Art Director; Brian Leitch-Copy
Chief; Ronni Ascagni-Art Director;
Michel Haddi-Photographer

"Zero To Go"

Image/Positioning Ad
Department Store
Over 500 mm

Gordon Cooke-Executive VP/Sale
Promotion; Wendy Levine-Media
Director; John C. Jay-Sr
VP/Art Director; Brian Leitch-Copy
Chief; Jill Glover-Stylist

Winner

CVS
Woonsocket, RI
"Little Mermaid"

Action/Price Ad
Drug Stores
Over 500 mm

Heidi Leccesse-Advertising Sales
Promotion Director; Michelle
LeBlanc, Robert Felber-Designers;
PRODUCTION: LIGHT
MECHANICS: Photographer

Winner

CUB FOODS
Stillwater, MN
"Open Season"

Action/Price Ad
Food Retailers
Over 500 mm

Maureen Hooley-Advertising
Director
AGENCY: CHUCK RUHR
ADVERTISING: Bill
Johnson-Creative Director/Copy
Chief; Brien Spanier-Art Director;
Trip Johnson, Josh Denberg,
Randy Hughes-Copy Chiefs

MACY'S AFTER-EASTER SALE & CLEARANCE STARTS TOMORROW SAVE 20% TO 50%

FOR HER: DRESSES, SUITS, BLOUSES, SWEATERS, SHOES, HANDBAGS & MORE

FOR HIM: SUITS, SPORTCOATS, TIES, DRESS SHIRTS, SPORTSWEAR, SHOES & MORE

FOR KIDS: SAVINGS FOR BOYS, GIRLS, INFANTS, TODDLERS

FOR THE HOME: CELLAR SAVINGS, SILVER, CHINA, LUGGAGE & MORE

CLOSED TODAY EASTER SUNDAY

*Intermediate price reductions may have been taken. Colors and collections vary by store. Use your Macy's charge.

Winner

MACY'S NORTHEAST
New York, NY
"After Easter Sale"

Action/Price Ad
Department Store
Over 500 mm

Steven Kornajcik-Marketing Sales Promotion Director; Howard Adler-Advertising Director; Nan Cooper/Robin Hall-Creative Directors

Finalist

ABRAHAM & STRAUS
Brooklyn, NY
"Swim Break"

Campaign
Department Store
Over 500 mm

Steven Cohen-Creative Director; Luba Hanuschak-Art Director; Shen Henricks-Copy Chief; Dottie Pfeiffer-Copywriter

20%-50% OFF EVERY 1990 SWIMSUIT

ANNE COLE · ANNE KLEIN
ADRIENNE VITTADINI
BILL BLASS · CALVIN KLEIN
COLE OF CALIFORNIA
CATALINA · ESTHER WILLIAMS
GOTTEX · JANTZEN · LA BLANCA
PIERRE CARDIN · ROBBY LEN
ROXANNE · ROSE MARIE REID
OSCAR DE LA RENTA
TOO HOT BRAZIL

IT IS TO DIVE FOR!

A&S

E MBELLISHED BROCADE FROM EVAN-PICONE

ROBINSON'S

T HE NEW SHORT TRENCH BY DKNY

ROBINSON'S

T HE LONG PURE WOOL JACKET BY LINDA ALLARD FOR ELLEN TRACY

ROBINSON'S

Winner

ROBINSON'S
Los Angeles, CA
"DKNY, Ellen Tracy, Picone, &
Anne Klein"

Campaign
Department Store
Over 500 mm

Judy B. Farris-Senior VP; Marcia
Cotner-Vice President; Tula
Pregler-Division Vice President;
Agnes Davies-Copy Chief; Ginger
Hollender, Dick Cooper-Art
Directors
AGENCY: HARRISON SERVICES:
Lisa Shapot-Account Executive

ANNE KLEIN II GRAND BAROQUE

Anne Klein II sets the level of sophistication again in softest velvet and draped jacquard. From her dressy collection for Fall, we feature the velvet acetate/rayon cowl drape blouse. $156. Grand baroque drape jacquard skirt sparked with Lurex® in wool/silk. $176. Both, 4-14, in basic black. Imported. Available in Bridge Sportswear, selected stores. ☎ To order, please call 1-800-777-8910 toll-free, 24 hours a day. We're open later every Sunday from 11 a.m. to 7 p.m.

ROBINSON'S

Winner

NORDSTROM
Seattle, WA
"Paramus Store Opening"

Campaign
Apparel Specialty Store
Over 500 mm

Cindy Demme-Sales Promotion
Director; Linda Toschi
Finn-Advertising Director; Randy
Mecham-Copy Chief; Cheryl Fujii
Zahniser-Corporate Art Director

Wrap up your

shopping in style.

THE NEW YORK TIMES, FRIDAY, JULY 13, 1990   A5

If the shoe fits,

you've already

discovered Nordstrom.

Winner

BRITCHES
Herndon, VA
"...By Britches"

Campaign
Apparel Specialty Store
50-100 mm

Susan Wallert Rushford-Marketing
Sales Promotion Director; Donna
Reid Nogay-Advertising Director;
Kim Gallagher-Copy Chief; Janet
Daniel-Art Director; Emily
Russell-Assistant Art Director
AGENCY: EXTENSION 229:
Suzanne K. Egan-Account
Executive; Laura
Ciccone-Production Manager
PRODUCTION: CANGEMI
GRAPHIC: Helen
Norman-Photographer

REGATTA SWEATERS by Britches.

Our Striped Henley Sweater. 100% cotton, S-XXL. $69.50

Clothing for Life

TEAM SHIRTS By Britches.

Our Baseball Henley Tee, $35. 100% Washed Cotton Jersey. Rubber Buttons. Natural/Ink/Ruby, Ink/White/Gold, Jade/Purple/Black.

Clothing for Life

Bridgewater Commons

HARRY'S FIRST ANNUAL (AND HOPEFULLY LAST) BUSINESS IS BRUTAL SALE

"Things couldn't be worse," moaned Harry from his end of the boardroom table, tired brow buried in his hands, last week's sales figures flashing through his mind like a bad dream.

"Must be the weather," offered a sweating suit buyer as spring sunshine glanced off every corner of the room.

"Economy's taking it in the ear," observed another, backing it up by quoting today's interest rates.

"Tough all over," opined yet another seer with a knowing nod.

"Rubbish!" Harry rose. "We missed a few too many boats. Too many sweaters, too few jackets. Not enough denim. In short, there is no spring in our spring. About the only thing that'll bring customers through the doors is the opportunity to bag some bargains of a lifetime."

"Sharpen your pencils, people. We're going on sale."

And so the call went out to Harry's stores across the land. Mark down select groups of merchandise by at least 20% below the norm. Suits. Jackets. Slacks. Dress shirts, casual shirts and most certainly those sweaters.

"Please Harry, not my ties," pleaded the neckwear buyer, proud of his resplendent array.

"Everything but the ties," ordered Harry, hating to see a grown man cry.

"But I'll promise you one thing. If this stuff doesn't start to move soon, I'll be fitting you all with a different style of neckwear."

Please. Come in to Harry's and buy something.

HARRY ROSEN

TORONTO: 11 Adelaide St. W., 117 Richmond St. W., 82 Bloor St. W., Eaton Centre, Fairview, Oakville Place, Scarborough Town, Sherway, Yorkdale, Square One. MONTREAL: Fairview Shopping Centre, Rockland Centre, Carrefour Laval. QUEBEC: Place Ste-Foy. OTTAWA: Rideau Centre, Bayshore Centre. LONDON: Galleria London. WINNIPEG: Polo Park. EDMONTON: Eatonmaus Centre, West Edmonton Mall. CALGARY: South Centre, Toronto-Dominion Square. VANCOUVER: Oakridge Centre, Pacific Centre. BUFFALO: Walden Galleria.

REGRETFULLY, HARRY'S BUSINESS IS BRUTAL SALE CONTINUES

"It's the strangest thing," puzzles Harry. "We run an ad saying all is not rosy at Rosen's and that we're cutting prices on a selection of merchandise by at least 20%…and what happens?

"Vancouver gobbles up everything in sight. Calgary opens their wallets. Winnipeg likewise. London and Oakville carry off stuff by the ton. Ditto in Montreal, Quebec City and our Toronto suburban stores. But in downtown T.O. we laid an egg.

"What is it with the denizens of Bay Street? Too proud to save a buck? Are they all out buying yen?"

With that, Harry's favourite daily journal lands on his desk. 'Toronto ranked as most expensive city in Western Hemisphere,' he reads.

"Heck, they can't blame us," he says, holding up the headline for all to see.

"But just to be on the sale side, let's mark some more stuff down. Suits, jackets, shirts."

"Right across the country?" queried one of the assembled brainstrustees.

"You bet. Why should Calgary lose out just because they came in sixth?"

HARRY ROSEN

TORONTO: 11 Adelaide St. W., 117 Richmond St. W., 82 Bloor St. W., Eaton Centre, Fairview, Oakville Place, Scarborough Town, Sherway, Yorkdale, Square One. MONTREAL: Fairview Shopping Centre, Rockland Centre, Carrefour Laval. QUEBEC: Place Ste-Foy. OTTAWA: Rideau Centre, Bayshore Centre. LONDON: Galleria London. WINNIPEG: Polo Park. EDMONTON: Eatonmaus Centre, West Edmonton Mall. CALGARY: South Centre, Toronto-Dominion Square. VANCOUVER: Oakridge Centre, Pacific Centre. BUFFALO: Walden Galleria.

HARRY'S 'BUSINESS IS MUCH BETTER THANK YOU' SALE

The sun shone with renewed brightness through the windows of Rosen's execuloft atop his Scotia Plaza store. "It just goes to show you that honesty is the best policy," Harry smiled, looking up from last week's sales charts.

As much of better-dressed Canada knows, Harry had gone on-sale a touch earlier than usual.

Truth be told—and it was—the new things for spring weren't selling with the accustomed Rosen rapidity.

Ignoring the doomsayers who blamed the downturn on everything from high interest rates to the hole in the ozone, Harry grabbed the bull by the horns."Cut the prices by at least 20% on select merchandise," he ordered.

And you responded. Spring suits and jackets and shirts and sweaters were gobbled up at tasty savings.

Now if you were among the few who did not take advantage of Harry's benevolence-out-of-necessity, you may take heart in knowing that the sale continues with the same great savings. But be forewarned that the selection is dwindling.

While Harry may have been one of the few retailers willing to admit in print that business was brutal, he may be the only retailer able to admit that his business is better.

HARRY ROSEN

TORONTO: 11 Adelaide St. W., 112 Richmond St. W., 82 Bloor St. W., Eaton Centre, Fairview, Oakville Place, Scarborough Town, Sherway, Yorkdale, Square One. MONTREAL: Fairview Shopping Centre, Rockland Centre, Carrefour Laval. QUEBEC: Place Ste-Foy. OTTAWA: Rideau Centre, Bayshore Centre. LONDON: Galleria London. WINNIPEG: Polo Park. EDMONTON: Edmonton Centre, West Edmonton Mall. CALGARY: South Centre, Toronto-Dominion Square. VANCOUVER: Oakridge Centre, Pacific Centre. BUFFALO: Walden Galleria

OPENING IN MARKVILLE SHOPPING CENTRE, MARKHAM, IN AUGUST 1990 AND HAMILTON EATON CENTRE, IN OCTOBER 1990.

At Up To 60% Off, It's Standing Room Only.

Incredible savings on the latest looks, styles and colours.
Pants. Regular $40. *Now 15.99.* Sweaters: Regular $40. *Now 15.99.*
Blouses. Regular $40. *Now 15.99.* Skirts. Regular $45. *Now 19.99.*

FAIRWEATHER

There's Only One Thing More Important Than The Party. The Dress.

Stunning velvet dress with satin ruffle sleeve. Regular $185. Sale $148. And right now you can save 20% on all holiday dress wear.

Offer ends Saturday.

FAIRWEATHER

Winner

FAIRWEATHER
Toronto, Canada
"1989 Christmas"

Campaign
Apparel Specialty Store
100-250 mm

Sally Edmonds-VP-Marketing Director; Mark Steinberg, Advertising Manager; Teresa Losggio-Art Director; Denise Grimes-Advertising Co-ordinator AGENCY: SAFFER ADVERTISING: Trevor Goodsoll-Creative Director; Paul McClimond-Art Director; Mickey Burns-Copy Chief; Elizabeth Yeung-Account Executive; Heather Epple-Production Manager; Anita Saliss-VP-Account Director; Earl Richter-Photographer

We Wanted To Say Merry Christmas, So We Put It In The Paper.

We'd like to wish you all a safe, happy holiday and all the best in the year ahead.

FAIRWEATHER

Winner

FLYGFYREN
Norrtalje, Sweden
"Leve Livet"

Campaign
Food Retailers
10-50 mm

Rolf Holmberg-Marketing Sales
Promotion Director
AGENCY: JACK WAHL AB: Jack
Wahl-Creative Director; Claudio
Pizzelli-Art Director; Johan
Kylander-Copy Chief; Ulf
Ahlstrand-Account Executive;
Johan Carlson-Photographer

Winner

BROOKS
Pawtucket, RI
"Before It Goes Into Your
System, It Goes In Our System"

Image/Positioning Ad
Drug Stores
Over 500 mm

Douglas Palmacci-VP/Advertising
Director; Ron Mancyak-Creative
Director
AGENCY: MARIANI,
HURLEY/CHANDLER: Tom
Chandler-Art Director; Bob
Mariani-Copy
PRODUCTION: CYTAFEX
STUDIOS: Larry Larusso

Winner

DAYTON'S HUDSON'S
MARSHALL FIELD'S
Minneapolis, MN
"Southdale Opening"

Image/Positioning Ad
Department Store
Over 500 mm

Stew Widdess-Marketing Sales
Promotion Director; Jack
Mugan-Advertising Director;
Connie Soteropulos-Executive Art
Director; Eric Erickson-Copy
Chief; Todd Knaeble, Dyer
Davis-Copywriters; Lisa
Henkemeyer-Art Director

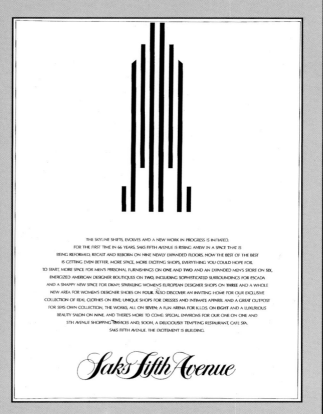

THE SKYLINE SHIFTS, EVOLVES AND A NEW WORK IN PROGRESS IS INITIATED. FOR THE FIRST TIME IN 66 YEARS, SAKS FIFTH AVENUE IS RISING ANEW IN A SPACE THAT IS BEING REFORMED, RECAST AND REBORN ON NINE NEWLY EXPANDED FLOORS. NOW THE BEST OF THE BEST IS GETTING EVEN BETTER. MORE SPACE, MORE EXCITING SHOPS, EVERYTHING YOU COULD HOPE FOR. TO START, MORE SPACE FOR MEN'S PERSONAL FURNISHINGS ON ONE AND TWO AND AN EXPANDED MEN'S STORE ON SIX. ENERGIZED AMERICAN DESIGNER BOUTIQUES ON TWO, INCLUDING SOPHISTICATED SURROUNDINGS FOR ESCADA AND A SNAPPY NEW SPACE FOR DKNY. SPARKLING WOMEN'S EUROPEAN DESIGNER SHOPS ON THREE AND A WHOLE NEW AREA FOR WOMEN'S DESIGNER SHOES ON FOUR. ALSO DISCOVER AN INVITING HOME FOR OUR EXCLUSIVE COLLECTION OF REAL CLOTHES ON FIVE, UNIQUE SHOPS FOR DRESSES AND INTIMATE APPAREL AND A GREAT OUTPOST FOR SFA'S OWN COLLECTION, THE WORKS, ALL ON SEVEN; A FUN ARENA FOR K.I.D.S. ON EIGHT AND A LUXURIOUS BEAUTY SALON ON NINE. AND THERE'S MORE TO COME: SPECIAL ENVIRONS FOR OUR ONE ON ONE AND 5TH AVENUE SHOPPING SERVICES AND, SOON, A DELICIOUSLY TEMPTING RESTAURANT, CAFE SFA. SAKS FIFTH AVENUE. THE EXCITEMENT IS BUILDING.

Saks Fifth Avenue

IN MATTERS EUROPEAN, SAKS FIFTH AVENUE EMERGES AT THE FOREFRONT OF DESIGNER FASHION WITH LOOKS THAT SIGNAL A CHANGE IN THE ATMOSPHERE. FIND COLLECTIONS THAT INTERPRET THE UNEXPECTED WITH UNCOMMON FINESSE AND ARE STAMPED WITH THE UNIQUE IMPRIMATUR OF SFA. FROM GIORGIO ARMANI, ENJOY MODERN SILHOUETTES AT EASE WITH THE MOMENT IN A PRESENTATION THAT IS WITHOUT PEER. THIS FALL, SEE ALL THAT IS NOW GIORGIO ARMANI, ENSCONCED IN OUR ELEGANT NEW SHOP ON THREE, AT SFA.

Saks Fifth Avenue

GIORGIO ARMANI'S GOLD SILK AND POLYESTER METALLIC LACE STRIPED JACKET FOR SIZES 4 TO 12, AND BLACK SILK CREPE SIDE WRAP SKIRT FOR SIZES 4 TO 12. THE COLLECTION FROM $700 TO $3,200. EUROPEAN COLLECTIONS ON THREE. NEW YORK STORE ONLY.

NEW YORK, INQUIRIES: 753-4000. OPEN MONDAY THRU SATURDAY, 10 A.M. TO 6:30 P.M.; THURSDAY TIL 8 P.M. • WHITE PLAINS, SPRINGFIELD & GARDEN CITY OPEN MONDAY & THURSDAY TIL 9 P.M. BERGEN OPEN WEEKDAYS TIL 9:30 P.M.; STAMFORD TIL 9 P.M.; SATURDAY TIL 6 P.M. SPRINGFIELD, GARDEN CITY & STAMFORD OPEN SUNDAY, 12 TO 5 P.M.; WHITE PLAINS 12 TO 6 P.M.

THE SEASON REVS UP FOR A FRESH START AS SAKS FIFTH AVENUE TAKES A LOOK AT EUROPE'S MOST PRIZED OFFERINGS AND SHOWCASES THEM IN SHOPS THAT ARE CLEARLY A CUT ABOVE. MODERN, SOPHISTICATED AND ESSENTIALLY EUROPEAN, OUR BOUTIQUES ON THREE PRESENT THE FINEST ALL HAVE TO OFFER FROM THE MOST EXEMPLARY NAMES IN FASHION. AT THE START, ENAMORED ONESELF WITH LOOKS THAT MARK HIM AS SEPARATE AND DISTINCT, BACK, WITH AN AFTER-FIVE THAT RECLAIMS ITSELF A WINNER. IT REMAINS THE BEST OF CLASS IN A DESIGNER PRESENTATION THAT IS SHOWCASE IN AN INTERPRETATION NOW, ENJOY ALL THE GLORIES OF EUROPE BROUGHT TO YOU BY SAKS FIFTH AVENUE.

Saks Fifth Avenue

FASHION CUTS TO THE QUICK. THIS FALL WITH IMPORTS THAT ARE ENTICING, EXCITING AND ON THE EDGE. NOW SAKS FIFTH AVENUE HAS THE LATEST FROM CLAUDE MONTANA, ONE OF EUROPE'S MOST ADVANCED CREATORS, AND BRINGS YOU OUR SELECTIONS ON THREE WITH ALL OF THE EXPERT SKILL AND KNOWLEDGE OF OUR TOP-NOTCH SALES STAFF. IT'S A PRESENTATION DESIGNED TO HIGHLIGHT THE DESIGNS, AND YOU AS WELL, IN A MOST FAVORABLE LIGHT. WHEN WHAT YOU WANT IS SOMETHING OUT OF THE ORDINARY, COUNT ON SAKS FIFTH AVENUE TO FIND YOU WHAT'S EXTRAORDINARY.

Saks Fifth Avenue

DAMASK'S ENGARD'S BLACK AND WHITE WOOL HARLEQUIN JACKET. GOLD EDGED BLACK SILK BLOUSE AND GOLD METALLIC LEATHER SKIRT, ALL FOR SIZES 4 TO 12. THE COLLECTION FROM $800 TO $3,200. EUROPEAN COLLECTIONS ON THREE. NEW YORK STORE ONLY.

FROM CLAUDE MONTANA, THE SCULPTED FLOSSIA WOOL SUIT FOR SIZES 4 TO 10. THE COLLECTION, FROM $300 TO $4,300. ADVANCED DESIGNER COLLECTIONS ON THREE. NEW YORK STORE ONLY.

Finalist

SAKS FIFTH AVENUE
New York, NY
"Saks Fifth Avenue Tower Opening"

Image/Positioning Ad
Apparel Specialty Store
Over 500 mm

William Berta-Marketing Sales Promotion Director; Bette Chabot-Advertising Director; Rebecca Wong Young-Creative Director; Susan Alai-Copy Chief; Gary Lowe-Art Director; Ross Bonanno-Production Director; Suzanne Pandjiris-Styling Manager; Nana Watanabe-Photographer

Macy's
Welcomes The
New Kid On The Block

It is a source of great pride that Macy's

has been able to play a part in the

growth of this special community.

We are delighted that Nordstrom is now

joining us, adding vitality and diversity

to Paramus and the Garden State Plaza.

WE'RE A PART OF YOUR LIFE

We have only one thing to say to Chicago Place and the new Crate & Barrel on Michigan Avenue.

Welcome

Water Tower Place and The 900 North Michigan Shops

Winner

JMB/URBAN PROPERTIES
Chicago, IL
"Welcome"

Image/Positioning Ad
Shopping Center

Helen De Witt-Marketing Sales
Promotion Director
AGENCY: KEROFF/ROSENBERG
ADVERTISING: Dan Oditt-Creative
Director; Pat Valone-Art Director;
Christina Calvitt-Copy Chief;
Deborah Karabin-Account
Supervisor; Mike
Chaplick-Production Manager;
Lisa Solomon-Assistant Account
Executive

Winner

MACY'S NORTHEAST
New York, NY
"Macy's Welcomes Nordstrom
To Garden State Plaza"

Image/Positioning Ad
Department Store
Over 500 mm

Steven Kornajcik-Marketing Sales
Promotion Director; Howard
Adler-Advertising Director; Nan
Cooper/Robin Hall-Creative
Directors

Winner

LAMPERTS
St. Paul, MN
"Sale On Everything From A-Z
Including The Kitchen Sink"

Insert/Section Ad
Other Specialty Store
50-100 mm

Frank Wetzel-Advertising Director;
Randy Lied-Art Director; John
Brandon-Copywriter;

Winner

DAYTON'S HUDSON'S
MARSHALL FIELD'S
Minneapolis, MN
"Chicago View Fall '89"

Insert/Section Ad
Department Store
Over 500 mm

R. Cappelli-Marketing Sales
Promotion Director; Janet
Garrott-Advertising Director;
Thomas Smallwood-Creative
Director; Lenora Rand-Copy Chief

COMING SEPTEMBER 30TH,
THE TARGET GREATLAND GRAND OPENING.

DON'T MISS IT.

Drop in to the Target Greatland Grand Opening and you'll discover a storeful of shopping conveniences that clearly hit the mark. Starting with wider aisles. Bigger, smarter carts. Plenty of super-efficient checkout lanes, featuring quick, dual-cashier service. And a gigantic parking lot with ID signs to help you find your car from wherever you are.

You'll also fall for our full-scale food court, photo processing while you shop, expanded pharmacy—plus fast, friendly service and lots more of the high quality, low price Target products you've come to expect. The Target Greatland Grand Opening, Sunday 9 am to 9 pm, County Road 42 and Cedar Avenue in Apple Valley. Come on down.

TARGET
Greatland

SOMETIMES YOU JUST NEED A BIGGER TARGET.

Special Merit Award

TARGET
Minneapolis, MN
"Don't Miss It"

Image/Positioning Ad
Mass Merchandiser
Over 500 mm

"At Target Center"

Insert/Section Ad
Mass Merchandiser
Over 500 mm

Target Advertising

Different Spokes For Different Folks.

GIRLS' HUFFY
20" BMX "BAHAMA"
Single speed with coaster brake and one rear side-pull brake, 20 X 1.75" white unidirectional tires, full pad kit. Made in USA. Professionally assembled. Great Buy priced at **89.99**

BOYS' ROADMASTER
20" BMX "BLACK ICE"
Single speed, coaster brake with dual caliper side-pull brakes, padded anatomic ATB saddle, 20 X 2.125" black knobby tires. Professionally assembled. Great Buy priced at **89.99**

TARGET
RIGHT. ON THE MONEY.

Special Merit Award

TARGET
Minneapolis, MN
"Different Spokes"

Action/Price Ad
Mass Merchandiser
Over 500 mm

Target Advertising

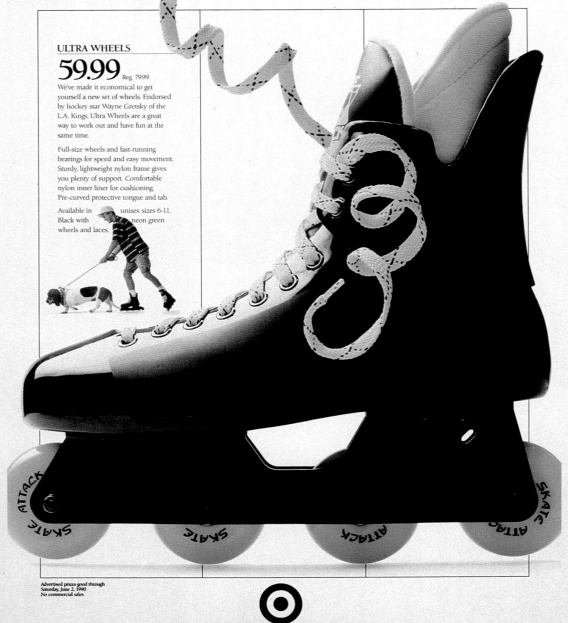

Deals On Wheels.

ULTRA WHEELS

59.99 Reg. 79.99

We've made it economical to get yourself a new set of wheels. Endorsed by hockey star Wayne Gretsky of the L.A. Kings, Ultra Wheels are a great way to work out and have fun at the same time.

Full-size wheels and fast-running bearings for speed and easy movement. Sturdy, lightweight nylon frame gives you plenty of support. Comfortable nylon inner liner for cushioning. Pre-curved protective tongue and tab.

Available in unisex sizes 6-11. Black with neon green wheels and laces.

Advertised prices good through
Saturday, June 2, 1990.
No commercial sales.

TARGET
RIGHT. ON THE MONEY.

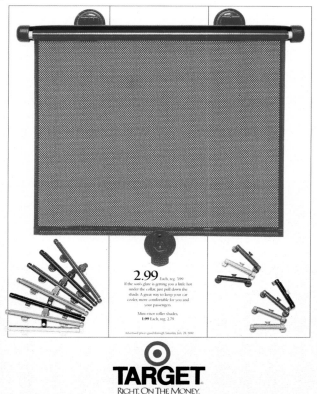

Special Merit Award

TARGET
Minneapolis, MN
"Sunscreen, Just A Shade
Under $3"

"Get Mower For Your Money"

Action/Price Ad
Mass Merchandiser
Over 500 mm

Target Advertising

CREATIVITY

You're the top!
You're the Colosseum.
It is easy to imagine Cole Porter, at a grand and glittering party, sitting at a block-long concert grand piano and simply saying to music . . .
You're the top!
You're the Louvre museum.
You're the melody from a symphony from Strauss,
You're a Bendel bonnet,
A Shakespeare sonnet,
You're Mickey Mouse.*

If there is a hall-of-fame list for creativity, Cole Porter is surely at its top. Someone commented to Cole that it must be a wonderful feeling, being so creative that sophisticated words and music poured effortlessly out of him. Cole answered, that far from being effortless, creating was donkey-work: difficult and grueling — hammering out notes and words, one at a time.

I chose Cole Porter to illustrate what creativity means to me for a number of reasons. Listening to his music, and understanding how it was created, explains the most important one: His sheer genius for words and storytelling. Another is his commitment to his work and his ability to master the painful process of creativity.

Cole's first Broadway musical opened in 1916, three years after he graduated from college. Success came early and stayed. It made him rich and famous. Cole then spent most of the Twenties, seemingly as an expatriate playboy, in Europe. He actually invested his years in Europe learning about life, sharpening his skills and honing his talent.

As the Twenties ended Cole returned to America, ready to make his mark. While the country plunged into a deep depression — Cole was far from depressed. The Thirties were his period of greatest creativity. His amusing, exhilerating, sometimes touching songs brought cheer to a cheerless nation. It was as if he took the words Americans wanted to say to each other, then set them to music.

The best creative work always seems natural — as if done with no visible effort. Similarly, the best actors always seem to simply talk to the audience. It seems true creativity, in whatever medium, always speaks to its audience with a natural and comfortable voice.

Like good music, much of the creative advertising work you will enjoy in this book has a natural quality. Those who created it were prepared, like Cole Porter — with a thorough grasp of the subject; a broad knowledge of available tools and forms; and a sharp focus on the audience — and with a willingness to work hard to achieve excellence.

It's the top.

*Copyright 1934, Warner Bros., Inc.

Tom Holliday

Outdoor

Winner

TARGET
Minneapolis, MN
"Greatland Grand Opening"

Mass Merchandiser
Over 500 mm

Target Advertising

Finalist

CROSSROADS PLAZA
Salt Lake City, UT
"Back to School '90"

Shopping Center

David A. Zukowski-Marketing
Director
AGENCY: HARRIS-VOLSIC
CREATIVE: Debra Harris- Creative
Director; David Volsic-Art
Director; Dan Murray-Account
Executive

Finalist

ZUBAZ
Roseville, MN
"Snake Charmer"

Vendor
10-50 mm

Dan Stock-Vice President; Bob
Truax-President
AGENCY: PETERSON PEARSON
MILLA: Dave
Peterson-Creative/Art Director;
Joe Milla-Copy Chief; Tim
Pearson-Account Executive; Barb
Knoche-Production Manager
PRODUCTION: ARNDT
PHOTOGRAPHY: Jim
Arndt-Photographer; Craig
Gjerness-Producer

Finalist

BLOCKBUSTER VIDEO
Ft. Lauderdale, FL
"Star Gaze Tonight"

Other Specialty Store
Over 500 mm

Brian Woods-Marketing Sales
Promotion Director
AGENCY: BERNSTEIN REIN: Clair
Reizer-Account Executive; Bruce
Butcher-VP/Management
Supervisor

C R E A T I V I T Y

"Every act of Creativity is first an act of destruction."
— Picasso

If creativity first begins with destruction, then we're at the beginning of what promises to be one of the most creative eras in retail history. Change abounds all fronts of our industry, and if you look closely you'll see that it's not the strong that are surviving, but the creative.

We've seen old-line department store chains go under and "category killers" emerge. That's not all. An estimated 300 retailers filed for Chapter 11 in 1990. There's no doubt that the industry has been redefining itself — or rather, that the customer has been redefining the industry.

Consumer spending patterns can best be described as a mirror of the collective consumer psyche, and since good retail advertising has emotional appeal, it's important to look at the factors influencing buying behavior.

The free spending 1980s have given way to the more pragmatic 1990s, which should not be surprising if you follow the growing pains of the baby boom generation. Right now, consumer debt is at an all-time high while consumer confidence is at an all-time low, driving a phenomenon that *Barrons* calls "trading down." We like to call it "enlightened" practicality.

While this picture may look rather grim, kids will still need back-to-school clothing, gifts will still be purchased for the holidays, but it's going to take more effort to convince shoppers to walk through your doors. You're going to have to be more CREATIVE!

It's always difficult to discuss creativity. Once you define something you put a limit on it. So, at Target creativity has no definition, no limit.

In advertising we tend to think of creativity in terms of copywriting and art direction, but to communicate at the most effective levels, boundaries must be crossed. As marketers we need a broad perspective to understand our customers. That understanding becomes the foundation for truly great advertising. In fact, a recent article in *The Harvard Business Review* said that the ability to think across boundaries, lateral thinking, will be one of the most critical business skills for the future.

The retail industry provides one of the best opportunities to think laterally. At every intersection, from product development to visual merchandising, there is an opportunity to creatively cross boundaries.

As retail marketers, it's not enough to create clever price-item advertising. We have to be able to empathize with the consumer at every juncture — to transcend price-item thinking. How many product development ideas have we had? What visual merchandising recommendations have we made? And when was the last time store hours and return policies were discussed? If you think that any of the above are not in your job description, think again. Each of these issues communicates to the customer, which is at the heart of what we do.

Looking ahead, although it may appear that everything in our industry will be different, beneath the surface nothing will really change. The ability to anticipate and meet the needs of our customers will continue to determine success and failure, so our thinking needs to be like our customers — multi-dimensional.

— John Pellegrene

Multi-Media

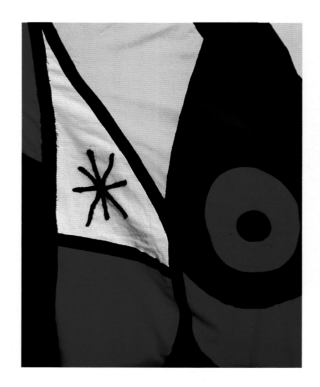

Winner

BLOOMINGDALE'S
New York, NY
"Spain Europe's Rising Star"

Department Store
Over 500 mm

Gordon Cooke-Executive VP/Sale
Promotion; Wendy Levine-Media
Director; John C. Jay-Sr
VP/Art Director; Brian Leitch-Copy
Chief; Jill Glover-Stylist; Kirsti
Kroener-Designer; Michel
Comte-Photographer; Robert
Valentine-Graphics

EUROPE'S RISING ✦ STAR

spain

bloomingdale's

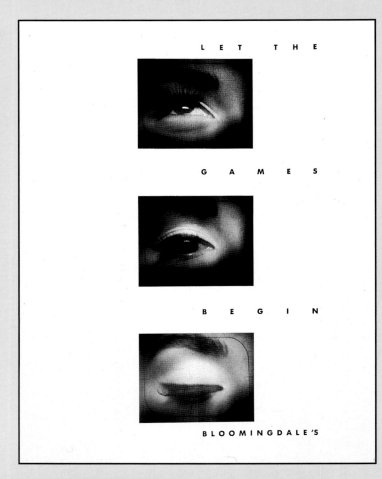

LET THE

GAMES

BEGIN

BLOOMINGDALE'S

Winner

BLOOMINGDALE'S
New York, NY
"Sport Story"

Department Store
Over 500 mm

Gordon Cooke-Executive VP/Sale
Promotion; Wendy Levine-Media
Director; John C. Jay-Sr
VP/Art Director; Brian Leitch-Copy
Chief; Jill Glover-Stylist

DONNA KARAN

bloomingdales

S P O R T   S T O R Y

FOR THE LOYAL FANS OF OSCAR DE LA RENTA. Shrugging off the competition with a glamorous new game plan, the drama of duchesse satin and deeply piled velvet, in sportswear shapes. Here, his hooded short 'stadium' topper in iridescent loden/cranberry, with a ruby cashmere sweater and slim brown velvet skirt with satin belt. Demonstrating an athletic prowess on Boulevard Four, New York. And selected stores. Bloomingdale's offers you the pinnacle of professional shopping assistance: Call Hope Golden in 'Hope's Corner' at (212) 705-3375; or June Selig in 'At Your Service' at (212) 705-3135. They can help with a wide variety of Fall fashion wardrobe needs.

Winner

BERGD0RF GOODMAN
New York, NY
"Bergdorf Goodman
Men-Opening"

Apparel Specialty Store
100-250 mm

Marilyn Levey-Marketing Sales
Promotion Director; Charles
Bumgardner-Creative Director; Ron
Dignnairo-Copy Chief; J. P.
Williams-Art Director

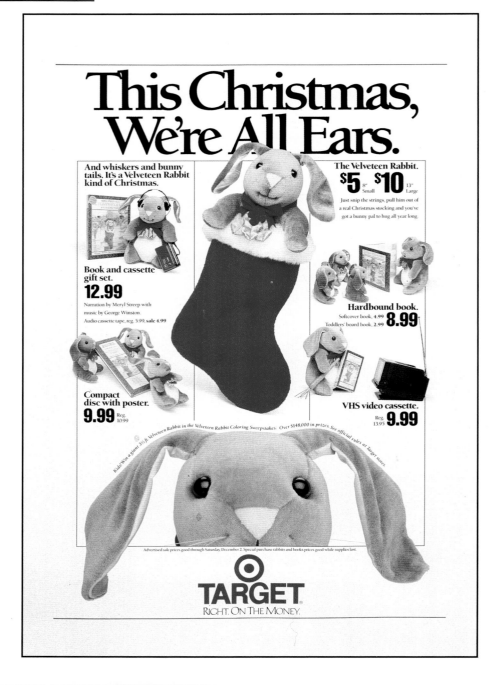

Finalist

TARGET
Minneapolis, MN
"Velveteen Rabbit"

Mass Merchandiser
Over 500 mm

Target Advertising

The VELVETEEN RABBIT

Once, there was a Velveteen Rabbit. On Christmas morning, he sat in the Boy's stocking, the best gift of all.

One day in the nursery, he asked the wise old Skin Horse, *"What is REAL?"* *"Love makes you Real,"* replied the Skin Horse. *"When a child grows to love you, then you become Real."*

That night, the Rabbit slept with the Boy. **At first it was uncomfortable,** for the Boy hugged him very tight. But soon he grew to like it.

When the Boy fell ill with scarlet fever and was bedridden, the little Rabbit never left his side.

After the Boy was well, the doctor said the Velveteen Rabbit was to be burned with everything else that had been in the Boy's bed.

Alone in the rubbish heap, the sad ragged Rabbit thought of the Boy and how happy they had been. Then a tear, a real tear fell to the ground.

Where the tear had fallen, a flower grew. Inside was a magic fairy. *"I take care of the playthings that children have loved. When they are worn out, I turn them into REAL."*

She kissed the little Rabbit and changed him altogether...he was a REAL RABBIT at last!

Love Makes You Real.

CHRISTMAS '89

"Love Makes You Real™"

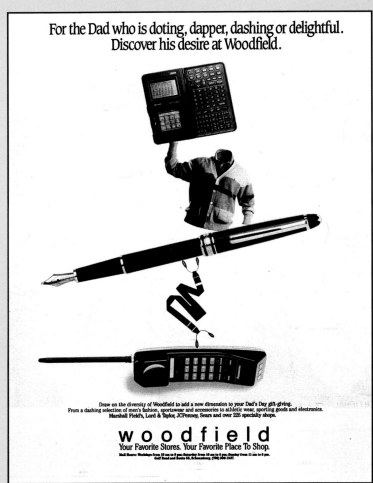

Winner

WOODFIELD SHOPPING
CENTER
Schaumburg, IL
"Alliteration"

Shopping Center

Betty Bryant-Marketing Director
AGENCY: SAFFER/USA
ADVERTISING

Seize the season with smart, sleek, sensational style! Slip into something stunning at Woodfield.

Spring is in full swing at Woodfield with a spectacular selection from all your favorite designers. Choose from over 80 stores that specialize in women's fashion and footwear. **Marshall Field's, Lord & Taylor, JCPenney, Sears and over 225 specialty shops.**

woodfield
Your Favorite Stores. Your Favorite Place To Shop.

Golf Road and Route 53, Schaumburg. (708) 330-1537.

Helping your home reach heroic new heights. It's all here — at Woodfield.

From the timeless elegance of the traditional to the quick-witted sophistication of the modern. . .enjoy an extensive selection of furniture, accessories and accents for every room in the home at more than 20 stores at Woodfield. **Marshall Field's, Lord & Taylor, JCPenney, Sears and over 225 specialty shops.**

woodfield
Your Favorite Stores. Your Favorite Place To Shop.

Golf Road and Route 53, Schaumburg. (708) 330-1537.

Smart students set out for school with style. Start studying at Woodfield!

Start with the ABC's of basics, then learn all about the latest looks for fall at our Back to School Fashion Show this Saturday at 1 & 3 PM. Units presents ''Unique, Universal Units'' on August 18, 1:30 PM. And then JCPenney hosts the ''Seventeen Live'' Fashion Show on August 19, 2 PM. Studying was never this easy! **Marshall Field's, Lord & Taylor, JCPenney, Sears and over 225 specialty shops.**

woodfield
Your Favorite Stores. Your Favorite Place To Shop.

Mall Hours: Weekdays from 10 am to 9 pm, Saturday from 10 am to 6 pm, Sunday from 11 am to 6 pm. Golf Road and Route 53, Schaumburg. (708) 330-1537.

Finalist

ATHLETE'S FOOT
Atlanta, GA
"Where To Look For A Good
Tennis Shoe"

Other Specialty Store
250-500 mm

James Hutchinson-Advertising
Director
AGENCY: GROUP 243: Eddie
Snyder-Creative Director; Gregg
Meade-Art Director; Dave
Nelson-Copy Chief; Lee
McComb-Account Executive

WHAT TO LOOK FOR IN A GOOD TENNIS SHOE.

WHERE TO LOOK FOR A GOOD TENNIS SHOE.

Foot and leg problems are some of the most common injuries reported by tennis players. Many of these can be prevented with the proper shoes. And the more you know what to look for in a good shoe, the better your chances of preventing injury and achieving maximum comfort when you play.

Since 1971, The Athlete's Foot® has developed a strong following among serious tennis players across the country. Not only because of our shoe selection, but because of the passion we share with you for your sport.

In that spirit, we present this guide to help you pick the right tennis shoe. The way we see it, better you learn it here than out on the court.

DURABILITY. BECAUSE YOU DRAG YOUR SHOES ALL OVER THE COURT.

The first thing to look at in a court shoe is the outsole. Today's better shoes use outsoles composed of rubber or polyurethane.

Design of the outsole is important for proper traction and durability. Nike® uses Durathane, an extra long-lasting material around the toe and forefoot for increased durability in its high performance shoes. It also uses a herringbone outside pattern for better traction.

CUSHIONING. HOW TO KEEP FROM TAKING A POUNDING.

If you're an aggressive player, chances are you're often airborne and move in quick spurts. As a result, your body can produce a force 2 to 4 times your weight. That's a tremendous shock to your feet and legs.

The midsole is one of the most important areas of the shoe for cushioning. Refer to the literature that

comes with most shoes and look for midsoles composed of compression molded ethyl vinyl acetate (EVA) or polyurethane. These compounds are preferred because of their light weight and cushioning properties.

Midsole design, however, is where manufacturers have made the greatest strides lately. Nike's patented Air-Sole® cushioning is a good example.

The Nike-Air® midsole is an excellent unit because it retains its original shape and cushioning properties even after hours of pounding.

Another part of the shoe that helps cushion your feet is the removable insole. It's also the first to break down. So we recommend you replace the insole halfway through the life of your shoe. You'll feel the difference.

STABILITY. FANCY FEATURES FOR FANCIER FOOTWORK.

The continuous side-to-side movement in tennis calls for a stable shoe. The latest advance in this area is

NIKE

the contoured midsole. Contoured midsoles are molded at the factory to allow your heel and/or forefoot to sit down into the unit. This not only provides support, but it helps the fit of the shoe as well. Nike uses contoured midsoles in many of its court shoes.

A relatively new design feature is the footframe. This is a polymer unit that supports the upper and runs along the side of the shoe.

There are other features that make a shoe more stable. To minimize rear-foot motion, look for a firm, resistant heel counter.

If you have weak ankles, you might opt for what many of the pros use—a padded ¾ cut. And rear-quarter stability straps with plastic eyelets

will give you a little more support during lunges and quick stops.

FIT. HOW DO YOU KNOW?

To determine the proper shoe length, use the "rule of thumbnail." There should be a space the width of your thumbnail (not the salesperson's) between the end

of the toebox and the tip of your longest toe on your longer foot. Make sure you can freely wiggle your toes. The heel should be snug, but not tight. Constant play in warm weather can expand your feet in width and length up to a half size. Which means too-tight shoes in the store can be killers on the court.

Above all else, get your feet remeasured every time you buy new shoes. Your size can actually change as a result of the aging process or injuries.

THE WEARTEST CENTER KEEPS US IN STEP WITH COURT SHOES.

The Athlete's Foot is the only retailer in the country with its own independent facility like the WearTest Center.

Located on the campus of North Central College in Naperville, Illinois, the center evaluates the major manufacturers' court shoes for a variety of foot types based on flexibility, durability, cushioning and motion control. The staff there then passes the information along to our stores along with the latest updates on shoe technology and recent sports medicine findings.

So next time you need a new pair of tennis shoes—from Nike or any other major brand—you have a choice.

You can go to any of a dozen mainstream-oriented stores you'll find on just about any corner.

Or you can go to the athlete-oriented store you'll find on the next page.

NOBODY KNOWS THE ATHLETE'S FOOT LIKE THE ATHLETE'S FOOT.

Winner

TARGET
Minneapolis, MN
"Kids for Saving Earth"

Mass Merchandiser
Over 500 mm

Target Advertising

CREATIVITY

"If You Could Change the World . . ."

On a chilly February R.A.C. afternoon the founder and the director of Esprit, Suzie Tompkins, asked us all a question. "If you could change the world, what would you do. . ."

The folks at Esprit are asking this question of their customers, too. Inviting their comments via a user friendly postcard. And they fully intend to do something with and about the customer comments.

Why, you ask? Because Esprit is a wonderfully creative company. A company concerned with our world. Concerned with values. Suzie shared their values with us, because many of our stores and our customers love Esprit . . . what they make and what they represent.

In Suzie's words, "Esprit represents good values." Making a difference in today's world. Postcards and hangtags on recycled paper. Models that represent their image because they are Esprit employees. Words like "volunteering" and "eco-audit" are part of their everyday business vocabulary.

Creativity is a passion with these folks. "We are aware. And we are involved. We are informed. And that gives us inspiration."

During a recent lecture in their eco-park next door to San Francisco headquarters, Anita Roddick (of The Body Shop International) told them:

"You educate people by their passions. Especially young people. You find ways to grab their imagination. You want them to feel that they're doing something important, that they're not a lone voice. That they are the most powerful, potent, people on the planet."

John Jay of Bloomingdale's, who introduced all the creativity speakers that afternoon, singled out Esprit. He spoke warmly of their "soul" and championed their values. Because so very often they put their philosophy to work through their creative product.

I took away a lot of fine ideas that afternoon. A perfect case study of business in action. For Suzie Tompkins it all starts at home. With Esprit. She believes the consumer rebellion will lead to a new retail activism. And that we have a responsibility. We have a responsibility to our employees and to our customers. That good values lead to making a difference. And that difference will make us part of the solution.

Kathleen Holliday

Other/New
Media

Winner

DAYTON'S HUDSON'S
MARSHALL FIELD'S
Minneapolis, MN
"Spring Shopping Bag"

Department Store
Over 500 mm

Stew Widdess-Marketing Sales
Promotion Director; Jack
Mugan-Advertising Director;
Connie Soteropulos-Executive Art
Director; Eric Erickson-Copy
Chief/Writer; Cheryl Watson-Art
Director; Vicky Rossi-Writer

Finalist

DAYTON'S HUDSON'S
MARSHALL FIELD'S
Minneapolis, MN
"Bridal Registry"

Department Store
Over 500 mm

Stew Widdess-Marketing Sales
Promotion Director; Jack
Mugan-Advertising Director;
Connie Soteropulos-Executive Art
Director; Eric Erickson-Copy
Chief; Elizabeth Baldwin-Art
Director; Lisa Christensen-Writer

Winner

MACY'S SOUTH/BULLOCK'S
Atlanta, GA
"A Distance Beyond
Autumn/Scotland 1990"

Department Store
Over 500 mm

Helane Blumfield-Creative
Director; Joseph Garbarino-Sr
VP/Sales Promotion Director

Finalist

BRITCHES
Herndon, VA
"The World's Biggest Bomber"

Apparel Specialty Store
50-100 mm

Susan Wallert Rushford-Marketing
Sales Promotion Director; Donna
Reid Nogay-Advertising Director;
Kim Gallagher-Copy Chief; Emily
Russell-Assistant Art Director;
Ramon Matheu-Illustrator
AGENCY: EXTENSION 229:
Suzanne K. Egan-Account
Executive; Laura
Ciccone-Production Manager
PRODUCTION: WESTLAND

Finalist

EDWARD J. DEBARTOLO
Youngstown, OH
"Good Neighbors"

Shopping Center

Mary B.
Rutkoski-Director/Shopping
Center Marketing
AGENCY: G S & B ADVERTISING:
Julio Blanco, Bruce
Fitzgerald-Creative Directors;
David Forest-Copy Chief; Evan
Contorakes-Account Executive;
Rudy Estripeaut-Production
Manager; Illustrator-Rhonda Voo

Finalist

DAYTON'S HUDSON'S
MARSHALL FIELD'S
Minneapolis, MN
"College Recruiting"

Department Store
Over 500 mm

Stew Widdess-Marketing Sales
Promotion Director; Jack
Mugan-Advertising Director;
Connie Soteropulos-Executive Art
Director; Eric Erickson-Copy
Chief; Matt Eller-Art Director

Finalist

SAKS FIFTH AVENUE
New York, NY
"Cross-Cultures"

Apparel Specialty Store
Over 500 mm

William Berta-Marketing Sales
Promotion Director; Bette
Chabot-Advertising Director;
Rebecca Wong Young-Creative
Director; Susan Alai-Copy Chief;
Larry Lobaugh-Art Director;
Marilyn Bai-Producer/Director;
Suzanne Pandjiris-Styling
Manager; Beth Wagshul-Copywriter

Finalist

DAYTON'S HUDSON'S
MARSHALL FIELD'S
Minneapolis, MN
"Evan Picone Fall '90"

Department Store
Over 500 mm

Kristin Staubitz-In Store Media
Manager/Executive Producer;
Brenda Locher-Associate Producer;
PRODUCTION: THINMAN: Geoffrey
Madeja-Director Producer

 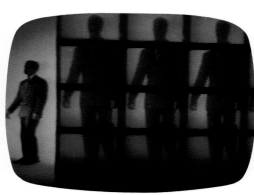

C R E A T I V I T Y

We're wondering today if anyone in the business has any misconceptions about the importance of imagination and the value of good talent (art and copy) in advertising. How high do you rate these qualities? Where do they stand in relation to the purpose of advertising?

The key to this controversy is in the word "purpose." (Yes, there is a controversy.) There are people in high places in our craft who lack the gift of imagination . . . and are shy on talent. And, because they haven't personal attributes in these directions, they do not understand those who have. That stands to reason. A six-year-old may stand before Rembrandt's "Night Watch" and have no real feeling for what he sees. And, if he has any comment to make, might say, "Look at that funny man." In so saying, he will have made a truthful observation. The point is, there is more than that to the subject.

We've all heard it said that the average mentality of our newspaper audience rates at eleven years. That's a cliche and a libel. It has done much to disparage good advertising in this otherwise enlightened United States. We continually *under*-estimate our audience if we hold to this concept. Moreover, we have no quarrel with people who insist they must create advertising at a child's mental level. We think an eleven-year-old will react without inhibition to elements of drama and imagination. We quarrel violently with those in our midst who insist on filling white space with endless dullness, drab and deadly, and calling it advertising. They say, "It sells." "It tells the facts." "It describes the merchandise."

We need not elaborate that no printed message, in coarse 60-line screen, black on newsprint, can *ever* "describe the merchandise" or "tell the facts." How can an advertisement do justice to the smooth, silky, deluxe finish of a superb white refrigerator? Only physical touch and sight can begin to understand the "facts" or appreciate the details. An advertisement at its superlative best is only a shadow, a reflection of the real thing. The real thing *sells*. Heaven is kind to us because it has given humans the power of imagination. And, as we present shadows in newspaper space, our imaginative readers visualize the reality in store for them. So they come to see, to feel, to be pleased, to be *sold. In the store* . . . where sales are made.

So much for the nonsense of insisting that advertising can do anything, but anything, beyond generating and creating enough persuasion to go down and see the merchandise. It's so utterly shortsighted for anyone to go on and on insisting that advertising has to "sell." Advertising can't sell. The only thing advertising can sell is *the idea* that very possibly this merchandise fulfills my need and therefore I'm persuaded to find out. That's *all* we can do. When we talk about the *purpose* of advertising we mean just this. If advertising can accomplish *this purpose* it has done all that can be expected of a printed message on newspaper stock.

Let's have no mistaken notions. The importance of descriptive copy and factual illustrations cannot be overestimated. We have to be realistic and honest in our approach to our readers. We have to supply the basis on which the reader builds via his own imagination, the desire for this merchandise.

There's absolutely nothing complicated about this. Those advertisers who can influence the readers' imagination most effectively are the ones who get their merchandise sold. Not that the physical advertisement made the sale. Not at all. It provided the basis. It set the wheels in motion. It stimulated the imagination. It awakened the desire.

M. Seklemian
(circa 1955)

Television

Winner

BLOOMINGDALE'S
New York, NY
"Sale TV"

Action/Price Ad
Department Store
Over 500 mm

Gordon Cooke-Executive VP/Sales
Promotion; Wendy Levine-Media
Director; John C. Jay-Sr
VP/Creative Director; Jill
Glover-Stylist
AGENCY: GREY ADVERTISING:
Doug Bartow-Art Director; Ed
Taussig-Copy Chief; Nina
Kessler-Account Executive; Susan
Marber-Account Supervisor
PRODUCTION: Douglas
Kieve-Director

Winner

BLOOMINGDALE'S
New York, NY
"Sport Story"

Action/Price Ad
Department Store
Over 500 mm

Gordon Cooke-Executive VP/Sales
Promotion; Wendy Levine-Media
Director; John C. Jay-Senior
VP/Creative Director; Jill
Glover-Stylist
AGENCY: GREY ADVERTISING:
Doug Bartow-Art Director; Ed
Taussig-Copy Chief; Nina
Kessler-Account Executive; Susan
Marber-Account Supervisor;
Michel Comte-Director

Winner

MACY'S NORTHEAST
New York, NY
"White Flower Day"

Action/Price Ad
Department Store
Over 500 mm

Steven Kornajcik-Marketing Sales
Promotion Director; Don
Marner-Copy Chief; Rose Mus-Art
Director; Ed Sheehan-Post
Production Producer

 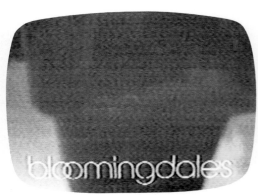

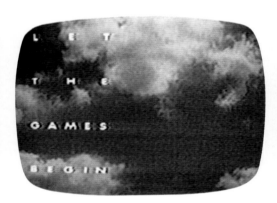

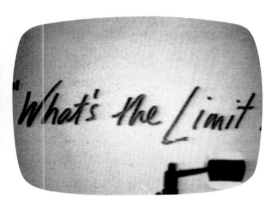

Winner

TARGET
Minneapolis, MN
"Thanksgiving"

Action/Price Ad
Mass Merchandiser
Over 500 mm

Target Advertising

Finalist

UPTONS
Norcross, GA
"Two Day Sale Archie, Archie"

Action/Price Ad
Department Store
100-250 mm

Ruth Hines-Sales Promotion
Director; Rosa Ravelo-Creative
Manager; Melinda
Martin-Assistant
Manager/Broadcast; Clara
Banas-Executive Producer; Michael
Paxton-Producer/Editor

Winner

WOODFIELD SHOPPING
CENTER
Schaumburg, IL
"Time Honored"

Cable
Shopping Center

Betty Bryant-Marketing Director
AGENCY: SAFFER/USA: Eric
Revels-Art Director; Sandra
Soczyk-Copy Chief; Kim
Gryka-Account Executive; Colleen
Griffin-Production Manager

Finalist

SAM GOODY
Minneapolis, MN
"Country to Blues, Comedy To
Drama, Adventure to Horror"

Cable
Other Specialty Store
Over 500 mm

Bonnie J. Burton-VP/
Advertising/Marketing; Mike
Stadelman, Wayne Wilcox-Creative
Directors
AGENCY: PETERSON PEARSON
MILLA: Dave
Peterson-Creative/Art Director;
Joe Milla -Copy Chief; Tim
Pearson-Account Executive; Ardie
Kramer-Production Manager
PRODUCTION: JONES
PRODUCTIONS: Jim Lynd-Director

Winner

BLACK PHOTO
Markham, Canada
"1989 Christmas"

Campaign
Other Specialty Store
100-250 mm

Bryan Black-Marketing Sales
Promotion Director
AGENCY: SAFFER ADVERTISING:
Trevor Goodgoll-Creative Director;
Cam Levalk-Copy Chief John
Auriemma-Production Manager
PRODUCTION: AIR COMPANY:
Terry O'Kelly-Producer/Director;
Bruce Fleming-Engineer

Finalist

BP AMERICA
Cleveland, OH
"Fireworks; Skydevils;
Spectacle"

Campaign
Other Retailer
Over 500 mm

Nancy Heinen-Advertising Director
AGENCY: W. B. DONER: John
DeCerchio-Creative Director; Joe
Minnella-Art Director; Mike
Sullivan-Copy Chief; David
DeMuth-Account Executive; Rob
DeMilner-Production Manager;
Dale Silverberg-Writer
PRODUCTION: IAN MCDONALD

144

Winner

CANADIAN TIRE
Toronto, Canada
"Hockey, Paint,
Soap Box"

Campaign
Other Retailer
Over 500 mm

Tony Scala-Advertising Director;
Laurie Cook-Managing
Director/Advertising
AGENCY: W. B. DONER: Dan
Hackett-Creative/Art Director;
Mike Rutka-Creative
Director/Copy Chief; Tony Gaudin,
Stephen Pytel-Art Directors; Dave
Michalak, Steve Platto-Copy
Chiefs
PRODUCTION: PARTNERS: Phillip
Borsos-Director

Winner

HIGHLAND SUPERSTORES
Plymouth, MI
"Symposium; Lady's Man;
Boogie Man"

Campaign
Other Specialty Store
Over 500 mm

Frank Ferriolo-Advertising
Director
AGENCY: W. B. DONER: Dan
Hackett-Creative Director; Grant
Priehs-Art Director; Charles
Borghese-Copy Chief; Ross
Lerner-Account Executive; Hugh
Broder
PRODUCTION: STORY PICCOLO
GULINER: Mark Story-Director

Finalist

ECKERD DRUGS
Largo, FL
"In The Real World"

Campaign
Drug Stores
Over 500 mm

Betsi
O'Neill-Director-Advertising/Sales
Promotion; Julie
Gardner-Manager-Advertising/Mar
keting Services
AGENCY: W. B. DONER

Highland's low price guarantee says that we'll beat any competitor's price on anything we sell or it's yours free.

See store for details.

With a guarantee like this, can you afford not to look at Highland?℠

For those of us in the real world who need help looking good under pressure, there's Eckerd.

Winner

CUB FOODS
Stillwater, MN

"Western Lean,
Cub Cuisine, Produce/Apples"

Campaign
Food Retailers
Over 500 mm

Maureen Hooley-Advertising
Director
AGENCY: CHUCK RUHR
ADVERTISING: Bill
Johnson-Creative Director/Copy
Chief; Doug Lew-Art Director;
Arleen Kulis-Production Manager

Winner

JCPENNEY
Dallas, TX
"Fashion Comes
To Life"

Campaign
Department Store
Over 500 mm

AGENCY: AYER SOUTHWEST: Jim
Hradecky-Management Director
Creative Service; Matt
Manroe-Creative/Art Director; Don
Sedei-Creative Director; Holly Bea,
Shep Kellam-Copy Chiefs; Sally
Hotchkiss-Production Manager
PRODUCTION: DECTOR HIGGINS
COMPANY: Thom
Higgins-Director; Kenny
White-Music/Crushing

Finalist

MERVYN'S
Hayward, CA
"Cluster II, Cheetah Shoes"

Campaign
Department Store
Over 500 mm

Sue Sprunk-VP-Sales Promotion;
Pat Holt-Advertising Director;
Steven Proffitt-Creative Manager
AGENCY: COHEN/JOHNSON:
Howie Cohen-Creative Director;
George Roux-Art Director; Brier
White-Account Supervisor; Beverly
Chamberlain-Copywriter
PRODUCTION:
RAWI/SHERMAN/IPS: David
Herrington-Photographer; Phil
Brown-Producer; George
Roux-Director

Winner

KOHL'S DEPARTMENT STORE
Menomonee Falls, WI
"The Big One"

Campaign
Department Store
Over 500 mm

Don Oscarson-VP Marketing; Glen
Guszkowski-VP Advertising;
Kirsten Karraker-Broadcast
Manager
AGENCY: WILLIAM EISNER: Bill
Eisner-Creative Director; Tim
O'Brien-Copy Chief; Wyn Becker,
Michael Fratantuno-Account
Executives; Kristine Masta, Cathy
Braun, John Tanner-Others
PRODUCTION: MARX
PRODUCTION CENTER: Bill
Eisner-Director

Winner

NORDSTROM
Seattle, WA
"Menswear"

Campaign
Apparel Specialty Store
Over 500 mm

Cindy Demme-Sales Promotion
Director; Linda Toschi
Finn-Advertising Director; Randy
Mecham-Copy Chief; Cheryl Fujii
Zahniser-Corporate Art Director
AGENCY: ELGIN SYFERD: Pamela
Mason Davey-Creative Director;
Leann Ebe-Account Executive;
Trish Murray-Production Manager

Finalist

PARISIAN
Birmingham, AL
"Spring Image"

Campaign
Apparel Specialty Store
250-500 mm

Patty Bystrom-Marketing Sales
Promotion/Advertising Director
AGENCY: STEINER/BRESSLER:
John Zimmerman-Creative
Director/Copy Chief; Ginger
Sims-Account Executive/Producer;
Jeff Steinborn-Photographer

Winner

RED ROOF INNS
Hilliard, OH
"The Wall, Sousa, Desk Clerk"

Campaign
Other Retailer
250-500 mm

D. Wible-Advertising Director
AGENCY: W. B. DONER: Mike
Sullivan-Creative Director; Chris
Lozen-Art Director; Greg
Marchi-Account Executive; Dan
Barbieri-Production Manager;
Mark Beyer, Bary Wolfson-Others
PRODUCTION: HIGHLIGHT
COMMERCIALS: David
Steinberg-Director

Finalist

SEARS
Chicago, IL
"House One"

Campaign
Mass Merchandiser
Over 500 mm

Velta Kopocek-Producer
AGENCY: OGILVY & MATHER: John
Gottschalk-Art Director; Phil
Bodwell-Producer; Ruth
O'Boyle-Writer

Winner

CUB FOODS
Stillwater, MN
"Western Lean"

Image/Positioning Ad
Food Retailers
Over 500 mm

AGENCY: CHUCK RUHR
ADVERTISING: Bill
Johnson-Creative Director/Copy
Chief; Doug Lew-Art Director;
Arleen Kulis-Production Manager

Winner

FAN FAIR SHOES
Elm Grove, WI
"Six Monks"

Image/Positioning Ad
Apparel Specialty Store
10-50 mm

Keith Harmon-Marketing Sales
Promotion Director
AGENCY: MCDONALD DAVIS:
Chuck Schiller-Creative Director;
Peter Klabunde-Art Director; Joe
Locher-Copy Chief/Production
Manager; Larry Swanlund-Account
Executive
PRODUCTION: STRIPES/DIVISION
OF PARTNERS

Winner

TARGET
Minneapolis, MN
"High Dive"

Image/Positioning Ad
Mass Merchandiser
Over 500 mm

Target Advertising

Winner

TOYS "R" US
Paramus, NJ
"I Don't Want To Grow Up I'm a
Toys "R" Us Kid"

Image/Positioning Ad
Other Specialty Store
Over 500 mm

Ernie Speranza-VP/Marketing
Sales Promotion; Pam
Troxel-Advertising Director
AGENCY: J. WALTER THOMPSON:
Linda Kaplan-Creative Director

Winner

TWIN VALU/ SHOPKO STORES
Green Bay, WI
"It's Just You; Ceramics;
Lettuce"

Image/Positioning Ad
Other Retailer
50-100 mm

Gene Bankers-Advertising Director
AGENCY: W. B. DONER: Dan
Hackett-Creative/Art Director;
Mike Rutka-Creative Director;
Dave Michalak, Gail Offen-Copy
Chiefs; Monica Tysell-Account
Executive; Kurt Kulas-Production
Manager
PRODUCTION: STORY PICCOLO
GULINER: Mark Story-Director

Finalist

BAYSHORE MALL
Whitefish Bay, WI
"Where Can I Go"

Image/Positioning Ad
Shopping Center

Rebecca Powell-General Manager;
Michael Jonas-Marketing Director
AGENCY: WILLIAM EISNER: Bill
Eisner-Creative
Director/Photographer; John
Tanner-Copy Chief; Jan
Frank-Account Executive; Kristine
Masta, Cathy Braun-Others
PRODUCTION: EISNER
RECORDING STUDIO: John
Tanner-Composer; Bill
Eisner-Producer/
Director

Finalist

ZELLERS
Montreal, Canada
"Worker"

Image/Positioning Ad
Mass Merchandiser
Over 500 mm

Garnet
Kinch-VP/Sales-Promotion; Dave
Middleton-Advertising Director
AGENCY: PADULO ADVERTISING:
Doug Moen-Creative Director;
Raymond Dion-Art Director; Gord
Steventon-Account Director;
Johnny Chambers-Producer
PRODUCTION: PAINTED HORSE:
Stephen Bower-Cinematographer;
Andrea Hubert-Producer; Paul
Cade-Director

Finalist

NUVISION
Flint, MI
"Chuck Hildebrand"

Image/Positioning Ad
Other Specialty Store
10-50 mm

George Ramos-Advertising Director
AGENCY: W.B. DONER: Gary
Wolfson-Creative Director; Mark
Freeman-Art Director; David
Vawter-Copy Chief; Vera
Yardley-Account Executive; Dan
Barbieri-Production Manager
PRODUCTION: MICHAEL DANIEL
CO.: Mark Pisnarski-Director

Finalist

BELLEVUE CENTER
Nashville, TN
"Believe It"

Image/Positioning Ad
Shopping Center

Pat Ledford-Marketing Sales
Promotion Director
AGENCY: ERICSON MARKETING
COMMUNICATIONS: Arthur
Taylor-Creative Director; Martica
Griffin-Art Director; Tom
Chmielewski-Copy Chief; Phil
Martin-Account Executive;
PRODUCTION: HOMEMADE
FILMS: Randy
Towers-Photographer; Joe
Ramey-Producer/Director

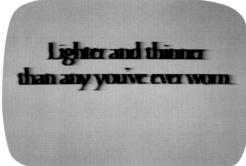

CREATIVITY

We're all so busy plying our trade . . . that sometimes we obligate ourselves too much to what's corporately known as "measurable, productive work." We thus neglect seeking creative inspiration from outside sources.

If you have found yourself in such a rut . . . then, *break out!* If you want your advertising ideas to remain fresh . . . if you ponder that the sources for ideas seem to be drying up . . . then it's time to go out on a creative binge. Get theater tickets — for on- or off-Broadway. Is a touring company or ballet corp. coming through your town for a limited engagement? Make time to attend. Use a weekend . . . take an extra day. Travel to someplace else in these vast 50 states . . . and get a new perspective on things.

Have you been to any of our parks? Yosemite? Zion? Grand Canyon? You've never been to Santa Fe, New Mexico? Whether you make it during the summer Opera Festival or not . . . you'll still be overwhelmed by the landscape, colors, pottery, paintings, crafts . . . the town, the architecture, the people. You'll feel inspired to make your copy — poetry . . . and your layouts, works of art.

One very extraordinary source of inspiration is just halfway between San Diego and Los Angeles in Laguna Beach. Every summer (for over 50 years), at an outdoor amphitheater, cooled by breezes from the Pacific Ocean . . . master works of great artists and artisans are re-created upon the stage: In full life-size and featuring live, human models.

The annual two-month event (July and August) is called "The Pageant of the Masters," presented by the Festival of Arts of Laguna Beach, CA.

Try to imagine Claude Monet's "Boat at Giverny." The music begins (a full polished and professional orchestra) . . . the curtain parts, and the impeccably designed lighting reveals the masterpiece in stunning lifesize proportions. The three women depicted in the boat are real people — costumed and "painted" so they appear as integral parts of the Monet's own brushstrokes.

You raise your binoculars to your eyes. You want to see if any of the women move . . . or blink. How can they stay so still? Where does her arm and the brushstrokes of the sleeve begin?

Over two dozen pieces of art are presented in this manner. Not only paintings. There were Victorian Valentines, a piece of Steuben glass, Gene Moore's Tiffany Circus Collection, an Etruscan fresco and an intricate Egyptian necklace. (Yes all . . . life size . . . and alive.)

If you can't make it to Laguna, then find an arts festival that's within driving distance of your address. Check the culture calender of your newspaper or your "city" magazine and find some event you never ever would have thought to attend. Experience something that ordinarily would never be your cup of tea; because it might just help you do a better job of earning your bread and butter!

Ideas and inspiration are everywhere. You need only seek them out. Often . . . you need only be alert and pay attention. Watch people. Listen to conversations. If you bury your head in a book when you travel, that's a no-no. Talk to people — especially those who appear to come from places or backgrounds that are unfamiliar. You'll get new insights and new ideas. And more than that — you'll be surprised at what a good time you'll have.

And yes . . . (if you are not already doing this) . . . *always carry a pen and a small notebook in your pocket.* On a bus, on a plane, at a bar, near your bed, in your bathroom. When the creative idea comes — you'll want to capture it at the moment of inspiration!

Joan Salb

Radio

"Self Help"

ANNCR:	Hi, once again I'm inviting everyone in America to 7-Eleven's Open House. A whole month of fun, great deals and more. Today, I'm calling David Moss from Royal Oak, Michigan.
SFX:	PHONE RINGING
MAN:	Hello, Self-Help Hotline. Can I help you?
ANNCR:	Oh, sorry. Wrong number.
MAN:	No, don't hang up. I want to help.
ANNCR:	Actually I was calling about 7-Eleven's Open House and what a great time it is.
MAN:	It sound's to me like you're reaching out for help.
ANNCR:	No, no . . . see at our Open House, you can discover one of the best and freshest cups of coffee around.
MAN:	Really, perhaps you'd care to probe deeper and find out why you feel that way.
ANNCR:	Well, at 7-Eleven, every pot's brewed fresh from carefully selected coffee beans ground in the store.
MAN:	Now why don't you tell me why you really called?
ANNCR:	Listen, this is crazy.
MAN:	I prefer not to use that word.
ANNCR:	I'm sorry . . . I'm just . . . I'm just (BREAKS DOWN) working so hard.
MAN:	I know. I know.
ANNCR:	Do you? Do you know what it's like to call everyone in America?
MAN:	Hey, I'm here for you.
ANNCR:	Don't miss 7-Eleven's Open House. Where you're invited to save on a 20-ounce cup of fresh-brewed coffee for just 69 cents. At participating stores for a limited time only.

"Class Reunion"

ANNCR:	And now, Perry Drug presents yet another reason to Make It Easy: Precious Memories.
SFX:	RESTAURANT AT LUNCHTIME
WOMAN 1:	Hi. Sorry I'm late but I had to stop at Perry.
WOMAN 2:	Oh, whadja get?
WOMAN 1:	Pictures of last weekend's class reunion which you missed.
WOMAN 2:	Oooh, I'm dying to see.
WOMAN 1:	You're gonna die alright. Look at this one. Carl Fanzer and Sandy Troutweiler . . .
WOMAN 2:	Geek alert, geek alert!
WOMAN 1:	It's a great picture, though.
WOMAN 2:	Yeah, it's gotta be hard to reproduce skin that pale.
ANNCR:	Perry Drug Photo Processing uses only the Kodak Colorwatch System and Kodak paper, for colors as vivid as your memories.
WOMAN 1:	Here's a blast from *your* past. Glenn Underwood.
WOMAN 2:	Oh, noooo.
WOMAN 1:	Shamu, Shamu, it's feeding time . . .
ANNCR:	And Perry's photo experts are always close at hand, to help make your pictures look great . . . whether you want them to or not.
WOMAN 1:	Oh, and look. Here's Gail Offenhauser, Legend in Her Very Own Mind.
WOMAN 2:	Gee. She looks better than ever doesn't she?
WOMAN 1:	I know. Not a wrinkle anywhere . . .
BOTH:	BURN IT!!
ANNCR:	So for top quality photo processing, make it easy. Make it Perry.

Winner
HIGHLAND SUPERSTORES
Plymouth, MI
"Can't Get No"

Action/Price Ad
Other Specialty Store
Over 500 mm

Frank Ferriolo-Advertising
Director
AGENCY: W.B. DONER: Dan
Hackett, Mike Rutka-Creative
Directors; Mark Simon, Michael
Zadoorian-Copy Chief/Producers;
Ross Lerner-Account Executive

Winner
ECKERD DRUGS
Clearwater, FL
"Connoisseur"

Action/Price Ad
Drug Stores
Over 500 mm

Julie Gardner-Advertising Director
AGENCY: W B DONER: Dan
Hackett, Mike Rutka-Creative
Directors; Michael
Zadoorian-Copy Chief/Production
Manager; Mark Simon-Copy Chief;
Shelly Manes-Account Executive

"Can't Get No"

ANNCR:	Highland Superstore's Blockbuster Weekend Of Savings is so big, we wanted someone really big to promote it. Someone like THE ROLLING STONES! But they refused. So, without further ado, please give it up for: Mick Jagorski & The Strolling Tones.
SFX:	ACCORDION BEING PLAYED
STAN:	(SINGING TO A POLKA BEAT) Can't get no, can't get no, can't get no savings like these. A weekend of big savings on brand name stuff like this. On Sony, on Kenwood, on Panasonic, Bose, Mitsubishi, G.E., RCA, JVC.
	(SPOKEN) That's right friends, now thru Saturday, you can save like dis: (:10 INSERT) Hey, hey, hey, dat's what I say.
ANNCR:	Highland's Blockbuster Weekend of Savings. With prices like these, can you afford not to look at Highland?
STAN:	No, no, no
SFX:	(ACCORDION FINISH)
STAN:	C'mon mates, let's trash the place!

"Connoisseur"

	(CLASSICAL MUSIC OVER OPENING)
ANNCR:	Eckerd presents "The Connoisseur." Today we speak to sun tan lotion connoisseur, Sebastian Paba.
SEBASTIAN:	Well, first off, we have a little domestic lotion. Bouncy, yet intriguing. I'll open it. (SFX: POP) Would you care to smell the cap?
ANNCR:	It's okay. Now what would this lotion go well with?
SEBASTIAN:	It's a good basic lotion. (SFX: SNIFF) I'd say it's about an SPF 15. It goes well with boating, picnics, the beach, most of your outdoor activities.
ANNCR:	Now you can get this lotion pretty much anywhere?
SEBASTIAN:	Sir, you mock me with your insensitivity. The finest selection of lotions are, of course, at Eckerd. This week at Eckerd, get $1.00 off any of the fine Bain De Soliel products, creams, gel, oils and savings. They're luxuriously light, yet robust.
ANNCR:	That's good through June 2.
SEBASTIAN:	Yes, yes, whatever. Let's try another. (SFX: POP) Ah, an import. Full bodied, but also introspective. Would you like to try some?
ANNCR:	No, no thanks.
SEBASTIAN:	I insist!
SFX:	(SQUIRT)
ANNCR:	That was my best suit!
SEBASTIAN:	Hmm, I should have let it breathe first.
(:09 TAGS)	

Winner

LAMONTS
Bellevue, WA
"Pardon Me"

Action/Price Ad
Apparel Specialty Store
100-250 mm

Brent Frerichs-VP
Advertising/Marketing/Writer
PRODUCTION: STEVE LAWSON

Winner

DAYTON'S HUDSON'S
MARSHALL FIELD'S
Minneapolis, MN
"Eternity"
13 Hour Sale

Action/Price Ad
Department Store
Over 500 mm

Stewart Widdess-VP/Marketing;
Jack Mugan-Creative Director
AGENCY: DAYTON HUDSON
PRODUCTION: PIDGIN: Gary
Jensen-Director/Producer
MUSIC: The Coast

"Pardon Me"

(We hear sounds of the English countryside. Birds singing, possibly a flute or violin in the background. We hear two cars approaching each other and come to a stop.)

ENGLISH GENTLEMAN 1
Pardon me, but do you have Lamonts grey coupon?

ENGLISH GENTLEMAN 2
Why, yes I do.

(Cut away to background music of violins)

ANNOUNCER: (British accent)

People absolutely everywhere are clamoring for the exquisite savings of Lamonts $10 on $25 grey coupon.

Lamonts grey coupon is a $10 savings on any purchase of Lamonts regular, sale or clearance merchandise totalling $25 or more.

For example, if a particular item was already sale priced, and your purchase totalled at least $25, you would save another $10 in addition to sale prices.

Lamonts $10 on $25 grey coupon is so special, so extraordinary that the offer is valid Saturday only, and only from 9 a.m. until 1 p.m.

Lamonts $10 on $25 grey coupon . . . $10 savings on any purchase $25 or more, Saturday only, at Lamonts.

(Cut violin background . . . go to background noise of train travelling across tracks, as if heard from inside the train. Distant train whistle.)

ENGLISH GENTLEMAN 1
Pardon me, but do you have Lamonts grey coupon?

WOMAN 1
Buy your own newspaper, buddy, and quit mooching off the kindness of others, why don't you?

(Cut back to violin music)

Lamonts $10 on $25 grey coupon. You'll find it in today's newspaper.

(Violin strings out)

"Eternity"

MUSIC:	"Tick" . . . "Tock" . . . "Tick" . . . "Tock" . . . (Sung like a gregorian chant, extremely slowly paced, opens spot and then continues under announcer)
ANNCR:	Thirteen hours. Sometimes it can seem like an eternity. Imagine thirteen hours in the car with your children.
	(Tick . . . Tock)
	Thirteen hours listening to your neighbor's dog.
	(Tick . . . Tock)
	Thirteen hours waiting for the IRS to complete your audit.
	(Tick . . . Tock)
	But there's one time when thirteen hours seems like no time.
	(Singers transition to soprano with an jazz-like sound. They continue to go "Tick . . . Tock" more frantically.)
	Marshall Field's / Dayton's / Hudson's Thirteen Hour Sale. All you've got is thirteen hours to find incredible buys in select departments throughout the store. Thirteen hours that seem to pass all too quickly.
	So hurry into Marshall Field's / Dayton's / Hudson's Thirteen Hour Sale. If you miss it, it could be a long wait for the next one.
MUSIC:	(singers return to slow pace. Gregorian chant returns as soprano's fade out). "Tick" . . . "Tock" . . . "Tick" . . . fade under)
ANNCR:	The Thirteen Hour Sale at Marshall Field's / Dayton's / Hudson's.
	Starts Wednesday (Thursday) (Friday) Ends Wednesday (Thursday) (Friday)
MUSIC:	Marshall Field's. Marshall Field's (fade out) Dayton's tick, tick, tickity knows you. Hudson's tick, tick, tickity knows you.

Finalist

KOHL'S DEPARTMENT
STORES
Menomonee Falls, WI
"Game Show"

Action/Price Ad
Department Store
Over 500 mm

Don Oscarson-Senior
VP/Marketing; Glen
Guszkowski-VP Advertising;
Kirsten Karraker-Broadcast
Manager

AGENCY: WILLIAM EISNER: Bill
Eisner-Creative Director; Tim
O'Brien-Copy Chief; John
Tanner-Production Manager; Wyn
Becker, Michael
Fratantuno-Account Executives
PRODUCTION: EISNER
RECORDING STUDIO:Tim
O'Brien-Producer

"Game Show"

GAME SHOW HOST: Our final category . . . famous land-marks. For 100, where is le Terra Burra de la . . . BEEP.

MAN: Bulgaria.

HOST: Very good. And where would one find the Mount Car . . . BEEP.

WOMAN: Bangledesh . . .

HOST:: The country where . . . BEEP.

WOMAN: Bolivia.

HOST: The Kohl's Department Store . . . BEEP . . . Bob?!

MAN: Yes?

HOST: You hit the buzzer.

MAN: I did?

HOST: Now come on folks. Where can you find great savings on hundreds of brand name items in every department. BEEP

WOMAN: Kohl's!

MAN: Yes. Kohl's IS the place for great savings . . . but where can you *find* Kohl's. BEEP

WOMAN: Uh, the French Sierra?

HOST: Uh, no. We're talking about the Grand Rapids Kohl's. BEEP

MAN: Grand Rapids.

HOST: Yes but where in Grand Rapids.?!!!

WOMAN: Touchy . . .

HOST: Here's a hint. Woodland. BEEP

MAN: The Forest?

HOST: No. The Woodland *Mall.* BEEP

WOMAN: In Woodland Mall.

HOST: Close. BEEP

MAN: By Woodland Mall.

HOST: Closer . . . BEEP

WOMAN: Atop Woodland Mall?

HOST: Right!!! And what do we have for them Johnnie?

ANNCR: For everyone, it's great savings on hundreds of brand name items . . . Lees, Levis, Reeboks, Nike, Sony, Cherokee, Healthtex . . . plus great gifts for Father's Day. At the amazing Kohl's Department Store . . . behind the Woodland Mall in GR . . . BEEP

WOMAN: FADING OUT Grand Rapids.

HOST: Good. But the game is . . . BEEP

MAN: Over?

HOST: Cute . . . yes that's very . . . BEEP

WOMAN: funny? . . . BEEP

MAN: Maddenning?

Winner

CUB FOODS
Stillwater, MN
"Fresh Walleye"

Action/Price Ad
Food Retailers
Over 500 mm

Maureen Hooley-Advertising
Director
AGENCY: CHUCK RUHR
ADVERTISING: Bill
Johnson-Creative Director; Josh
Denberg-Copy Chief

Winner

BERGNER'S
Milwaukee, WI
"Back To School Sale"

Campaign
Department Store
Over 500 mm

Patti Washcovick-VP Creative
Services Director

"Fresh Walleye/Greenbay"

SFX:	Mosquito buzzing
ANNCR:	There are two ways to get fresh Walleye Pike from Wisconsin's lakes this summer.
	The first way is to get up at the crack of dawn put on your fishing gear, pack the car, hitch the boat, drive to the lake, and swat mosquitos. Stop for bait, get your license, swat mosquitos, launch the boat, swat mosquitos, rig your rod, swat mosquitos, cast your lure, swat mosquitos, sit on your duff, swat mosquitos, swat a horsefly, sit on your duff, swat the guy next to you, hook a fish, fight the fish, fight mosquitos, land the fish and hope it's a walleye big enough to bring home.
	Or, you could go to Cub Foods where we've done all that for you. So the fish are fresh, there are no hassles and of course . . .
SFX:	(Swat)
ANNCR:	There are no mosquitos.
ANNCR:	Land fresh Walleye Pike filets this week at Cub Foods for only $3.99/lb. That's right, just $3.99/lb. for great tasting Walleye filets. Filets thru May. The Cub Foods on East and West Mason Street in Greenbay and next to Shopko in Appleton.
	Quantity rights reserved.

"K-I-D-Z/#1"

RICHIE:	Welcome back to (SING CALL LETTERS) K-I-D-Z, Kids Radio. I'm Richie comin' at ya live from my rec. room. (SFX: BICYCLE BELL) Today's topic: "Cool at School." You're on the air . . .
AMY:	Richie help! My mom's so uncool. She talkin' "cute dresses" . . . y-y-y-uck!
RICHIE:	Easy . . . Just take her to Bergner's Back-To-School Sale for 30% Off Girl's Lee Jeans. An', if she says **anything** like "sensible shoes" . . .
AMY:	Oooh, gro-o-ss!!!
RICHIE:	. . . get her to 25% savings on all kid's backpacks and bags.
AMY:	Richie, you're awesome.
RICHIE:	(SING) K-I-D-Z . . . stay tuned for more cool news from Bergner's Back-To-School Sale.

"K-I-D-Z/#2"

RICHIE:	Hey . . . Richie here on (SING CALL LETTERS) K-I-D-Z Kids Radio, live from my rec. room. (SFX: BICYCLE BELL) Today's topic: "School Cool" . . . you're on the air . . .
JASON:	Hey Dude . . . I tell my mom I have to look totally bodacious and she gives me this weird look.
RICHIE:	Easy . . . tell her it's like "groovy" and take her to Bergner's Back-To-School Sale for 25% savings on all boys Levi separates.
JASON:	Radical!
RICHIE:	Then head for Hush Puppy fleece separates . . . all 20% Off.
JASON:	Richie, you're my main man.
RICHIE:	(SING) K-I-D-Z . . . stay tuned for more cool news from Bergner's Back-To-School Sale.

"K-I-D-Z/#3"

RICHIE: Hey . . . live from my rec. room, it's (SING CALL LETTERS) K-I-D-Z Kids Radio, I'm Richie . . . (SFX: BICYCLE BELL) . . . Today's topic: "Cool for School" . . . you're on the air . . .

HORACE: Richard, I can't spend another semester as a nerd but my mother just doesn't understand cool.

RICHIE: Easy . . . just chill out and take your mom to Bergner's Back-To-School Sale for 25% savings on all boys "Bugle Boy" bottoms.

HORACE: Interesting.

RICHIE: Then butter her up with 30% Off all Buster Brown playwear.

HORACE: Bodacious, man!

RICHIE: What a dude! (SING) K-I-D-Z . . . stay tuned for more cool news from Bergner's Back-To-School Sale.

"Young Men's #2"

(SFX: CAR ENGINE & HORN HONK)

MATTHEW: Hey, man . . . your Dad's new wheels . . . Too cool! So, good summer?
(SFX: CAR TAKING OFF, HOLD ENGINE SOUND UNDER)

KEVIN: Camp's sure different when you're a counsellor. You?

MATTHEW: In a word . . . (DREAMY) Melanie . . . I'm in love . . .

KEVIN: You got it bad, man. Better get to Bergner's and clean up your act. We'll start with Young Men's Levi 505's and 501 button flys at 20% Off.

MATTHEW: Did I tell you she has green eyes?

KEVIN: Then we'll hit the Santana sandwash shirts . . . just $18.99. And check out the awesome new finishes on Levi 505 fashion silhouettes . . . are you with me?

MATTHEW: Now if we happen to see Melanie at Bergner's Back-To-School Sale, we're cool . . . get it? . . . very together . . . no goofy stuff . . .

"Juniors"

(SFX: STORE B.G. SOUNDS UNDER THROUGHOUT)

GAIL: Wow . . . with Bergner's, we're gonna be s-o-o "in" for school. Melanie . . . check out these turtlenecks and fleece separates for juniors . . . just $11.99!

MELANIE: I wonder what Matthew's favorite color is?

GAIL: Him again? Yesss! . . . knit leggings, $15.99.

MELANIE: I like these cotton blend sweaters . . . $19.99 . . . Ma . . . Math . . . Gail, I'm going to faint . . . it's HIM!

GAIL: Him who?

MELANIE: (DESPERATELY TRYING TO BE CASUAL) Oh, hi Matthew . . . um, Bergner's Back-To-School Sale's . . . um . . . pretty awesome, huh?

GAIL: I used to have this best friend who I always shopped with . . .

"Young Men's #2"

(SFX: STORE B.G. SOUNDS UNDER THROUGHOUT)

KEVIN: Are we going to be the coolest dudes at school, or what? Man, Bergner's has great stuff. These Bojo pants are too much . . . $35.99 on sale.

MATTHEW: I wonder if Melanie likes movies?

KEVIN: Her, again? Yo, Matt . . . we're supposed to be getting cool.

MATTHEW: Well, I like . . .

KEVIN: Concrete textured sweaters . . . $29.99 . . . Yesss!

MATTHEW: Oh man, Kev . . . i-it's HER!

KEVIN: Her who?

MATTHEW: Melanie . . . uh, hi . . . you, um, look great . . .

KEVIN: Matt, I thought we came to Bergner's Back-To-School Sale to . . . Oh, hi there . . . you're? (OBVIOUSLY TAKEN WITH HER) . . . Gail . . . Gail . . . uh, Gail . . . so, (FADE) what school do you go to?

Winner

BURGER KING
Miami, FL
"Cowboy Moe;
Willie; Crystal; Twins"

Campaign
Food Retailers
Over 500 mm

AGENCY: UNIWORLD GROUP:
Creative Director; Valerie
Graves-Director-Creative Services;
Bill Allen-Copywriter; Robert
Shaffron, Radio Band-Agency
Producers; Darlene Samuels,
Carmine Johnston
PRODUCTION: RADIO BAND OF
AMERICA: (Harley Flaum, Dan
Price-Writer, Producer, Director;
Engineer: RBA's Alan Warner at
Penny Lane Studios

"Cowboy Moe"

SFX:	(STATIC, SOUNDS OF CHANNELS BEING SCANNED)
SINGERS:	B.K. Radio
FEMALE ANNCR:	Big Daddy B.K. He loves to break the rules.
BIG DADDY:	Let's go to the phones.
CALLER:	Hey, Big Daddy . . .
BIG DADDY:	That's me.
CALLER:	(LAUGHS) What do you get when you cross a kangaroo in a bikini with a singing orthodontist?
BIG DADDY:	A dial tone.
SFX:	(DIAL TONE)
SINGERS:	Big Daddy!
BIG DADDY:	Now, here's Willy with the weather.
WILLY:	Today, some sun, and tonight, deep, deep darkness.
BIG DADDY:	Very deep, Willy. Now for a traffic report with our eye in the sky, Accujack.
ACCUJACK:	(UNINTELLIGIBLE SOUNDS OF TRAFFIC REPORT OBSCURED BY PROPELLER NOISE)
BIG DADDY:	Thanks, Accujack.
SINGERS:	B.K. Radio
BIG DADDY:	Well if it isn't our friend, Cowboy Mo!
SFX:	(COWBOY MUSIC, HORSE NEIGHS)
COWBOY MO:	I'm ridin' out to Burger King for B.K. Doubles, beautiful double cheeseburgers with a choice of tasty toppings. You know in the old days, all we could do was throw Jack Cheese on a couple of steers and try to bite 'em as they passed. Talk about fast food.
BIG DADDY:	Got it, Mo. Get B.K. Doubles.
SINGERS:	B.K. Radio
SFX:	(STATIC, SOUNDS OF CHANNELS BEING SCANNED)

"Willie"

SINGERS:	BK Radio!
WOMAN:	Now, breaking all the rules all the time — Big Daddy BK!
BID DADDY:	First, here's Willie with weather.
WILLIE:	This morning, dawn broke.
SFX:	Glass shatters.
WILLIE:	Come sundown, night will fall . . .
SFX:	Sandbag thump!
BIG DADDY:	Very heavy, Willie.
SINGERS:	Big Daddy!
ANNC:	We interrupt this program for a *few words* from Burker King. Two Burgers for a Buck. Now back to our regular programming.
VOICE ON PHONE:	. . . she said "It takes three!" One to hold the lightbulb and two to hide the flashlight!
SFX:	Canned laughter.
BIG DADDY:	This just in. A deranged billionaire has been spotted giving away crisp hundred dollar bills on the corner of —
ANNC:	We interrupt this program to yet *more* words from Burger King. Two Burgers for a Buck at participating restaurants. Now back to our regular programming.
BIG DADDY:	Here's today's horoscope with Futura C.
MUSIC:	Sitar.
FUTURA:	Thank you Big Daddy. Aquarius, beware of —
ANNC:	We interrupt with *still more words* from Burger King. Two juicy, flame-broiled Burgers for one buck is for a limited time only.
BIG DADDY:	Somebody say limited time? I'm outta here.
VOICE::	In the middle of the broadcas—
ANNC:	We interrupt with *one final group of words* to say: Sometimes you gotta break the rules!
SFX:	Channel switching.

"Crystal"

SFX:	CHANNELS SWITCHING.
MUSIC:	BK Radio!
WOMAN:	Breaking hearts while he's breaking rules — Big Daddy BK!
BIG DADDY:	First, one of my favorite hits!
SFX:	SMACK!! (Ooowww!)
BIG DADDY:	Now, Mike at the movies.
MIKE:	Went with my wife last night. Action! Adventure! Rage! Drama!
BIG DADDY:	No kidding?
MIKE:	Then we go to the movies.
SONG:	BIG DADDY!
MUSIC:	NEW AGE, CHIMES, ETC.
CRYSTAL:	Ooommm...
BIG DADDY:	It's Crystal Karma! What's now?
CRYSTAL:	A delicious now sandwich has entered the collective consciousness, Big Daddy. The new BK Broiler at Burger King. Flame broiled all white meat chicken, with lettuce, tomato and ranch sauce on an oat bran bun, in an ecologically responsible package.
BIG DADDY:	Sounds good.
CRYSTAL:	And for a limited time at participating Burger King restaurants, buy one BK Broiler after 4PM, and get another for just 99¢ ... Very good karma, numerologically speaking.
BIG DADDY:	BK Broiler, huh?
CRYSTAL:	Best thing I've tasted. In this life.
BIG DADDY:	Sometimes, you've gotta break the rules.
SONG:	BK RADIO!
SFX:	CHANNEL SWITCHING.

"Twins"

SFX:	Channels Switching
MUSIC:	BK Radio!
WOMAN:	Breaking rules to beat the band — Big Daddy BK!
BIG DADDY:	Got a call on the "Looking for Love" line!
WOMAN ON PHONE:	Hi. I'm an SBW seeking an SBM with MBA or a PHD and two BDR's for TLC ASAP.
BIG DADDY:	Hope he can spell.
MUSIC:	Big Daddy!
MAN ON PHONE:	Bonjour, Big Daddy.
BID DADDY:	Leapin' Lizards, it's Larry the Linguist. Whatcha got?
LARRY:	New phrase I learned in French. "Je ne sais pas."
BID DADDY:	Tasty. What's it mean?
LARRY:	I don't know.
BIG DADDY:	Call back when you do!
MUSIC:	BK Radio!
TWINS (Unison):	Hi Big Daddy!
BIG DADDY:	It's the Thomas twins, Tommy and Tony! Where you been?
TWINS:	Burger King. We just had the new BK Double. The Mushroom Swiss Double Cheeseburger. Two flame broiled patties with sauteed mushrooms and two slices of processed Swiss cheese.
BIG DADDY:	Sounds too good. Mushroom Swiss, huh?
TWINS:	Yep.
BID DADDY:	Hey, which twin is Tony!
TWINS:	I am.
BIG DADDY:	Sometimes you've gotta break the rules.
MUSIC:	BK Radio!
SFX:	Channels switching.

Winner

XEROX
Rochester, NY
"What'd He Say?; Hunky
Dory; Salesman; Stodgy"

Campaign
Vendor
Over 500 mm

Chuck Blackmon-Marketing Sales
Promotion Director
PRODUCTION: RADIO BAND OF
AMERICA: Harley
Flaum-Producer/Writer; Dan
Price-Director/Writer; Alan
Vaner-Engineer

"What'd He Say?"

ANNC:	Before Xerox introduced the new 62 Series Typing System, making revisions was not so simple. And not very quiet either.
SFX:	Noisy typing pool . . . IBM's clacking up front . . .
SFX:	Buzz.
MALE:	(filtered) Attention typing pool: Do we have those *revisions* on my *report* yet?
FEMALE #1:	What'd he say?
FEMALE #2:	He said everywhere it reads "decisions" change it to "support."
GROUP:	Right!
ANNC:	The new 62 Series is a technological breakthrough that makes revisions easier. Because it's quiet. Unlike the ones in *this* office.
SFX:	Buzz
MALE:	Everywhere you typed the word "gross," change it to "net."
FEMALE #2:	Replace the word "toast" with the word "jet"!
GROUP:	Right!
ANNC:	And the new Xerox 62 Series Typing System makes every document you create simply perfect.
MALE:	Before you leave today, I'll need an original, and a copy.
FEMALE #2:	He wants a dirigible . . . and make it sloppy!!
GROUP:	(pause) . . . a what . . . huh . . . what . . . ?
ANNC:	The new Xerox 62 Series. The quiet typing system that makes document revisions easier. On everyone.

"Hunky Dory"

BOSS:	Gentlemen, the Hunky Dory Copier Company is in deep clam dip.
SALESMAN:	Boss?
BOSS:	Ms. Brotwurst from Research will fill us in.
MS. BROTWURST:	Our small business clientele is learning that, compared to *our* copiers, Xerox 50 Series offers deeper longterm tangibles.
BOSS, SALESMAN, MAN:	Huh?
MS. BROTWURST:	They're a better value.
BOSS, SALESMAN, MAN:	Oh.
BOSS:	How 'bout *our* 90 Day Warranty?
MS. BROTWURST:	Contextually piteous.
BOSS, SALESMAN, MAN:	Huh?
MS. BROTWURST:	Stinks.
BOSS, SALESMAN, MAN:	Oh.
MS. BROTWURST:	Xerox 50 Series Copiers have a *3-year* warranty. And *that* is *12 times* longer than *our* warranty.
SALESMAN:	*You're* forgetting our 15-Day cartridge warranty-
MS. BROTWURST:	And *you* are forgetting that Xerox guarantees your copies will be great from the first to the 10,000th or they'll replace the cartridge!
BOSS:	In a nutshell, Xerox is making like less than hotsy-totsy for Hunky Dory.
MS. BROTWURST:	I feel we can expect the prolongation of a non-munificent down-turn.
BOSS, SALESMAN, MAN:	Huh?
MS. BROTWURST:	We're in deep clam dip.
BOSS, SALESMAN, MAN:	Oh.
FADE	
ANNC	See your authorized Xerox agent now and learn more about the Xerox 50 Series desktop copiers.
LOGO	

"Salesman"

SFX:	Shop bell.
SALESMAN:	Good morning.
MAN:	Yes. I need a fax machine.
SALESMAN:	(Used car type): Well here's one that uses curly, messy, impossible-to-write-on paper.
MAN:	Uh . . . how about one that just uses *plain* paper . . . like Xerox?
SALESMAN:	Ah, but Xerox faxes don't curl up.
MAN:	Right . . .
SALESMAN:	Wrong! Faxes are *supposed* to curl up!
MEN:	Who says so?
SALESMAN:	It's right here in the *Book Of Curly Faxes.* Quote: "Faxes are supposed to curl up and be waxy and fuzzy, so don't buy a Xerox plain paper fax."
MAN:	You just made that up.
SALESMAN:	Did not. Here's another one, and I quote: "The salesman never makes things up."
MAN:	Oh, let me see that . . .
ANNC:	Xerox plain paper faxes come out fast, flat, clean and crisp on ordinary copier paper. So you can use your faxes right out of the machine without having to copy them first. Plus every Xerox fax is backed by our exclusive Satisfaction Guarantee.
SALESMAN:	Wait, I'm quoting again: "A curly fax in the hand is worth two in the bush . . ."
MAN:	. . . see you around . . .
SALESMAN:	Here's another one: "There once was a fax from Nantuckett . . ."
	AD LIB FADE
ANNC:	Plain paper. The Xerox fax. Plain and simple.
	XEROX LOGO
ANNC:	The document company.

"Stodgy"

SFX:	People milling, talking . . .
BOSS:	People, people, look at this fax? It's on plain paper!
ALL:	(At once) I didn't do it.
BOSS:	People . . . what's our company name?
ALL:	Stodgy, Stuffy, Stulted & Moldy, sir.
BOSS:	And our motto?
ALL:	We hate change. We hate it. Hate it. Hate it.
BOSS:	So where's our old waxy, curly fax machine?
TOM:	We bought a new Xerox plain paper fax machine, sir.
BOSS:	Did I hear the word *new*? People hold your tongues!
ALL:	(Holding tongues). You mean like this?
ANNC:	Xerox plain paper faxes come out fast, flat, clean and crisp on ordinary copier paper. So you can use your faxes right out of the machine without having to copy them first. Plus every Xerox fax is backed by our exclusive Satisfaction Guarantee.
BOSS:	Okay, people, a Xerox plain paper fax it is.
ALL:	Good choice sir . . .
BOSS:	After all, when it comes to business I never want to be considered even a little behind.
DOUG:	Oh you'll always be a *big* behind to us sir.
JOE:	That's right . . .
ANNC:	Plain paper. The Xerox fax. Plain and simple.
	XEROX LOGO
ANNC:	The document company.

Winner
KIDS "R" US
Paramus, NJ
"BTS; Wig; Mother-In-Law"
Campaign
Apparel Specialty Store
250-500 mm

Ernie Speranza-VP/Marketing;
Corey Romao-Advertising Director
AGENCY: GEER DUBOIS

"Wig"

ANNCR: At Kids "R" Us, we make it easy to shop for kid's clothes. Because we've got the largest selection of brand name kid's clothes, footwear and accessories around. All at everyday low prices. Shop at Kids "R" Us, and you can outfit an entire kid in just one stop. Shop someplace else, and it could take all afternoon just to find the right size.

And if it takes all afternoon, you're gonna leave that store in a pretty bad mood.

And if you leave that store in a bad mood, you won't be paying attention to your driving.

And if you're not paying attention, you might back into a fire hydrant.

And if you back into a fire hydrant, you'll have to wait for the police.

And if you have to wait for the police, you'll be late for your hairdresser.

And if you're late for your hairdresser, he'll be angry.

And if your hairdresser's angry, he could ruin your hair.

And if he ruins your hair, you're gonna need a wig.

Kids "R" Us or a wig! The choice is yours!

V/O: Choose Kids "R" Us. With our huge selection of brand name kids' clothes, all at everyday low prices, it obviously doesn't make sense to shop anyplace else.

"Mother-In-Law"

ANNCR: There's no better place to shop for kids' clothes than Kids "R" Us. Because at Kids "R" Us, we've got the largest selection of brand name kids' clothes around. And everything we sell, from clothing to footwear to accessories, is priced low everyday. Which means, if you don't shop at Kids "R" Us, you're gonna end up paying full price somewhere else.

And if you have to pay full price somewhere else, you're not going to have a lot of extra money.

And if you don't have a lot of extra money, you can't buy a new car.

And if you can't buy a new car, you'll have to keep your old one.

And if you keep driving that old thing, it'll eventually end up in the shop.

And when you take it to the shop, you're gonna need a lift home.

And if you need a lift home, you may have to call your mother-in-law.

And when your mother-in-law finds out your car's broken, she'll want to stay until it's fixed.

And that could take forever.

V/O: Kids "R" Us. With our huge selection of brand name kid's clothes, all at everyday low prices, it obviously doesn't make sense to shop anyplace else.

"Grand Opening"

ANNCR: A new Kids R Us is about to open near you. So you'll soon be able to shop from the world's largest selection of brand name kid's clothes, all at everyday low prices. So whether your newborn or your twelve year old needs anything from shoes or socks to shorts or shirts, you can find it at Kids R Us. And that's a good thing. Because, without a Kids R Us store near you, you'd probably have to shop in a department store.

And if you have to shop in a department store, you could have a hard time just finding the children's department.

And if you finally find the children's department, you'll be lucky if they've got what you're looking for.

And if they do happen to have what you're looking for, chances are it won't be in the right size.

And if you do find the right size, you'll never find your favorite color.

And if you do find the right color, and the right size . . . well . . . then you're gonna have to wait in line to check out.

And if you have to wait in line in a department store . . . that'll probably take . . . the rest of your life.

V/O: Kids R Us. With our huge selection of brand name kids' clothes, all at everyday low prices, it obviously doesn't make sense to shop anyplace else.

"Philosophy"

ANNCR: When it comes to shopping for kids' clothes, no other store can compare to Kids R Us. Because at Kids R Us, we've got the largest selection of brand name kids' clothes around. Like Levi's, Palmetto's, O.P., Osh Kosh and lots more. And our stores are so big and so well-stocked, you always find the right size and the right color.

So, if you can't find what you're looking for at Kids R Us, chances are it doesn't exist.

And if you're looking for something that doesn't exist, you must be a philosopher.

And if you're a philosopher, then you're probably related to Socrates.

And if you're related to Socrates, you must be from Greece.

And, if you're Greek, then you know what people are talking about when they say, "It's all Greek to me."

And if you understand that, then you probably understand this commercial.

And if you understand this commercial, then you already know why you should shop at Kids R Us.

V/O: Kids R Us. With our huge selection of brand name kids' clothes, all at everyday low prices, it obviously doesn't make sense to shop anyplace else.

Winner
BEST BUY
Bloomington, MN
"New Concept: Shark,
Checking, Name Brands"

Campaign
Other Specialty Store
Over 500 mm

Julie Engel-Advertising Director;
Kevin Gordon-Creative Director;
Lou Johnson-Copy Chief

"Shark"

BOSS	Here at Video Valueland you're on straight commission.
GUY:	I know.
BOSS:	It don't pay sell loss leaders.
GUY:	Nope.
BOSS:	'Cause you don't make a dime on the low-ball items in the ad.
GUY:	I know it.
BOSS:	Still want the job?
GUY:	Yes sir.
BOSS:	Then show me your stuff, kid.
GUY:	Well, I grab the first couple through the door. I ask the old lady if she's, by chance, Liz Taylor's younger sister. Then, I trade some war stories with the old man and steer 'em toward cheapo corner.
BOSS:	Then what?
GUY:	I show 'em the lima bean-colored TV and tell 'em it's real practical 'cause lima bean's a color that goes with anything.
BOSS:	Then?
GUY:	Then they tell me they want wood-grain instead, plus a remote. And I say, "I think we might just have that and . . .
BOSS:	*And* WHAT?
GUY:	And I sell 'em the most profitable TV we got and you owe me fifty bucks. (FADING) and I'm worth it 'cause I can sell anything — to anybody. I'm a killer, I'm invincable.
ANNCR:	(COME IN OVER FADING GUY) If you're tired to be "helped" by store like this, come to Best Buy. At Best Buy, we don't have high pressure salespeople.
	We do have an electronic and appliance supermarket full of name brand products at low prices, and answer centers staffed with friendly people who only help if you want them to.
	That's Best Buy . . . no high pressure, no high prices.
LIVE TAG:	Best Buy is now open next to Shopko at East Town Mall in East Madison.

174

"Checking"

SFX:	Store ambience throughout
GUY:	I'd like to buy this VCR please.
SALES:	Alright, I'll just . . .
SFX:	(Clicking sounds of a computer keyboard)
SALES::	Check the computer.
SFX:	(Audible computer blip)
SALES:	Oh, I am sorry, it's out of stock.
GUY:	Okay, I'll just take this one.
SALES:	I'm afraid not. We have to keep that one on hand to show.
GUY:	(a tad snide) That you can't sell.
SALES:	(giving it right back) That we can't sell.
GUY:	(okay kink I'll try again) Okay, I'll take this one.
SALES:	(all business) Let's see what the warehouse says.
SFX:	(clicking computer sounds again . . . immediate blip)
SALES:	(almost glad) Not today.
GUY:	(growing impatience) Alright, I'll take that one on the back shelf. (beat) The dusty one.
SALES:	(not fazed a bit) Checking on . . . the dusty one.
SFX:	(computer blip)
SALES:	(with a smile) Bad news again.
GUY:	(angry) Alright, I'll take that refrigerator.
SFX:	(computer blip)
SALES:	(smug now) Out of stock
GUY:	(I'd just like to know) Look, answer me one thing.
SALES:	Of course, sir.
GUY:	(Hot) Why do you have all this stuff on display if you won't sell it?
SALES:	(smarty pants) To demonstrate the selection we offer.
ANNCR:	If you're tired of experiences like this, come to Best Buy. Best Buy is full of name brand electronics and appliances. And most merchandise is right out on the shelf. So it's easy to find what you want, pick it up and buy it. That's Best Buy . . . low prices, no hassles, just helping you help yourself.

"Name Brands"

SFX:	Small store ambience — jumbled TV audio in background.
GUY:	(pleasant) I'd like to buy an RCA TV.
SALES:	(matter of fact) Okay I can show you a couple of consoles, but our best seller is the FUNGI, which I, personally, consider to be a cut above the RCA.
GUY:	Do you have any other TVs?
SALES:	We got the full GEEKY line, from Sri Lanka.
GUY:	Oh. (trying again) Say, could I see a Zenith? Or a Panasonic? Or a Sony?
SALES:	I'll check in back, but take a look at this ZOLTAN, from Romania. (getting into it) These babies are really well built, like a filing cabinet.
GUY:	Ah, no thanks, I'll look someplace else.
SALES:	You won't find a better price on a Zoltan anywhere.
GUY:	Yah, well thank you.
SFX:	Door opens to street sounds.
SALES:	(raises voice to compete with traffic sounds) Come back. Be a little open minded. Look, we're talking about an internationally-known brand here, the Zoltan is Albania's best seller.
ANNCR:	(come in over ends of scene) There are name brands and there are name brands. At Best Buy we carry a big selection of the brands you want, brands that you'll recognize, all at low prices. Best Buy, no hassles, no high pressure, just helping you help yourself.
LIVE TAG:	Best Buy grand opening now next to Shopko at East Town Mall in East Madison.

"Sales Help"

SFX:	(STORE AMBIENCE UNDER THROUGHOUT)
SALES:	Can I help you with a TV today?
LADY:	No thanks, just looking.
SALES:	We have lots of different sizes.
LADY:	I can see that.
SALES:	Quite a variety of features.
LADY:	Yeah, thank you.
SALES:	Many come with remote controls.
LADY:	I know.
SALES:	A remote lets you control your TV from your chair.
LADY:	Yes, I know.
SALES:	We've got everything from pocket size TV's to big screens.
LADY:	I can see that.
SALES:	Many have stereo sound.
LADY:	I know.
SALES:	They come with two speakers . . . the stereo ones.
LADY:	You don't say.
SALES:	Made your selection yet?
LADY:	Er, no, not yet.
SALES:	Well, take your time. It's up to you.
LADY:	Thank you.
SALES:	Just let me know when you want me to write up your sales slip.
ANNCR:	(COME IN OVER FADING GUY) If you're tired paying for "advice" you don't want or need, come to Best Buy. We're an electronic and appliance supermarket full of name brand products at low prices, with answer centers for help . . . if you want it. That's Best Buy . . . no high pressure, no high prices, just helping you help yourself.
LIVE TAG:	Best Buy is grand opening now next to Shopko at East Town Mall in East Madison.

Finalist

SOFT WAREHOUSE
Dallas, TX
"PC Modem & Bob"

Campaign
Other Specialty Store
250-500 mm

Chuck Kremers-Marketing/Sales
Promotion Director; Dina
Santschi-Advertising Director;
Steve Brownrigg-Creative Director
AGENCY: AXCESS: Carmen
Italia-Creative Director; Beatrice
Leemhorst-Copy Chief/Production
Manager; Victor Allen-Account
Executive; Christian
Epting-Copywriter

"P.C. Modem & Bob"

BOB: I'm here with P.C. Modem, the computer genius from Soft Warehouse. P.C., what are those photographs you're looking at?

P.C.: Bob, these are pictures of Soft Warehouse, taken from outer space. We wanted to give people an idea of how big it is.

BOB: Boy, they're incredible. And look at all those locations around the United States!

P.C.: That's right, Bob. And look here, you can even see the stacks of printers, computers, monitors, software . . .

BOB: Yeah, and what's that little blue area near the software section?

P.C.: Lake Michigan.

BOB: Wow. And P.C., I can also read here on those little signs: "Everything's 30 to 80 percent off, everyday."

P.C.: Heck of a camera they're using these days, Bob.

BOB: Does it come with a case?

P.C.: Yes it does. Now, it's even easier to see that Soft Warehouse is the biggest computer store in the whole world.

BOB: Guess that's why they call Soft Warehouse the computer superstore, P.C. Hey look, there we are! We look like ants.

P.C.: Those *are* ants, Bob, that's how great this camera is.

BOB: Wow, and what's that big area that looks like the Soft Warehouse parking lot?

P.C.: Asia Minor.

BOB: Oh.

BOB: Well, here he is, Mr. P.C. Modem, the computer genius from Soft Warehouse. What's new P.C.?

P.C.: Bob, I've come up with a new idea for a game show.

BOB: Really? What is it?

P.C.: Computer Quiz. Want to play?

BOB: Sure.

P.C.: Ok, first question; how many software titles does Soft Warehouse carry?

BOB: Uh . . . six?

P.C.: Not even close, Bob. The correct answer is 2000.

BOB: Oh, I was way off.

P.C.: You sure were. Next question. What program from Borland offers superior spreadsheet power?

BOB: Oh, that's easy. The Quattro Pro. makes spreadsheets quicker and easier to do with multi-page and free-form consolidation, impressive graphics and text.

P.C.: The Quattro Pro is correct, Bob. Last question: Where can you find the Quattro Pro along with 5000 other products, from hardware to software, all 30 to 80 percent off everyday?

BOB: Uh . . . Ed's World of Things?

P.C.: (Buzz) Wrong, Bob. It's Soft Warehouse, the computer superstore. I'm afraid you're not going to go to the semi-finals.

BOB: You mean, I don't win fabulous cash prizes?

P.C.: No.

BOB: Can I meet the woman who points to the furniture?

P.C.: Sorry, Bob, Marcella is my main squeeze.

BOB: Here's P.C. Modem, the computer genius from Soft Warehouse.

P.C.: Hello, Bob. How are you?

BOB: Not very good, thanks. My printer is possessed.

P.C.: What's that, Bob?

BOB: Possessed, P.C. Something horrible and demonic has taken up residence inside it.

P.C.: Why would you think that, Bob?

BOB: Because it makes bizarre noises. Sounds like Shangrilas. And it's printing in tongues. I think I need an exorcist.

P.C.: Actually, Bob, I think you need a new printer.

BOB: Oh.

P.C.: Yes, Bob. A new printer from Soft Warehouse. May I suggest the Panasonic 9-pin dot matrix printer.

BOB: You may, P.C.

P.C.: Very well, Bob. This Panasonic offers many high-end features, but is highly affordable. With an EZ set operation panel, versatile paper handling and superior resolution.

BOB: It can't levitate, can it?

P.C.: No, Bob, I don't think it comes with that feature.

BOB: Good.

P.C.: And Bob? This Panasonic printer is just one of the 5000 computer-related items available at Soft Warehouse. Where everything is 30 to 80 percent off everyday. You see Bob, Soft Warehouse is the computer superstore. Uh . . . who are you calling?

BOB: Rome. Gotta cancel that exorcism. Oh darn . . . I got their answering machine again. Yeah, yeah, I know; wait for the beep.

BOB: We're here with Mr. P.C. Modem, the computer genius from Soft Warehouse. Now, P.C., you know everything about computers and can solve any problem, right?

P.C.: That's correct, Bob.

BOB: Ok, try this one: I'm at the office, been working at the computer for *hours* — when suddenly, I get that darn eye strain. Everything's getting blurry and I can't tell my rocket launches from my defense shields! What's a guy to do?

P.C.: Uh-oh. Well, Bob, eye strain is a common problem. But there is a simple solution: an Anti-glare Screen. Fits on to the front of your monitor, cuts the glare and improves contrast.

BOB: That's not going to make me sterile, is it?

P.C.: No way, Bob. And Anti-glare Screens are just a tiny fraction of the things you'll find at Soft Warehouse. Over 5000 different items, from hardware to software, supplies, to furniture. And here's the best part, Bob: everything at Soft Warehouse is 30 to 80 percent off . . . everyday.

BOB: Wow. I guess that's why they call Soft Warehouse the computer superstore, huh P.C.?

P.C.: That's correct, Bob. Now, let's get back to work.

BOB: Ok, how 'bout a game of demonoids in space?

P.C.: Ok, but you gotta drive.

Winner
PARISIAN
Birmingham, AL
"Fall Image"
Campaign
Apparel Specialty Store
250-500 mm

Patty Bystrom-Marketing Sales
Promotion/Advertising Director
AGENCY: STEINER BRESSLER:
John Zimmerman-Creative
Director/Copy Chief; Lee
McBride-Production Manager;
Ginger Sims-Account Executive
PRODUCTION STUDIO: BOUTWELL

"The Wedding"

MUSIC:	(Establish theme)
MAN:	(Fifty-ish) So there I was, at the church, an hour before my wedding and I spilled a whole cup of coffee down the front of my shirt. The most important day of my life, and my shirt and tie are ruined.
SINGER:	There comes a time, In every life, When you should feel like Somebody special.
MAN:	Well, I'm about to panic when my son says "Relax, Dad, I'll take care of it." Half an hour later this guy that I've never seen before shows up at the chapel with a new shirt and tie. Turns out he'd called Jerry at Parisian who picked the stuff out and brought it over himself. Not only was it the right size, but he'd had it pressed, so it looked great. To tell the truth, the shirt and tie Jerry brought over looked better than the ones I put on that morning. I had never even met him and he treated me like I was his best customer.
SINGER:	You're somebody special at Parisian.
MAN:	Thanks, Jerry.

"Meet the Parents"

MUSIC:	(establish theme)
WOMAN:	Last week, I visited my boyfriend's house to meet his family for the first time. I wanted to look nice, but not too dressy. Not like I was trying *that* hard.
SINGERS:	There comes a time In every life When you should feel like Somebody special
WOMAN:	So, I went to Parisian and this lady named Chris asked if she could help me. Well, I explained the situation, you know, I'm on a budget, meeting his family, the whole bit. She was wonderful. She showed me at least three or four different outfits — all in my price range. She even helped me find shoes, earrings and perfume. And you know, his mom even asked me where I got the dress. I said Parisian, and well, that helped a little.
SINGER:	You're somebody special at Parisian.
WOMAN:	Thanks, Chris.

"Back to Work Image"

MUSIC:	(establish theme)
WOMAN:	I had to go back to work right after having my baby. And, needless to say, I didn't feel much like shopping, but I really needed some new clothes.
SINGER:	There comes a time, In every life, When you should feel like Somebody special.
WOMAN:	Well, I called Wendy at Parisian. I've been going to her for years, so she's really like an old friend — I knew she would help. I told her about the baby, and that I needed new clothes for work, but I really didn't feel like shopping. When I got there, she had a whole dressing room already set up with everything: jackets, skirts, blouses even shoes. All I had to do was try things on and decide what I wanted. Best of all, I felt pampered at a time when I really needed it.
SINGER:	You're somebody special at Parisian.
WOMAN:	Thanks, Wendy.

Finalist

EATONS
Toronto, Canada
"Eaton's Surprise Sale/Space"

Campaign
Department Store
Over 500 mm

Richard Cherniuk-Marketing Sales
Promotion Director; John
Dawkins-Advertising Director
AGENCY: ROBINS SHARPE: Marc
Giacomelli-Creative Director;
Pauline Harper-Account Executive;
Mary Secord, Bernadette
Lowergan-Copy Chiefs

"Teddy Bear Image"

MUSIC:	(Establish theme)
WOMAN:	(60'ish) It was the day before my grandson's birthday, and I suddenly realized I had forgotten all about it. I couldn't go shopping for a present, and he lives in another city. I didn't know what to do.
SINGER:	There comes a time, In every life, When you should feel like Somebody special.
WOMAN:	I called some other stores for help, without any luck. So I called Parisian and talked to a young man named Scott. He really seemed glad to help, which kind of surprised me, because you just don't see that anymore. He must have described everything in the Children's Department. I honestly couldn't decide what to get when Scott said 'if *I* were your grandson, I'd wanta teddy bear.' Well, that settled it. He had that bear giftwrapped and sent in time for my grandson's birthday. And my daughter called to say that boy hadn't let go of his new bear all day.
SINGER:	You're somebody special at Parisian.
WOMAN:	Thanks, Scott.

"Surprise Sale/Space"

MUSIC:	Organ music.
SFX:	Rocket SFX
ANNCR:	Once again the Surprise Adventures of Captain Buck Saver and his faithful Space — Scottie, Re-Tail, as they make contact with alien balloon people.
BUCK:	Take us to your leader.
SFX:	Balloon voices. (Being rubbed together)
BUCK:	What are they saying Re-Tail?
RE-TAIL:	Arf Captain, I'm a dog, not a balloon.
ANNCR:	Look for the bright Red balloons at Eaton's Surprise Sale. One day only. Thursday, June 14th. 10-20% off selected regular-priced items. 10-50% off of clearance items. 1/2 price Interplanetary Specials.
RE-TAIL:	Arf!
SFX:	Air releasing from balloons.
BUCK:	Nice to see inflation hasn't caught up with them, Re-Tail.
RE-TAIL:	Arf (Eaton's.) we are, Canada's Department Store.
TALENT:	Buck — Robert Cait Re-Tail - Peter McCowin Anncr - Walter Soles

"Presents"

(Music throughout)

FEM. SINGER: It's a great time of year to be a Toys "R" Us Kid. (SFX: wrapping paper being torn off gift)

LITTLE GIRL: Mommy, look! She's beautiful! She's the best doll in the whole world!

FEM. SINGER: The presents all around the tree can make you flip your lid! (SFX: wrapping paper)

TWO SINGERS: And as we draw near to that one special day . . .

GIRL 2: (quietly, to herself) Oh, thank you, Santa, it's just what I wanted.

TWO SINGERS: Everyone at Toys "R" Us has just one thing to say . . .(SFX: wrapping paper)

BOY 2: Mom! Dad! You got it! I don't believe it!

ALL SINGERS: To all the children who don't want to grow up, and all the grown-ups who never did . . . (SFX: wrapping paper)

DAD: Hey, kids, this is great! Let's go try it out!

ALL SINGERS; Have a very Merry Christmas . . .

FEM SINGER: All you wonderful Toys "R" Us kids.

"What's Your Name Baby?"

SING:	What's your name baby Mama told me what to do She said if you know what you want Go out and get it I'm here and I'm hungry for you What's your name baby What's your name
ANNCR:	The name is Mr. Sub. A big bite for the money, with buns always baked fresh. Choose white or new wholewheat.
SING:	The name of Mr. Sub Mr. Submarine
SINGER TALKS:	Great buns.

Finalist

CWT SPECIALTY STORES
South Attleboro, MA
"Junior Sale"

Image/Positioning Ad
Apparel Specialty Store
100-250 mm

Ame Thompson-Marketing Sales
Promotion Director
AGENCY: RETAIL ADVERTISING
GROUP: Florence Tischler-Creative
Director; Joan Bender-Copy
Chief/Producer; Maureen
Munnelly-Account Executive
PRODUCTION: BEE VEE SOUND:
Engineer: Bruno MUSIC: Richard
Berg

Winner

KEYSTONE MOTORS
Berwin, PA
"Meditation"

Image/Positioning Ad
Other Retailer
10-50 mm

Al Stein-Advertising Director
PRODUCTION:DICK ORKIN'S
RADIO RANCH: Christine
Coyle-Director/Writer; Dick Orkin,
Steve Hammel

"Junior Sale"

MUSIC UNDER
You know, I used to think that Mary Jane Connely was my very best friend. But that was until she started dating Tommy. So now I have a new best friend. And guess what, my new friend has 3 names, too. Cherry, Webb and Touraine. Anyway CWT is a store that really knows what I'm all about. And to prove it they're having a sale on the hottest junior clothes, shoes and accessories. Absolutely everything I want. They know I've been working out, so there's lots of stretchy Lycra stuff on sale. And there's tons of sweaters and lacy tops because a girl just needs zillions of them. And they even have big, slouchy boyfriend jackets (but as long as it's not Tommy's I'm fine.) CWT always seems to know what's important to me — like loyalty, a friendly attitude and sensible prices. But best of all they won't steal my boyfriend!

ANNCR: Sale ends Sept. 3rd. Don't miss it!

"Meditating"

GAL: Okay, class, in order to achieve inner harmony, close your eyes, and picture a place that represents peace and tranquility to you. Christine, what are you picturing?

CHRIS: A field brimming with wildflowers...

GAL: Good. And Roger?

ROG: I'm picturing the beautiful and spacious lots of Ed Chovanes Ford in San Leondro...

GAL: Roger, perhaps picturing a sky filled with fluffy clouds...

ROG: I'm walking through Ed Chovanes Ford's lot. It's filled with beautiful Ford cars and trucks ...

GAL: Roger, meditating requires a mental image that's relaxing and...

ROG: Now one of their relaxed, friendly salespeople is greeting me.

GAL: Roger, picture a place that's pleasant, a quiet oasis, A—

ROG: Ed Chovanes Ford is an oasis amongst auto dealers. No pressure. No hype. A nice, pleasant experience car buying experience—

GAL: Kay, Roger. Have it your way. Now class we'll choose our mantra — a word that represents peace and harmony. Christine?

CHRIS: Mine will be Bluebird. (begins repeating!) Bluebird, Bluebird...

GAL: And Roger?

ROGER: Ed Chovanes Ford ... Ed Chovanes Ford ... Ed Chovanes Ford...

GAL: Roger! (talk out)

ANNCR: Experience Ed Chovanes Ford in San Leondro. Thirty-six years of great prices, great service and a great reputation.

"Styles to Fit Every Me/You"

1. I like to wear a lot of short mini skirts and then tight pants under them.
2. I have to dress comfortably.
3. They carry all sizes.
4. But I have to look professional.
5. They got the latest looks at Fashion Bug.
6. I feel special.
7. Paisley prints, oversized knit tops.
8. I saw this awesome leather jacket, it was great.
9. I came today to buy something for my daughter.
10. I shop at Fashion Bug because of the prices, styles and convenience.
11. You scoot in and you scoot back out.
12. They have everything under one roof.
13. They have socks in every color.
14. Heavy flannels for in the winter.
15. Light knits for in the summer.
16. Very sexy lingerie.
17. Quality is great.
18. Very, very sexy lingerie.
19. Fashion Bug has styles to fit every me.
20. Different styles for different occasions.
21. Fashion Bug has styles to fit every you.
22. I wear a plus size.
23. Fashion Bug is the greatest.
24. I never leave Fashion Bug empty handed.
25. I love this place.

(Fashion Bug Jingle)
(:05 Station Tag for Locations)

"Styles/Really Really Short"

1. I'm gonna buy a pair of bright yellow neon sweat pant shorts.
2. My friends shop here.
3. Jackie — size 5, Jowell size 3.
4. Fashion Bug is reliable, reasonable, stylish.
5. Dawn size 7/8.
6. Purses, hats, scarves.
7. A nice business suit.
8. Fashion Bug has styles to fit a woman any age.
9. You get great prices at Fashion Bug.
10. Everyone can shop at Fashion Bug no matter what size.
11. I'm a size 16.
12. Or what age..
13. I'm 47.
14. 43.
15. I'm a mommy.
16. I'm 26.
17. My mom looks great in Fashion Bug clothes and so do I.
18. I love the quality.
19. I buy a lot of earrings here.
20. Everything is laid out for you.
21. I don't stick with just one style.
22. Professional wear.
23. Leathers.
24. Belts.
25. Hosiery.
26. Sweaters.
27. For $10.00.
28. That's amazing.
29. I found a little suit.
30. I'm a little person.
31. She's really, really short.
32. Fashion Bug is great.

(Fashion Bug Jingle)
(:05 Station Tag for Locations)

"Occupations"

1. I'm a receptionist.
2. A housewife.
3. A secretary.
4. I do accounting work.
5. Clothing enhances your self-esteem.
6. I look cute in Fashion Bug tops.
7. Nurse.
8. Cheerleader.
9. I come to Fashion Bug once a week.
10. I'm a hairdresser.
11. Play baseball.
12. I sell cosmetics.
13. Fashion Bug has styles to fit every you.
14. I love Fashion Bug.
15. No sale is final.
16. I never have a hassle or problem.
17. No aggravation.
18. When I have to return something.
19. All of my clothes last.
20. I love your shopping bags.
21. I love the prices here.
22. They carry all sizes from junior.
23. I have a little girl.
24. Misses.
25. Plus size women.
26. They have style and fashion in the larger sizes.
27. Hassle free.
28. This store is really beautiful.
29. The only place I can ever find the clothes that I like to wear.
30. I buy clothes for work.
31. I buy casual clothes.
32. A career look.
33. Coats.
34. Slacks.
35. Dresses.
36. Tops.
37. Jeans.
38. I wear great looking Fashion Bug clothes.
39. It makes me feel special.

(Fashion Bug Jingle)
(:05 Station Tag for Locations)

CREATIVITY

Creativity is art. — *Alec Rand, age 7.*

Creativity is something that you make that's beautiful. — *Kyle Grone, age 8.*

Creativity is when you make something that nobody else can make. — *Lauren Stamatis, age 7.*

Creativity is something that you do one time that you can't do the same way ever again. — *James Tang-Mills, age 8.*

Creativity is being creative by doing something that looks different. — *Stacey Ashton, age 7.*

Creativity is making something. You add stuff to it. — *Jacob Howerton, age 8.*

Creativity is something that you do that you think that another person would not do. — *Matthew Whitehurst, age 8.*

Creativity is when you do something all by yourself and you don't copy it. — *Alex Gotto, age 8.*

Creativity is something that you make up from new ideas. — *Bryan Macrie, age 7.*

Creativity is smart and having good ideas. — *Sierra Hannum, age 8.*

Creativity is smart ideas. — *Jennifer Oddo, age 7.*

Creativity is you make something up in your mind that doesn't copy someone else. — *Brian Petrovich, age 8.*

Creativity is something that you do by imagining it. — *Leslie Harris, age 8.*

Creativity is using your imagination and getting something new that you have never done before. — *Katie Calahan, age 8.*

Creativity is when you imagine it. Then you build it in your mind. And then you try to build it with tools. If it works, you keep on building them and building them and building them and building them. If you wait a day to build it, what you im-agined might change. You take a piece out of your mind, look at it, and build it. — *Scott Castle, age 7.*

Creativity is you build something. — *William Fox, age 8.*

Creativity is thinking what you do first and then doing it. — *Toni Puente, age 8.*

Creativity is good work because you think so hard. — *Betsy Palaschak, age 8.*

Creativity is that you do an activity. — *Wayne Waite, age 8.*

Creativity is having or showing what you can do. — *Alena Whitlock, age 8.*

Creativity is fun. You make pictures. — *J. Reid, age 8.*

Creativity is drawing something real neat. — *Sameer Kanabar, age 8.*

Creativity is when you draw something real good and then add something on to it. — *Theresa Brindisi, age 7.*

Creativity is unique and different because you have to make it unusual. — *Ben Bonsall, age 8.*

Creativity is being creative by using materials you have never used before. — *Katie Houck, age 8.*

Creativity is a piece of art that is very beautiful. — *Carol Gobus, age 8.*

Creativity is using your imagination and letting it run far off in a meadow. — *Kimmy Schulz, age 8.*

Creativity is...
as related to
Dr. Carole Gilmore
on March 19, 1991
by each of the children
in the second grade class
of Madison Simis School,
7302 North Tenth Street,
Phoenix, Arizona 85020.

RAMA Members

ABRAHAM & STRAUS
420 Fulton St
Brooklyn, NY 11201
Ph: 718/802-7247
Fax: 718/802-8188
Steven Cohen, Operating VP/
Creative Art Dir
Robert Cole, Operating VP
Ph: 718/802-7222
Joyce Dworkin, VP Brdcst/
Creative Mktg
Ph: 718/802-7249
Nancy Lee Ryan, VP-
Brdcst Adv
Martine Reardon, Dir Special
Events
Ph: 718/802-7224
Nancy Slavin, Operating VP-
Traffic Dir
Ph: 718/802-7267
Joseph Yewdell, Sr VP-Sls
Prom
Ph: 718/802-7246

ABRAMS & BUEHNER
156 Duncan Mill Rd, U#24
Don Mills, ON M3B 3N2
Canada
Ph: 416/391-0030
Fax: 416/391-0038
Manfred Buehner, President

ACME BEDDING
3800 S Division
Grand Rapids, MI 49548
Ph: 616/243-4342
Fax: 616/243-8420
Ron Zagel, President

**ACTCOM
WORLDWIDE**
200 Renaissance, #1000
Detroit, MI 48243
Ph: 313/446-8752
William Power, Pres/CEO

**ACTION NICHOLSON
COLOR**
6519 Eastland Rd
Brook Park, OH 44142
Ph: 216/234-5370
Fax: 216/234-7850
James Agrippe, VP Sls/Mktg

ACXIOM CORP
301 Industrial Blvd
Conway, AR 72032
Ph: 501/450-1422
Fax: 501/450-1415
Dave Wilson, Group Exec

**AD VANTAGE
COMPUTER SYSTEMS**
11027 Aurora Ave
Des Moines, IA 50322
Ph: 515/270-2600
Fax: 515/270-6161
Dennis Hays, President

AD DIRECT
285 Riverside Ave
Westport, CT 06880
Ph: 203/222-6614
David Cramoy, President
Eric Tolkin, Acct Supv
Ph: 203/226-2468

AD INFINITUM
PO Box 1232
San Juan, PR 00902
Puerto Rico
Ph: 809/721-6400
Fax: 809/721-4597
Ivan Diaz, Copywriter
Jim Minnich, Exec VP/
Creative Dir

**ADAMS OUTDOOR
OF ATLANTA**
732 Ashby St
Atlanta, GA 30318
Ph: 614/888-5900
Fax: 614/888-8825
Herb Neu, Dir-Client Services

ADAMS PUBLISHING
12 South 6 St, Ste 400
Minneapolis, MN 55402
Ph: 612/336-9226
Fax: 612/339-5806
Carri Tedstrom, Prod Dir

ADSPACE
527 W 34th St
New York, NY 10001
Ph: 212/330-0676
Fax: 212/330-0660
Richard Atkins, President
Diana Moore, Mgr Mkt Services
212/330-0682

ADVERTISING AGE
220 E 42nd St
New York, NY 10017
Ph: 212/210-0176
Judy Graham, Retail Reporter

ADVO SYSTEM
One Univac Lane
Windsor, CT 06095
Ph: 203/285-6100
Fax: 203/285-6233
Randy Antik, Exec VP-
Sls/Mktg
John Birk, Pres/COO
Ph: 203/285-6112
Fax: 203/285-6412

ALDEN PRESS
2000 Arthur Ave
Elk Grove Village, IL 60007
Ph: 708/640-6000
Fax: 708/640-6029
Don Carlson, VP-Field Sls Div
Ph: 312/640-6000
Warren Mueller, Sls Rep
John Van Horn, VP-
Planning/Mktg

**ALEXANDER/
YOSKOWITZ**
1901 Brickel Ave
Miami, FL 33129
Ph: 305/854-3753
Barry Yoskowitz, Exec VP

**ALEXIS NIHON
QUEBEC**
2 Place Alexis Nihon #1808
Westmount, PQ H3Z 3C1
Canada
Ph: 514/931-2591
Fax: 514/931-1618
Johanne Leclerc, Mktg Delg
Toni-Lynn Trottier, Shopping
Center Mgr

**ALL-CANADA
RADIO/TV**
1000 Yonge St
Toronto, ON M4W 2K2
Canada
Ph: 416/963-7820
Fax: 416/963-4367
John Gorman, VP-Gen Mgr
Jane Martindale, Research Dir
Carol Weir, Mgr-Mktg Services
Ph: 416/963-7822

**ALLIED GRAPHIC
ARTS**
1515 Broadway
New York, NY 10036
Ph: 212/642-9500
Fax: 212/819-1287
Arlene Hayden, VP-Creat Dir
John Mathewson, Sr VP
Vanetta Vancak, Acct Supv
Ph: 212/642-9529
Daniel Wies, Vice President
Ph: 212/642-9500
Fax: 212/819-1287

ALLIED GROUP
519 John St
Burlington, ON L7R 2L1
Canada
Ph: 416/681-7262
Fax: 416/681-7264
Bob Binkley, Admin

ALLING & CORY
27-17 Jackson Ave
Long Island City, NY 11101
Ph: 718/784-6200
Fax: 718/392-8726
Nicholas Viest, Sls Mgr

ALPERTS FURNITURE
100 Highland Ave
Seekonk, MA 02771
Ph: 508/336-6400
Fax: 508/336-3325
Stephen Barylick, Dir-Adv

**ALTMAN PROCKO
PRODUCTION**
20205 NE 15th Ct
Miami, FL 33179
Ph: 305/651-8258
Steve Procko, Dir/Cameraman

AM&A
389 Main St
Buffalo, NY 14205
Ph: 716/847-9608
Fax: 716/853-4046
Don Alexander, VP-Sls
Prom & Mktg
J Keith Alford, President
Teresa Campion, Asst Art Dir
Kathy Shaw, Copywriter Chief
Michelle Wells, Creative Art Dir
William Zalewski, Prod Mgr

**AMBROSI &
ASSOCIATES**
1100 W Washington
Chicago, IL 60607
Ph: 312/666-9200
Nicholas Ambrosi, President
Mark Pearson, VP

AMC & COMPANY
905 Hudson St
Hoboken, NJ 07030
Ph: 201/656-3391
Fax: 212/767-5606
Anna Mae Cashin, President

AMCENA
1114 Ave of the Americas
New York, NY 10036
Ph: 212/391-4141
Fax: 212/302-4381
Neal Tyler, VP-Strategic Mktg

AMERetail
14 Ticonderoga
Irvine, CA 92720
Ph: 714/651-9308
Laurence Straus, President

**AMERICAN COLOR
CORP**
2500 Walden Ave
Buffalo, NY 14225
Ph: 716/684-8100
Fax: 716/684-0274
John Adler, Sls Mgr

**AMERICAN COLOR
CORP**
3740 Stern Ave
St. Charles, IL 60174
Ph: 312/377-8660
Joanne Koessler, Sls Rep

AMERICAN EXPRESS
200 Vesey St
New York, NY 10285
Ph: 212/640-4707
Fax: 212/619-6738
Ivy Abrams, Mgr Retail
Industry Mkt
Donna Pagnutti, Mgr Retail
Industry Mkt
Ph: 212/640-3547
Patricia Alexander, VP-Retail
Headquarters Accts
Ph: 212/640-5291
Kathryn Russell, VP-Retail
Industry Mktg
Ph: 212/640-3102
Joel Ruzich, Retail Mktg Mgr
Ph: 212/640-3170
Emelie Smith, Mgr
Ph: 212/640-2696
Jennifer Gold, Dir Retail Mktg
Ph: 212/640-3535
Fax: 212/619-9835
Amy Davidson, Asst Mgr
Ph: 212/640-4781

AMERICAN EXPRESS
3 University Plaza Ste 614
Hackensack, NJ 07601
Ph: 201/343-3506
Fax: 201/343-4912
Maureen Moran, Retail AcctVP

AMERICAN EXPRESS
1870 Pacific Ave. #404
San Francisco, CA 91409
Ph: 415/472-1177 157
Patricia Ferrin, Mktg Mgr

AMERICAN EXPRESS
Two Forest Plaza
Dallas, TX 75251
Ph: 214/387-8134
Jo Hodgson, Industry Dir-
Retail

AMERICAN EXPRESS
300 S Riverside Plaza, #710
Chicago, IL 60606
Ph: 312/902-1499
Fax: 312/902-1335
Claudia Laupmanis, VP-Retail
Acct Develop

**AMERICAN EXPRESS
PUBLISHING**
541 N Fairbanks, Ste 2030
Chicago, IL 60611
Ph: 312/644-0952
Fax: 312/644-9096
Tracey Crane, Midwest Mgr

**AMERICAN
FURNITURE CO**
PO Box 3685, Station D
Albuquerque, NM 87190
Ph: 505/883-2026
Fax: 505/883-2498
Laura Smigielski, Mktg Dir

**AMERICAN OLEAN
TILE**
1000 Cannon Ave
Lansdale, PA 19446
Ph: 215/855-1111
Fax: 215/362-6050
Debra Kereczman, Mgr-Adv &
Prom

**AMERICAN
SIGNATURE**
6320 Denton Dr
Dallas, TX 75235
Ph: 214/358-1371
Fax: 214/353-2986
Robert Schick, Sr VP-Sls

AMERICAN STORES
709 E South Temple
Salt Lake City, UT 84102
Ph: 801/539-4514
Tony Sansone, Accountant

AMERICAN TV-R
353 West 46th St
New York, NY 10036
Ph: 800/289-2400
Fax: 212/246-1320
Tom Graff, President
Ann Armbruster, VP

AMES DEPT STORES
999 S Quaker Ln, #2625
West Hartford, CT 06110
Ph: 203/231-6389
Fax: 203/231-6549
Ellen Oland, Mgr Brdct Adv/
Sls Prom

AMW ASSOCIATES
10 Pine Ln
Ocean, NJ 07712-7242
Ph: 908/493-2764
Audrey Winograd, President

**ANDERSEN & BLAESB-
JERG REKLAMEBREAU**
Tigergaarden
Denmark, Holland
Ph: 66/12 14 19
Fax: 011/4566148419
Henry Rasmussen, Copywriter

ANDERSON LITTLE
502 Bedford St
Fall River, MA 02720
Ph: 508/676-1901
Fax: 508/675-5150
Oscar Chilabato, Adv Dir

CR ANTHONY
PO Box 25725
Oklahoma, OK 73125
Glenn Smith

ANTIOCH CENTER
5307 Center Mall
Kansas City, MO 64119
Ph: 816/454-1200
Fax: 816/454-0661
Stephanie Burkett, Asst Mktg Di
Linda Meyer, Asst Mktg Dir

**ANTIOCH
PUBLICATION**
5209 1/2 Antioch Rd
Kansas City, MO 64119
Ph: 816/741-7972
Carmen Nelson, Prod Supv

APOLLO RADIO
350 Park Ave, 10th Fl
New York, NY 10022
William Stakelin, Pres & CEO
Ph: 212/750-4592

ARBEIT & COMPANY
36 W 44 St, Ste 1111
New York, NY 10036
Ph: 212/575-5070
Fax: 212/730-4517
Stephen Arbeit, President

ARCATA GRAPHICS
1185 Ave of the Americas
New York, NY 10036
Ph: 212/827-2751
Fax: 212/869-2089
Robert Finn, Mgr
Carroll Thomas, Mgr
Ph: 212/827-2754
Arthur Tonucci, VP-
Publications Sls
Ph: 212/827-2764
Samuel Vail, VP-Sls
Ph: 212/840-6140

**ARCTIC HOME
FURNISHINGS**
153 Pine South
Timins, ON P4N 2T3
Canada
Ph: 705/264-5301
Paul Degilio, Mgr

ARIZONA REPUBLIC
120 E Van Buren
Phoenix, AZ 85004
Ph: 602/271-8447
Fax: 602/271-8500
Dennis Christensen, Retail
Sls Mgr

ARKADIA GROUP
41 W 25th St
New York, NY 10010
Ph: 212/645-6226
Fax: 212/206-9754
Greg Costello, Creative Dir
Fred DeCoursin, CEO
Richard Fairchild, VP
Bob Walker, Dir-Oper
Terry Williamson, VP Sls

ARMSTRONG WORLD
PO Box 3001
Lancaster, PA 17604
Ph: 717/396-4760
Fax:717/396-4426
Cynthia Clarkin, Mktg Supv
John Lachiusa, Sr Mktg Supv
Ph: 717/396-4459
Sherry Qualls, Adv Mgr-
Flooring
T. Raatikainen, Adv Mgr
Ph: 717/396-4368
Gerard Schouten, Mgr
Ph: 717/396-5931

ARMSTRONG WORLD
2500 Columbia, Bldg 402-MDC
Lancaster, PA 17604
Ph: 717/396-5918
Fax: 717/396-5923
Janice Henry, Sr Supv
Daniel McGinn, Sr Supv
Deb Rose, Sr Supv
Barbara Moncrief, Sr Supv
Ph: 717/396-5916

ARMSTRONG'S
3rd Ave & 3rd St
Cedar Rapids, IA 52401
Ph: 319/363-0201
Elsie Matteson, Adv Dir
Connie Thorson, Creative Dir

**ARMY & AIR FORCE
EXCHANGE**
Headquarter Aafes Europe
Apo, NY 09245
Ph: 214/780-2653
John Hanson, Chief/Sls Prom
Div/MK-O

**ARMY & AIR FORCE
EXCHANGE**
PO Box 660202
Dallas, TX 75266-0202
Ph: 214/780-2780
Inci Tepecik, Chief Adv Branch

ARONSON FURNITURE
3401 W 47th St
Chicago, IL 60632
Ph: 312/376-3400
Fax: 312/376-3831
Bob Cremer, President
Rhonda Schlesinger, Adv Dir

**ART & DESIGN
STUDIOS**
68 Merton St
Toronto, ON M4S 1A1
Canada
Ph: 416/481-6461
Michael George, VP-Adv

ART'S MUSIC SHOP
177 East Blvd
Montgomery, AL 36117
Ph: 205/271-2787
Paul Freehling, Gen Mgr

**ARVEY PAPER &
OFFICE PRODUCTS**
3351 W Addison
Chicago, IL 60618
Ph: 312/463-6423
Fax: 312/463-7776
Gary Jackson, Adv Supv
Katherine Steffen, Adv Mgr

ASBURY PARK PRESS
3601 Rt. 66/Box 1550
Neptune, NJ 07754-1550
Ph: 201/922-6000
Robert Koerner, Store
Develop Mgr
Susan Wajda, Major Acct Exec

How to get to where your future is taking you.

The world is changing. Overnight. Evolving every day. And with it so are the needs and opportunities of catalogers, publishers and many other users of information.

To help you reach your goals and the world you serve, we work hard to learn your markets. Anticipate your needs. Customize our services to fit your requirements. Target products to attract your consumers and advertisers.

Apply our technology and expertise to help ensure your competitive advantage.

As a result, we've become a global company. With facilities that go across the country, around the globe and into the skies. So we can help you get where your future is taking you--better and faster than you might get there otherwise.

R.R. DONNELLEY & SONS COMPANY

ADDING EFFICIENCY TO RETAIL ADVERTISING

708/574-3840

ASSOCIATED MERCHANDISING
1440 Broadway
New York, NY 10018
Ph: 212/536-4174
Jennifer Benepe, Research Dir

ASTER WINSLOW
147 W 26th St
New York, NY 10001
Ph: 212/645-2824
Fax: 212/929-2039
Helen Aster, VP
Ann Winslow, President

ATC
116 Inver
Englewood, CO 80112
Michelle Mason Beauchamp, Adv Sls Dir
Ph: 303/649-8015

ATHLETE'S FOOT
3735 Atlanta Indus Pkwy
Atlanta, GA 30331
Ph: 404/699-8200
James Hutchinson, Dir-Adv

FREDERICK ATKINS
1515 Broadway
New York, NY 10036
212/536-7012
212/719-3758
C Joseph Rivers, Sls Prom Dir

ATLANTA JOURNAL
72 Marietta St NW
Atlanta, GA 30303
Cathy Coffey, VP/Adv
Ph: 404/526-5256
Fax: 404/526-5258
Roy Sheppard, Retail Adv Mgr
Ph: 404/526-5275
Fax: 404/526-5895
Debbie Timbert, Sls Mgr
Ph: 404/526-5204

ATLANTIC TELEVISION SYSTEM
PO Box 1653
Helifax, NS D3J 2Z4
Canada
Ph: 902/453-4000
Fax: 902/454-3270
Colin Burns, Gen Sls Mgr
Nigel Fuller, Natl/Regl Sls Mgr

ATLANTIC TELEVISION SYSTEM
251 Bay Side Dr
St. John, NB E2J-1A7
Canada
Ph: 506/658-1010
David Reid, Regl Sls Supv

AUSTAD'S
4500 E 10th
Sioux Falls, SD 57196
Ph: 605/336-3135
Fax: 605/339-0362
Greg Neff, Retail Adv Mgr

AVANTI PRESS
13449 NW 42nd Ave
Miami, FL 33054
Ph: 305/685-7381
Fax: 305/688-3260
Joe Arriola, CEO
Debbie Filipe, Acct Exec Dir
Gene Martinez, President
Ph: 800-327-7481
Karen Powell, VP

AXCESS MARKETING GROUP
6135 Wilshire Blvd
Los Angeles, CA 90048
Ph: 213/937-3691
Fax: 213/937-0945
T. Bradley Kelly, President
David W.C. Riatti, COO

AYER WORLDWIDE
825 8th Ave
New York, NY 10019-7498
Ph: 212/474-5000
Fax: 212/474-5400
Chuck Meding, Dir-Natl Oper

LS AYRES
1 W Washington St
Indianapolis, IN 46204
Debra Hood, Brdcst Mgr
Ph: 317/262-2794

AZ MARKETING SERVICES
31 River Road
Cos Cob, CT 06807
Ph: 203/629-8088
Fax: 203/661-0920
Arlene Clanny, VP
Charles Orlowski, Exec-VP
Alice Zea, President

B & Q
121-141 Westbourne Terrace
London England, W2 6JR
UK
Ph: 01/262-5077
Fax: 01/258-3757
Bill Whiting, Mng Dir

BACHMAN'S INC
6010 Lyndale Ave
Minneapolis, MN 55419
Adrienne Weinstein, Adv Mgr
Ph: 612/861-7694
Fax: 612/861-7746

BACKER SPIELVOGEL BATES
2 St Clair Ave W
Toronto, ON M4V 1L5
Canada
Ph: 416/485-7400
Fax: 416/925-1206
Stephen Sussman, Gen Mgr-Retail Div

BACKER SPIERVOGEL BATES
405 Lexington Ave
New York, NY 10174
Ph: 212/297-7130
Randall Windschitl, Sr VP-Mgmt Rep

MAURICE BADLER
17 Cushing St
Newton, MA 02161
Ph: 617/964-4652
Gerard Badler, Mktg Dir

BAGDASARIAN PRODUCTIONS
13911 Ridgedale Dr, #451
Minnetonka, MN 55343
Ph: 612/591-1492
Fax: 612/591-1581
Marcia Marcus, VP-Sls & Mktg

BAIM & COMPANY
1 Embarcadero Ste #3400
San Francisco, CA 94111
Ph: 415/627-1003
Greg Potter, Mgr

BAL HARBOUR SHOPS
9700 Collins Ave
Bal Harbour, FL 33154
Ph: 305/866-1816
Enid Rosenthal, Mktg Dir

BALTIMORE SUN
501 N Calvert St
Baltimore, MD 21278
Ph: 301/332-6327
Fax: 301/783-2501
Claudia Arbaugh, Sls Mgr-Retail Adv
Irene Baker, Sls Rep
Ph: 301/332-6442
Brenda Jackson, Acct Exec
Ph: 301/332-6416
Megan Easton, Retail Ad Mgr
Ph: 301/332-6438
Fax: 301/783-2513
Regina Swearingen, Mktg-Research Mgr
Ph: 301/332-6245
Fax: 301/332-6670

JOS A BANK CLOTHIER
25 Crossroads Dr
Baltimore, MD 21117
Ph: 301/356-8515
Michael Waters, Exec VP-Mktg

BARGAIN TOWN
140 West Oxmoor Rd
Birmingham, AL 35209
Ph: 205/942-1234
Judy Bonzo, Adv Dir

F CURTIS BARRY
2104 Willowick Ln
Richmond, VA 23233
Ph: 804/740-8743
Curtis Barry, President

BASIC/BEDELL ADV SELLING IMPROVE
PO Box 30571
Santa Barbara, CA 93130
Ph: 805/683-5857
Fax: 805/963-1503
C Barrie Bedell, President

EDDIE BAUER
14850 NE 36th St
Redmond, WA 98052
Ph: 206/882-6616
Fax: 206/867-7729
Davia Kimmey, Div VP-Adv
Lori McFadden, Mgr-Graphic Services
Ph: 206/882-6162
Robert Prevost, Copy Chief
Ph: 206/882-6355
Lisa Lee, Mgr, Retail Adv
Ph: 206/882-6339
Fax: 206/882-9529
Robert Prevost, Copy Chief
206/882-6355

BAY/SIMPSONS
2200 Yonge St
Toronto, ON M4S 2C6
Canada
Ph: 416/440-7121
Fax: 416/440-7466
Dennis Kelman, Sls Prom Mgr
J Barry Agnew, VP-Sls Prom
Ph: 416/440-7119
Marianne Kennedy, Adv Mgr
Ph: 416/861-6757
Fax: 416/861-4517
Rick Sorby, VP
Ph: 416/440-7501
Kathy Winter, Sls Prom Mgr
Ph: 416/440-7380

BAY & SIMPSONS
2 Bloor St E 4th Fl
Toronto, On M4W 3H7
Canada
Ph: 416/972-4192
Fax: 416/972-4096
Stuart Fraser, VP-Exec

BAYER BESS VANDERWARKER
225 N. Michigan Ave, #1900
Chicago, IL 60601
Ph: 312/861-3883
Jean Morrison, VP-Acct Dir

BBDO
1285 Ave of the Americas
New York, NY 10019-6095
Ph: 212/459-5281
Fax: 212/459-6402
Jesse Garbowitz, Media Supv
Ph: 212/459-6746
Harry Tropp, VP-Assoc Media Dir

BCA ADVERTISING
6606 Tussing Rd
Columbus, OH 43216
Ph: 614/575-7432
Fax: 614/575-7285
Sharon Brink, Art Dir
Alex Nikifortchuk, President
Ph: 614/575-7281

BCE DEVELOPMENT
444 Cedar St
St. Paul, MN 55101
Ph: 612/291-8900
Fax: 612/297-6222
Dawn Dietrich, Retail Mgr

BEALL'S DEPT STORE
PO Box N
Bradenton, FL 34206
Ph: 813/747-2355
Fax: 813/746-1171
Jenny Babinski, Creative Dir
Michael Higgins, Adv Prod Mgr
Sherman Kirkpatrick, VP-Sls Prom
Janis Talbott, Adv Bus Mgr

BEALL'S DEPT STORE
1806 38th Ave E
Bradenton, FL 34206
Ph: 813/747-2355
Fax: 813/746-1171
Laura Jerard, Adv Bus Mgr
Allen Weinstein, VP-Gen Mgr

BEARD
6331 N Lakewood
Chicago, IL 60660
Ph: 312/465-0573
Alfrieda Beard

BEAVER CANOE CORP
1475 Dupont St
Toronto, ON M6P 3R9
Canada
Ph: 416/516-0911
Tracey Bourgon, Stores Admin

BEL-AIRE ASSOC
745 5th Ave
New York, NY 10151
Ph: 212/838-1060
Fax: 212/223-3153
Gregory Chislovsky, Exec VP
John Grubman, President
Donald O'Brien, VP-Mktg

BELK BROS CO
308 E 5th St
Charlotte, NC 28202
Ph: 704/377-4251
Fax: 704/375-9856
Bud Bergren, Sr VP

BELK BEERY
221 N Second St
Wilmington, NC 28401
Ph: 919/763-9912
Fax: 919/763-9912
Robert Alexander, Sls Prom Mgr

BELK BEERY
3500 Oleander Dr
Wilmington, NC 28403
Ph: 919/392-1440
Jack Harrell, Sls Prom Mgr

BELK BROTHERS
111 E Trade St
Charlotte, NC 28231
Ph: 704/377-4251
Tim Belk, VP-Sls Prom

BELK BROTHERS
308 E Fifth St
Charlotte, NC 28202
Ph: 704/377-4251
Fax: 704/375-9856
Bud Bergern, Sr VP
Denise Browning, Adv Mgr
Jan Carroll, VP-Sls Prom
Robert Idzakovich, Creative Dir
Jan Carroll

BELK DEPT STORE
PO Box 9828
Asheville, NC 28815
Ph: 704/298-4970
Fax: 704/298-1594
Micheal Dehart, Adv Mgr

BELK HUDSON LEGGETT
PO Box 111
Raleigh, NC 27602
Ph: 919/832-5851 x226:
Fax: 919/832-5851
Gene Ayscue, Sls Prom Mgr
Howard Walters, Jr/Sr VP-Sls & Merch

BELK IN THE TRIAD
PO Box 3017
Greensboro, NC 27402
Larry Smith, Group Sls Prom
Ph: 919/621-2800
Fax: 919/621-2800-489

BELK LINDSEY STORE
100 Colonial Plaza
Orlando, FL 32803
Ph: 407/898-2355
Fax: 407/895-5142
Judith Brett, VP-Sls Prom

BELK SIMPSON
PO Box 1628
Greenville, SC 29602
Ph: 803/297-9752
Fax: 803/297-5184
Gloria Chrietzberg, Sls Prom Mgr

BELK STORES SERVICES
2801 W Tyvola Rd
Ph: 704/357-1000
Fax: 704/357-1876
Charlotte, NC 28217-4500
James Eversole, VP-Sls Prom
Laurie Garner, Dir-Archdale Adv
Cindy Hunter, Adv Dir
J. David Huskey, Sr VP/Corp Sls Prom
Linda Pyle, Special Events Coord.

BELLMAR COLOR PRESS
PO Box 472
Nowata, OK 74048
Ph: 918/273-1950
Fax: 918/273-1041
JD Sanders, VP

LOUIS BENITO ADVERTISING
600 N Westshore Blvd
Tampa, FL 33609
Ph: 813/287-8200
Fax: 813/287-1462
Rebecca Hall, VP-Acct Grp Supv

BENO'S FAMILY FASHIONS
1620 S Los Angeles St
Los Angeles, CA 90015
Ph: 213/748-2222
Fax: 213/741-2329
Gregg Seaman, Adv Dir

BERENTER GREENHOUSE
233 Park Ave S
New York, NY 10003
Ph: 212/995-9500
Fax: 212/995-9836
Ted Pulton, Sr-VP Group
Acct Dir

BERGDORF GOODMAN
745 5th Ave
New York, NY 10019
Marilyn Levey, VP-Mktg
Ph: 212/872-8662

PA BERGNER & CO
331 W Wisconsin Ave
Milwaukee, WI 53203
Ph: 414/347-5329
Fax: 414/347-0728
John Beachum, Dir-Prom & Publicity
Stan Bluestone, Pres & CEO
Fax: 414/347-5340
Mary Ann Bouche, Copy Chief
Ph: 414/278-5732
Ann Chenoweth, Photo Studio Dir
Ph: 414/347-5340
Anne Danen, Catalog Estimator
Ph: 414/347-5054
Tom Fox, Exec Copy Dir
Ph: 414/347-5047
Jeani Marquis, Copy Chief-Direct Mail
Ph: 414/278-5731
Joyce Nelson, Newspaper Adv Mgr
Ph: 414/347-5353
Marian Trumble, Admin Plnr Dir
Ph: 414/347-5046
Patrice Ulschmid, Art Dir
Ph: 414/347-5340
Catherine Wood, Exec Art Dir
Ph: 414/347-5330
Edward Carroll Jr, Sr VP Sls Prom & Mktg
Ph: 414/347-5340
Fax: 414/278-5748
Bill Jansen, Mktg Mgr
Ph: 414/347-5316
Patti Washcovick, VP/Creative Services Dir
414/347-5340

BERNARD MARKS & ASSOCIATES
2970 Maria Ave Ste 206
Northbrook, IL 60062
Ph: 708/205-0636
Fax: 708/205-0949
Donald Ingwersen, Creative Dir

BEST BUY
PO Box 9312
Minneapolis, MN 55440
Ph: 612/896-2300
Fax: 612/896-1141
Bradbury Anderson, Exec VP-Sls/Mktg
Richard Schulze, Pres& CEO

BEST BUY
4400 W 78th St
Bloomington, MN 55435
Ph: 612/896-2330
Fax: 612/896-2422
Julie Engel, VP-Adv
Kevin Gordon, Creative Dir
Ph: 612/896-2334

BEST PRODUCTS
PO BOX 26303
Richmond, VA 23060
Ph: 804/261-2389
Fax: 804/261-6376
Daniel Hough, VP-Mktg/Adv
Paul Michelle III, Dir-Mktg/Adv
Ph: 804/261-2284
Fax: 804/261-2250

BESTINFO
1400 N Providence
Media, PA 19063
Ph: 215/891-6500
Fax: 215/891-0134
Jim Bessen, President

BIG APPLE ADVERTISING
33 W 10 St, Ste 710
Anderson, IN 46016
Ph: 317/649-3526
Fax: 317/649-3526
Judy Miller, VP

BIG SANDY FURNITURE
2 Box 409
South Point, OH 45680
John Suart, VP

Tired Of Getting Your Marketing News In Bits And Pieces?

It happens a lot. You open your mail to find that someone has clipped an article from *Advertising Age* for you. And it's usually a valuable piece of information.

But think about how much you miss.

After all, every week *Advertising Age* contains business news and marketing information that are often found nowhere else. Ad Age covers retail marketing, fast-food marketing, toy marketing, new product marketing, entertainment marketing — the *whole* world of marketing. That's why busy executives around the world regularly turn to *Advertising Age*.

Don't miss out on what the competition is doing—or *seeing*. Subscribe to Ad Age today. In fact, if you act now, you can save $51 off the cover price. Call 1-800-678-9595. It's a great marketing move.

Advertising Age
WHERE THE WORLD GETS THE WORD
On Marketing

BIG V PHARMACIES
3 Buchanan Ct
London, ON
Canada
Ph: 519/686-5081
Fax: 519/686-5514
John Muszak, Adv Mgr

BIGSBY & KRUTHERS
1750 N Clark St
Chicago, IL 60614
Ph: 312/440-1700
Carrie Brown, Adv Dir

BILL'S DOLLAR STORES
PO Box 9407
Jackson, MS 39286
Ph: 601/987-0667
Fax: 601/366-4823
David Kahlstorf, Dir- Sls Prom

BILL'S DOLLAR STORES
3800 I-55 North
Jackson, MS 39211
Ph: 601/981-7171
Mark Allen, Dir-Mktg
Cliff Treadaway, Adv Mgr

BISKIND DEVELOPMENT
4954 Great Northern Mall
Cleveland, OH 44070
Ph: 216/734-6304
Fax: 216/734-4365
Susan Hastings, Retail Mktg Dir

BLACK PHOTO CORP
371 Gough Rd
Markham, ON L3R 4B6
Canada
Bryan Black, VP-Mktg
Ph: 416/475-2777

BLACKER APPLIANCE
5023 E Cleveland
Caldwell, IA 83605
Ph: 208/459-0801
Fax: 208/459-0805
Jim Blacker, President

BLANKS COLOR IMAGE
2343 N Beckley
Dallas, TX 75208
Ph: 214/741-3905
Fax: 214/741-6105
Ken Encinas, Sls Rep
Ted Pospisil, VP Sls Mktg

BLOOMINGDALE'S
1000 Third Ave, 11th Fl
New York, NY 10022
Ph: 212/705-2410
Fax: 212/705-2516
Ronni Ascagni, Sr Home Furn Art Dir
Sophie Fermanis, Sr Home Furr Art Dir
212/705-2427
Brian Leitch, Copy Supv
212/705-2413
Carolyn Rothseid, Home Furn Copy
212/705-2414
John Jay, Sr VP-Creative Dir
Ph: 212/705-2427
Fax: 212/705-2516
Wendy Levine, Media Dir
Ph: 212/705-2429
Shawn Peacock, Men's Copy-writer
Ph: 212/705-2662

BLOOMINGDALE'S BY MAIL
155 E 60th St 2nd fl
New York, NY 10022
Ph: 212/705-2216
Fax: 212/832-0763
Gordon Cooke, CEO
Ph: 212/705-2434
Nancy Kaminsky, Dir- Prod
Lydia Munro, Creative Dir
Ph: 212/705-3832

BLOOMINGDALE'S
PO Box 5220/FDR Station
New York, NY 10150-5220
Ph: 212/705-3144
Fax: 212/705-2531
Francey Smith, Oper VP

BOMBAY COMPANY
550 Bailey, Ste 400
Fort Worth, TX 76107
Ph: 817/347-8228
Fax: 817/332-4872
Karen McKenzie, VP

190

THE BON MARCHE
3rd & Pine
Seattle, WA 98181
Ph: 206/344-8330
Fax: 206/344-8760
Marcia Broderick, Sr Art Dir
John Buller, VP-Sls Prom
Ph: 206/344-8759
Teresa Cicrich Powell, Copy Dir
Ph: 206/344-8771
Brian Walter, Brdcst Prod Mgr
Ph: 206/344-8775
Val Walser, Adv Oper Dir
Ph: 206/344-8759
Robert Raible, Sr Art Dir
Ph: 206/344-8776
Fax: 206/344-8761

BON TON DEPT STORES
2801 E Market St
York, PA 17402
Ph: 717/751-3160
Fax: 717/751-3245
Thomas Vranich, VP/Dir-Sls Prom

BOND
190 Fairway Dr
Pinehurst, NC 28374
William Bond, Consultant

BOOZ, ALLEN & HAMILTON
Three First Nat'l Plaza, 28 fl
Chicago, IL 60602
Ph: 312/346-3312
Mike Suchsland, Associate

BOSCOV'S DEPT STORES
4500 Perkiomen Ave
Reading, PA 19606
Ph: 215/370-3771
Fax: 215/370-3788
Frank Krandel, Dir-Adv
Kate Marvcco, Adv Mgr
Ph: 215/370-3773

BOSTON GLOBE
135 Morrissey Blvd
Boston, MA 02107
Ph: 617/929-2109
Fax: 617/929-3481
Gerard Cronin, Retail Adv Mgr
Elaine Mooney, Div Sls Mgr
Ph: 617/929-2124

BOSTON GLOBE
PO Box 2378
Boston, MA 02107
Ph: 617/929-2104
George Harden, Display Adv Mgr

BOSTON HERALD
One Herald Sq
Boston, MA 02106
Ph: 617/426-3000
John Nemerowski, Retail Adv Mgr

BOWMAN R&C PROJECTS
445 S Catherine
LaGrange, IL 60525
Ph: 708/482-3893
Carol Bowman, President

DALE BOWMAN ASSOC
9310 W Jefferson Blvd
Culver City, CA 90232
Ph: 213/837-8107
Fax: 213/837-2846
Joe Bowman, Mktg Dir
Dale Bowman, President

BOWRING DOWNTOWN
PO Box 4100
St. John's, NF A1C 5S6
Canada
Ph: 709/576-1539
Fax: 709/576-1874
Rosarii Mooney, Adv Dept

JEFFREY BOYLE
8725 NW 18th Terrace
Miami, FL 33172
Ph: 305/592-7032
Dan Aderhold, Acct Exec

BOZELL
201 E Carpenter Fwy
Irving, TX 75062
Ph: 214/830-2535
Fax: 214/830-2102
Ed Pitkoff, VP-Mgr/Retail Group

BPCC PLC
52 Fretter Ln
London, England EC4A1AA
UK
Ph: 01/377-4799
Varun Raj, Corp Sls Mgr

BRADLEES
One Bradlees Cir
Braintree, MA 02184
Ph: 617/380-5253
Fred Gelfand, VP/Dir-Mktg

BRANCH
841 Willow Ln
Hinsdale, IL 60521
Ph: 708/654-0937
Robert Branch

BRANHAM NEWSPAPER
444 N Michigan, #1110
Chicago, IL 60611
Ph: 312/321-0321
Fax: 312/321-0405
Georgia Evans, Sls Rep

BRENDLES, INC
1919 N Bridge St
Elkin, NC 28621
Ph: 919/526-6526
Andres Toro, Sls Prom Dir

BRESEES DEPT STORE
155 Main St
Onconta, NY 13820
Ph: 607/432-6000
Elaine Bresee, VP
Marc Bresee, VP

BRETT'S DEPT STORE
1575 Mankato Mall
Mankato, MN 56001
Ph: 507/625-6611
Janet Odden, Asst Art Dir
Lynne Schneider, Adv Dir
Donna Strand, VP-Mktg/Prom

BRETTONS
6535 Millcreek Dr, Unit 25
Mississauga, ON L5N 2M2
Canada
Ph: 416/821-8950
Fax: 416/821-3691
Kathryn Warren, Design Coord
Eilzabeth Williams, Copy Chief

BREWBACKER FURNITURE
401 Washington Ave
Onaway, MI 49765
Ph: 317/733-8595
Kathleen McConnell, Adv Dir

BRICK WAREHOUSE
#2500, 10060 Jasper Ave
Edmonton, AB T5J 3R8
Canada
Ph: 403/498-3124
Fax: 403/498-3168
Kim Odland, VP-Adv

BRITCHES OF GEORGETOWNE
544 Herndon Parkway
Herndon, VA 22070
Ph: 703/471-7900
Fax: 703/481-8733
Janet Daniel, Art Dir
Kim Gallagher, Copywriter
Ph: 703/834-6763
Fax: 703/481-8735
Lisa Hymes, PR Coord
Ph: 703/834-6766
Suzie Koones, Acct Supv
Ph: 703/834-6835
Susan Wallert, VP-Mktg
Ph: 703/834-6763

BROADWAY SOUTHWEST
4000 Fiesta Mall
Mesa, AZ 85202
Ph: 602/835-4500
Fax: 602/835-4582
Barbara Bailey, Sr VP-Mktg & Sls Prom
Terry Knoll, Exec Art Dir
Ph: 602/835-4547
Walter Knowles, VP/Adv Dir
Ph: 602/835-4545
Mary Jordan, Ad Home Art Dir
Ph: 602/835-4548
Susan Soto, Ad Copy Dir
Ph: 602/835-4552

BROADWAY
3880 North Mission Rd
Los Angeles, CA 90031
Ph: 213/227-2970
Leanne Mattes, Div VP-Adv Adm

BRODBECK ENTERPRISES
1035 E Highway 151
Platteville, WI 53818
Ph: 608/348-2343
Fax: 608/348-3345
Gary Fritz, Adv Dir

BROGAN & PARTNERS CO
3000 Towne Center, #475
Southfield, MI 48075
Ph: 417/353-9160
Fax: 417/353-4328
Marcie Brogan, President

BROOKS DRUG
75 Sabin St
Pawtucket, RI 02860
Ph: 401/724-9500
Douglas Palmacci, VP-Adv

BROWN PRINTER
122 E 42nd St, #1601
New York, NY 10168
Ph: 507/835-2410
Alisa Lograsso, Adv Mgr

BROWN PRINTING CO
3200 W End Ave, Ste 405
Nashville, TN 37203
Ph: 502/586-5773
Fax: 502/586-4558
Tom Williams, VP

BROWNE & BROWNE MARKETING
601 Lakeshore Pkwy, 10th fl
Minneapolis, MN 55343
Ph: 612/449-5116
Fax: 612/449-5101
Timothy Browne, President

BROWNS SHOE SHOPS
790 Begin St
Montreal, PQ H4M 2N5
Canada
Ph: 514/334-5512
Fax: 514/745-3250
Janis Brownstein, Adv Mgr

BRUNNING AGENCY
Queens Ct, 24 Queens St
Manchester England, M2 5HX
UK
Ph: 061/833-9999
Fax: 061/835-1319
Derek Linsley, Chief Exec
David Reid, Adv Mgr
Laurence Whittle, Joint Mgr Dir

BSB-DORLAND
121-141 Westbourne Terrace
London England,
UK W2 6JR
Ph: 011/44-1-262-5077
Fax: 01/258-3757
Brian Hovell, Retail Client Services Dir
John Stubbings, Deputy Mgr Dir
Ph: 011/44-1-262-5077
Fax: 01/258-3757

BUCKINGHAM, CIOFFI & ASSOC
37 Front St E, 4th Fl
Toronto
Ph: 416/360-3888
Brian Buckingham, President

BUCKS COUNTY COURIER
8400 Route 13
Levittown, PA 19057
Ph: 215/949-4120
Fax: 215/949-4114
Timothy Birch, Adv Dir

BUFFALO NEWS
One News Plaza, Box 100
Buffalo, NY 14240
Ph: 716/849-5470
Fax: 616/849-3409
Michael Squires, Retail Sls Mgr
David Stempkowski, Sls Rep
Ph: 716/849-5402

BUFFUM'S
301 Long Beach Blvd
Long Beach, CA 90802
Ph: 213/432-7000
Fax: 213/432-2356
Michael Mathews, VP-Sls Prom

BUILDERS EMPORIUM
40 Parker
Irvine, CA 92718
Lisa Burnand, Print Media Buyer
Ph: 714/454-6052
Fax: 714/454-6055
Tom Katada, Art Dir
Ph: 714/454-6048
Debra Scheibel, Dir-Adv
Ph: 714/454-6045
Fax: 714/454-6055

BULLOCK'S
800 S Hope St
Los Angeles, CA 90017
Ph: 213/612-5980
Fax: 213/612-5340
Mary Smart, Direct Mail Mgr

BURDINES
22 E Flagler St
Miami, FL 33131
Ph: 305/577-2400
Fax: 305/577-2032
David Campbell, Direct Mail Mgr
Linda Frankel, VP-Adv Dir
Ph: 305/577-1567
Jorge Lopez, OVP Adv Admin
Ph: 305/577-2706
Gilbert Lorenzo, DSSM Media Oper
Ph: 305/577-2726
Sally Moxham, Creative Dir
Ph: 305/577-2487

BURNETT DBA HALLMARK
PO BOX 538200
Orlando, FL 32853-8200
Ph: 904/734-0821
Robert Thompson, Exec VP

HE BUTT GROCERY
646 S Main
San Antonio, TX 78204
Ph: 512/270-8480
Fax: 512/270-8048
Melissa Stenicka, VP-Adv/Sls Prom

BWS ADVERTISING
37 Front St E, 4th fl
Toronto, ON M5E 1B3
Canada
Ph: 416/363-4485
Fax: 416/363-8533
Gerry Gaskin, VP-Gen Mgr

C & A
64 North Row, Marble Arch
London England W1A 2AX
UK
Ph: 011/629-1244
John AR Greene, Mktg Comm Mgr

CJCB - ATV
George St, Box 469
Sydney, NS B1P 6H5
Canada
Ph: 902/562-5511
Rick MacPherson, Mgr-Retail Bus Develop

CPC ASSOCIATES
33 Rock Hill Rd
Bala Cynwyd, PA 19004
Ph: 215/667-1780
Fax: 215/667-5650
Douglas Rose, Exec VP

CWO&O
866 Third Ave
New York, NY 10022
Ph: 212/750-4016
Fax: 212/935-9514
Jim Boynton, Sr VP-Retail Sls

CABLE TV ADVERTISING BUREAU
757 Third Ave
New York, NY 10017
Ph: 212/751-7770
Fax: 212/832-3268
Robert Alter, Pres & CEO

CABLE NETWORKS
260 Madison Ave
New York, NY 10016
Ph: 212/779-6108
Fax: 212/725-6949
James Dolan, VP
Peter Moran, Sr VP
Ph: 212/779-6108

CABOULI
230 W 55th St, 5D
New York, NY 10019
Ph: 212/582-3950
Fax: 212/974-4654
Pauline Cabouli, President

CACHET COMMUNICATIONS
17 N Sixth St
Geneva, IL 60134
Ph: 708/232-6644
Karen Newman, Creative Dir

CADILLAC FAIRVIEW
220 Yonge St, Ste 110
Toronto, ON M5B 2H1
Canada
Ph: 416/979-3300
Fax: 416/598-8607
Melaine Diamond, Dir-Natl Prom

CADILLAC FAIRVIEW
2145 Dunwin Dr Ste 15
Mississauga, ON L5L 4l9
Canada
Ph: 416/828-7151
Fax: 416/828-4838
Margaret Dickson, Mktg Dir

NOW AVAILABLE IN CANNES.

W.B. DONER & COMPANY

The work we do at Doner is seen every day in 28 countries around the globe. So, it's no surprise that our product is popular in Cannes, too. For the fourth straight year we've taken home more awards there than any other Detroit agency. 3 gold, 3 silver and 2 bronze lions. A pride we're proud of.

1987 Gold
Little Caesars
"Russians/Indians"

1987 Silver
Michigan Lottery
"Bilner"

1988 Gold
7-11
"Chickens/
Harvey/Mother"

1988 Silver
Sohio
"Wheels"

1989 Bronze
Canadian Tire
"Bike Story"

1989 Bronze
AAA
"Fire"

1990 Gold
Baltimore Symphony
"Baltimore's Other
Major League Team"

1990 Silver
Red Roof Inns
"The Wall"

CADILLAC FAIRVIEW
1200 Sheppard Ave E
North York, ON M2K 2R8
Canada
Ph: 416/495-7237
Fax: 416/495-9127
Giselle Doherty, Mktg Dir

CADILLAC FAIRVIEW
20 Queen St W, 4th fl
Toronto, ON M5H 3R4
Canada
Ph: 416/598-8570
Fax: 416/598-8607
John Garner, Mgr-Mktg & PR

CADILLAC FAIRVIEW
311-6th Ave, SW #1510
Calgary. AB T2P 3H2
Canada
Ph: 403/266-1066
Fax: 403/269-6966
Heather Hutley, Mktg Dir

CADILLAC FAIRVIEW
1800 McGill College, #810
Montreal, PQ H3A 3J6
Canada
Ph: 514/845-7111
Fax: 514/845-7350
Lisette Malo, Mktg Dir

CALDOR
20 Glover Ave
Norwalk, CT 06852
Ph: 203/849-2368
Fax: 203/849-2389
Paul Carlucci, Sr VP-Dir Mktg

CALGARY HERALD
215 16th St SE
Calgary, AB T2P 0W8
Canada
Ph: 403/235-7173
Fax: 403/235-8668
Gary Cobb, Retail Adv Mgr
Patrick Stadnyk, Sls Mgr Major
Retail Acct
Ph: 403/235-7184
Fax: 403/235-7113

CALGARY HERALD
PO Box 2400, Station M
Calgary. AB T2X 2Y6
Canada
Ph: 403/235-7174
Fax: 403/235-7113
Malcolm Gunn, Mgr-Multi-Mkt
Accts

**CAMBRIDGE
SHOPPING CENTRES**
95 Wellington St, Ste 300
Toronto, ON M5J 2R2
Canada
Ph: 416/369-1334
Fax: 416/369-1272
Stephen Szabo, Mgr Creative Ser
E Jane Walpole, Natl Mgr-Mktg
Ph: 416/369-1276

**CAMPBELL-MITHUN-
ESTY**
737 N Michigan Ave
Chicago, IL 60611
Ph: 312/266-5170
Fax: 312/226-5149
John Kroening, VP-Mgmt Supv
Jon Wylie, Sr VP-Mgmt Supv
Ph: 312/266-5160

CAMPING WORLD
650 Three Spring Rd
Bowling Green, KY 42102
Ph: 502/781-2718
Fax: 502/781-2775
Cathy Beard, Retail Mktg Mgr
Lisa Draughon, Retail
Mktg Mgr

CANADIAN TIRE CORP
2190 Yonge St
Toronto, ON M4P 2V8
Canada
Joanne Nicolson, English Copy/
Coord
Ph: 416/480-3684
Fax: 416/480-3843
Doug Webb, Mgr Retail Plnr
Ph: 416/480-3450
Andrea Ongaro, Mgr-Brdcst
Adv Prod
Ph: 416/480-3192
Fax: 416/480-3970
Tony Whitehouse, Mgr-Sls Prom
416/480-3129
Laurie Cook, Mgr Dir-Adv
Ph: 416/480-3096
Paul Renaud, Mgr Adv
Ph: 416/480-8052
Domenic Sanginiti, Creative
Sectionhead
Ph: 416/480-3438

192

CANADIAN AMERICAN
G-5115 Miller Rd
Flint, MI 48507
Ph: 313/733-1400
Fax: 313/733-1505
John Kupiec, President
Jim Williams, Exec VP-Mktg
Ph: 416/480-3000

**CANADIAN
BROADCASTING**
PO Box 500 Station A
Toronto, ON M5W 1E6
Canada
Ph: 416/975-7305

CANTERBURY TALES
544 Herndon Pkwy
Herndon, VA 22070
Ph: 703/834-6835
Fax: 703/481-8735
Suzanne Egan, Acct Exec
Patti Malone, Sr Art Dir
Ph: 703/834-6768

CARABINER
Box 1232
San Juan, PR 00901
Puerto Rico,
Ph: 809/721-6400

CARDINAL SERVICES
2101 W 37th Ave
Gary, IN 46408
Ph: 219/884-7000
Fax: 219/887-1541
Carol Dambrocia, Dir- Mktg

CARNATION MALL
2500 W State St
Alliance, OH 44601
Ph: 216/821-4447
Andrea Ferraro, Mktg Dir

CARPET ONE
One Harvey Rd
Manchester, NH 03103
Ph: 603/626-0333
Debi Blitzer, Asst Mktg

CARRIAGE HOUSE
1111 Ridge Rd
Lombard, IL 60148
Ph: 312/938-6500
Ronald Emanuel, President

CASAA
5520 N Hwy 169
New Hope, MN 55428
Ph: 612/535-6620 Ext-221
Chuck McKaige, Gen Mgr

CASE-HOYT
810 7th Ave, 18th Fl
New York, NY 10019
Ph: 212/489-1991
Fax: 212/498-0758
Jeff Benedict, Sls Rep
Elliot Greenberg, Sls Rep
Donald McCloskey, VP-
Catalog Sls

CASE-HOYT
1633 Broadway, 40th fl
New York, NY 10019
Ph: 212/307-0030
Fax: 212/307-4645
Bob Westover, Sls Mgr

CASTLE ADVERTISING
9340 Hazard Way, Ste A-1
San Diego, CA 92123
Ph: 619/569-9321
Fax: 619/571-7638
Chuck Castle, President

CATHERINE'S
1878 Brooks Rd, E
Memphis, TN 38116
Ph: 901/398-9500, 282
Fax: 901/398-9500, 279
Nina Miller, Dir Ad/Sls Prom

CATO CORPORATION
8100 Denmark Rd
Charlotte, NC 28210
Ph: 704/551-7220
Fax: 704/551-7554
Mare Ciarlante, Dir/Visual
Merchandising
Mary Saunders, Sls Analyst/
Media Plnr
Ph: 704/551-7328
Fax: 704/551-7521

CATO GOBE & ASSOC
411 Lafayette St
Ph: 212/645-6650
Fax: 212/979-8900
New York, NY 10003
Marc Gobe, Partner/Creative Dir

CB&S ADVERTISING
210 SW Morrison 3rd fl
Portland, OR 97204
Ph: 503/225-1200
Jim Card

CBA
50 Eisenhower Dr
Paramus, NJ 07652
Ph: 201/587-1717
Fax: 201/587-8308
Harold Matzner, VP

CBS ADVERTISING
1314 NW Northrup
Portland, OR 97242
Ph: 503/225-1200
Scott Bradley, VP

**CENTER ADVERTISING
AGENCY**
400 S Highway 169, Ste 800
Minneapolis, MI 55426
Ph: 612/525-1200
Fax: 612/525-2602
Mary Kiley, Sr VP

**CENTRAL
ADVERTISING**
279 Bayview Dr
Barrie, ON L4M 4W5
Canada
Ph: 705/728-6242
Kara Beaubien, Retail Adv Mgr
Peter Valiant, Adv Dir
Lori White, Supv Natl Adv

CENTRAL HARDWARE
5848 Wellington Farm Dr
St. Charles, MO 63303
Ph: 314/291-7000
Schultz Kurt, Dir-Adv

CENTRAL NEW JERSEY
123 How Lane, Box 551
New Brunswick, NJ 08903
Ph: 201/246-5612
Fax: 908/246-5518
Frank Savino, Retail Adv Mgr

**CEVETTE & COMPANY
ADVERTISING**
400 1st Ave N, Wyman Bldg,
Minneapolis, MN 55401
Ph: 612/338-1275
Fax: 612/338-1853
Patrick Strother, President

CFCF TV
405 Ogilvy Ave
Montreal, PQ H3N 1M4
Canada
Ph: 514/495-6100
Bruce Gornitsky, Retail
Sls Rep
Ron Robins, Sls Mgr
Peter Wright, Retail Sls Rep

CFCN TV
Box 7060 Stn E
Calgary, AB T3C 3L9
Canada
Ph: 403/240-5791
Glenn Grice, Retail Sls Mgr

CFMT TV
545 Lakeshore Blvd W
Toronto, ON M5V 1A3
Canada
Ph: 416/593-4747
Fax: 416/593-0629
Gary Bowmile, Dir Retail Sls

CHAPPELL'S
Northern Lights Mall
Syracuse, NY 13212
315/455-5711
Georgia Cuningham, Ad/Sls
Prom Mgr

CHARLES TUCKER
3750 N Lake Shore Dr
Chicago, IL 60613
Ph: 312/348-1411
Charles Tucker, Freelance
Consultant

**CHARLESTON DEPT
STORE**
1661 W Washington
St Charleston, WV 25312
Ph: 304/346-6793
Fax: 304/346-6797
Kelly Bartlett, Adv Dir

CHARMING SHOPPES
450 Winks Ln
Bensalem, PA 19020
Ph: 215/638-6764
Fax: 215/638-6699
Donna Brown, Asst to VP-Adv
Paul Toub, VP-Adv
Ph: 215/638-6761
Fax: 215/638-6699

CHARTERS MARKETIN
PO Box 127
Round Lake, NY 12151
Ph: 518/869-6913
Jeanne Charters, Dir-Mktg

CHC Advertising
61 Wilton Rd
Westport, CT 06880
Ph: 203/454-5585
Fax: 203/454-5589
Eric Tolkin, VP/Acct Dir

CHCH TV
163 Jackson St W, Box 2230
Hamilton, ON L8N 3A6
Canada
Ph: 416/522-1101
Fax: 416/523-3011
Richard Pudwell, Direct
Sls Mgr

JOHN S CHEEVER CO
105 Research Rd
Hingham, MA 02043
Ph: 617/749-8110
J. Kirby, Adv Dir

CHELSEA GROUP
641 Ave of the Americas
New York, NY 10011
Ph: 212/206-1780
Bernard McCabe, Creative Dir

CHIASSO
303 W Madison
Chicago, IL 60606
Ph: 312/419-1275
Keven Wilder, President

**CHICAGO APPAREL-
CENTER**
350 N Orleans
Chicago, IL 60654
Ph: 312/527-7770
Fax: 312/527-7897
Dorothy Fuller, Dir

CHICAGO MAGAZINE
414 N Orleans, #800
Chicago, IL 60610
Ph: 312/222-8999
Fax: 312/222-0699
Arlene Furey, Adv Dir/Assoc
Publisher

CHICAGO SUN-TIMES
401 N Wabash
Chicago, IL 60611
Ken DePaula, Group Sls Mgr
Ph: 312/321-2460
Fax: 312/321-3228
James Meyers, Sr VP-Mktg
Ph: 312/321-2029
Roger Saunders, Retail
Sls Mgr
Fax: 312/321-2422
Joe Sherman, Dir-Retail Adv Sls
Ph: 312/321-2455
Fax: 312/-321-9655

CHICAGO SUN-TIMES
156 W 56th St, Ste 1404
New York, NY 10019
Carole McClain, Sr Acct Mgr
Ph: 212/664- 1111
Fax: 212/664-1124

CHICAGO TRIBUNE
435 N Michigan Ave
Chicago, IL 60611
Ph: 312/222-4400
Fax: 312/222-3093
John Puerner, VP/Dir- Mkrt
Shirley Bradley, Retail Mktg
Supv
Ph: 312/222-3170
Fax: 312/222-3935
Beth Deputy, Sr Mktg Analysis
Ph: 312/222-3172
Dennis Grant, Natl/Retail
Ad Dir
Ph: 312/222-3915
David Murphy, Dir Retail Adv
Vincent Riordan, Sls Mgr
Ph: 312/222-2580
Patti Sullivan, Sr Mktg Analyst
Ph: 312/222-3172

CHILD WORLD
25 Littlefield St
Avon, MA 02322
Ph: 508/588-7300
Fax: 508/588-2019
Nancy Bildzok, Creative Dir
August Lodato, Dir-Adv

**CHORLEY &
PICKERSGILL**
121-141 Westbourne Terrace
London England, W2 6JR
UK
Michael Mitchell, Mngg Dir
Ph: 01/262-5077
Fax: 01/258-3757

BIRGER CHRISTENSEN
1300 Sherbrooke St W
Montreal, PQ H3G 1H9
Canada
Ph: 514/842-5111
Fax: 514/842-5111
Jim Killoch, Opers Mgr

CHUM GROUP TV
1315 Yonge St
Toronto, ON M4T 1Y1
Canada
Ph: 416/926-4150
Fax: 416/926-4156
Dan Hamilton, Supv Sls
Victor Rodriquez, Gen Sls Mgr
Don Cluff, General Manager
Ph: 416/961-0710

**CHUM REGIONAL
RADIO**
1315 Yonge St
Toronto, ON M4T 1Y1
Canada
Ph: 416/961-0710
Fax: 416/926-4156
John Wood, VP-Sls

CINCINNATI ENQUIRER
617 Vine St
Cincinnati, OH 45201
Ph: 513/369-1701
Fax: 513/369-1749
Jeni Wehrmeyer, Display Adv Dir

**CIOFFI &
ASSOCIATES**
1245 N Water St
Milwaukee, WI 53202
Ph: 414/276-1005
Fax: 414/276-3020
Susan Ciesiak, Media Mgr

CIOFFI & ASSOC ADV
744 Queen St, E
Toronto, ON M4M 1H4
Canada
Ph: 416/668-8882
Fax: 416/778-8879
Donna Pearl, Exec VP

**CIRCUIT CITY
STORES**
680 S Lemon Ave
Walnut, CA 91789
Ph: 714/869-7061
Larry Bier, Dir- Corp Adv

**CIRCUIT CITY
STORES**
9950 Mayland Dr
Richmond, VA 23233
Ph: 804/257-4228
Greg Jones, Asst VP-Mktg &
Adv

CITIBANK, NA
1 Ct Square, 28 fl
Long Island, NY 11120
Ph: 718/248-5280
Fax: 718/361-6622
Anne Brennan, VP

CKVR TV
PO Box 519
Barrie, ON L4M 4T9
Canada
Ph: 705/734-3300
Fax: 705/733-0302
John McCullough, Gen Sls Mgr
Fred Stacey, Retail Sls Supv
Ph: 705/726-9711
Fax: 705/726-4669

**CLEVELAND PLAIN
DEALER**
1801 Superior Ave
Cleveland, OH 44114
Ph: 216/344-4352
Fax: 216/694-6356
Stephen Casey, Retail Adv Mgr
David Nadeau, Asst Retail
Adv Mgr
Ph: 216/344-4997

**CLIFF FREEMAN AND
PARTNERS**
375 Hudsin St
New York, NY 10014
Ph: 212/463-2967
Fax: 212/463-3223
Bob Reed, Exec VP
David Srere, Sr VP
Ph: 212/463-3132

CLIPPER INC
1950 Spectrum Cir, Ste B300
Atlanta, GA 30067
Ph: 404/916-2020
404/266-1136
Fax: Liz Strickland, Mktg Asst

CLOTHESCARE
350 Main St
Binghamton, NY 13905
Ph: 607/798-7785
Jeff Schapiro

HARRISON SERVICES INC.

Service Is Our Middle Name

- **Marketing Concepts**
- **Creative Design**
- **Newspaper Ads**
- **In-Store Collateral**

- **In-House Photography**
- **Studio & Location**
- **In-House Typesetting**
- **Print Production**

New York Office: 8 West Thirty-Eighth Street, New York, NY 10018   (212) 302-1999
San Francisco Office: 170 Lombard Street, San Francisco, CA 94111   (415) 398-5666

CLOVER STORES
801 Market S, 9th fl
Philadelphia, PA 19107
Ph: 215/629-7721
Fax: 215/629-7197
Shirl Crowley, Adv Mgr
Rita McTighe, Asst to Adv Mgr
Ph: 215/629-7720
Barbara Neswald, Sls Prom Dir

CMA
1600 Hacienda Dr
El Cajon, CA 92020
Ph: 619/448-4885
Fax: 619/466-2335
Daniel Obst, President

CMF&Z
PO Box 2879
Cedar Rapids, IA 52406-2879
Ph: 319/395-6500
Fax: 319/395-6575
Diane Ramsey, Sr Acct Mgr

THE CNJ HOME NEWS
123 How Ln
New Brunswick, NJ 08903
Ph: 201/246-5618
Fax: 201/246-5518
Carol Hladun, Adv Sls Mgr

CO-OP ATLANTIC
123 Halifax St, Box 750
Moncton, NB E1C 8N5
Canada
Ph: 506/858-6290
Fax: 506/858-6373
Jonathan Andrews, Mdse Mgr
Steve MacDowall, Art Dir
Ph: 506/858-6046
Jennifer McMullan, Sr Artist
Ph: 506/858-6054
James Shane, Mgr- Adv
Services
Ph: 506/858-6046
Bob Stultz, Mdse Mgr-Food
Ph: 506/858-6046

**COAST TO COAST
STORES**
501 S Cherry St
Denver, CO 80222
Ph: 303/377-8400
Fax: 303/377-9638
Rollie Carlson, VP-Mktg
Carol Edinger, Adv Mgr
Gordon Johnston, Dir-Mktg
Patti Peri, PR Mgr
Ric West, Adv Prod Mgr
303/377-8400
303/377-9638

COHEN FURNITURE CO
336 S W Adams S
Peoria, IL 61602
Ph: 309/673-0711
Jeanne Dyer, Adv Dir

COHEN/JOHNSON
2029 Century Pk E, #1300
Los Angeles, CA 90067
Ph: 213/553-2300
Beverly Chamberlain, Assoc
Creative Dir
Brier White, Acct Supv

COHLMIA'S
5704 E 41st
Tulsa, OK 74145
Diane Posten

MM COHN
510 Main St
Little Rock, AR 72201
Ph: 501/372-8204
Velda Keeney, Sls Prom Dir

**COLBY'S HOME
FURNISHINGS**
3635 Touhy
Lincolnwood, IL 60645
Ph: 708/675-6767
Fax: 708/675-0178
Becky Walker, Adv Mgr

**COLONIAL
FURNITURE CO**
403 Bank St
Ottawa, ON K2P 1Y6
Canada
Ph: 613/236-9411
Sid Cohen, President

COLONY SHOP
PO Box 249
Wynne, AR 72396
Ph: 501/238-2381
Joe Dugan, President
Bob McMurtrey, VP-Opers

COLOPY DALE
208 Pine St
Pittsburgh, PA 15106
Ph: 412/429-0400
Fax: 412/429-0320
Robert Colopy, Partner

**COLOR TILE
SUPERMART**
515 Houston
Ft Worth, TX 76101
Ph: 817/870-9540
Ty Whorten, Adv Mgr

COLORCRAFT
3765 N 35th St
Milwaukee, WI 53216
Ph: 414/442-1344
Richard Johnson, VP-Sls

**COLOUR GRAPHICS
CORP**
3355 Republic Ave
Minneapolis, MN 55426
Ph: 612/929-0357
Fax: 612/929-1669
James Boosalis, VP

COLUMBIA FURNITURE
2125-27 W Chicago Ave
Chicago, IL 60622
Ph: 312/276-8100
Fax: 312/276-9261
Wally Papciak, Sls Mgr

**THE COLUMBIAN
NEWSPAPER**
701 W 8th St, Box 180
Vancouver, WA 98666
Ph: 206/694-3391
Fax: 206/699-6029
Christina Harmon, Major
Acct Mgr

**COLUMBIAN
PRINTING**
PO Box 180
Vancouver, WA 98666
Ph: 206/694-3391
William Strandy, Sls Mgr

COMFORT SHOP
11445 S Kedzie Ave
Merrionnette Pk, IL 60655
Ph: 312/385-0450
Thomas Bernar, Gen Mgr
David Roberts, President
Dick Willett, VP-Merchan/Mktg

**COMMERCIAL
GRAPHICS**
257 Park Ave S
New York, NY 10010
Ph: 212/477-9100
Fax: 212/505-8421
Barbara Buonocore, Acct Exec
David Christensen, President
Tracy Kimmel, Acct Exec
Vince Perrella, Creative Dir

**COMMUNICATION
GROUP**
7 Charnwood Crescent
St. Kilda Australia, Victoria
Australia
Ph: 03/537-2666
Michael Allen, Exec Dir

**COMMUNICATION
GROUP**
253 Sturt St
Adelaide S Australia, 5000
Australia
Ph: 08/211-7357
Kevan Scrimshaw, Exec Dir

COMPU-COLOR, INC
4655 Shallowford Rd
Chattanooga, TN 37411-1124
Ph: 615/892-5466
Don Benedict, Sls
Kent Harless, President

**CONDE NAST
PUBLICATIONS**
350 Madison Ave
New York, NY 10017
Ph: 212/880-8816
Fax: 212/880-8982
Gretel Schneider, Mktg Dir

**CONLON
COPYWRITING
COMMUNICATION**
825 Longmeadow Dr
Geneva, IL 60134
Ph: 708/232-9521
Richard Conlon

**CONSOLIDATED
STORES**
300 Phillipi Rd
Columbus, OH 43228
Ph: 614/278-6902
Fax: 614/278-6927
Ron Surgeson, Dir-Adv

CONSUMER VOICE
12825 Plum Hollow Dr
Oklahoma City, OK 73142
Ph: 405/841-8379
Fax: 405/841-8149
Carol Scroggins, President

**CONSUMERS
DISTRIBUTING**
62 Belfield Rd
Rexdale, ON M9W 1G2
Canada
Ph: 416/245-4900
Fax: 416/245-6905
Greg Antonacci, Prod Mgr
Janice Partington, Dir- Mktg

**CONTINENTAL
EXTRUSION**
2 Endo Blvd
Garden City, NY 11530
Ph: 516/832-8111
Taffy Benjamin, Mktg Mgr

**CORPORATE
PROPERTY**
305 E 47th St
New York, NY 10017
Ph: 212/421-8200
Fax: 212/319-9845
Lynn Blacker
Sherry Johnson, Corp Mkg Dir

COURIER-JOURNAL
525 W Broadway
Louisville, KY 40202
Ph: 502/582-4714
Fax: 502/582-7111
Gail Bardenwerper, Major
Accts Mgr
James Lobas, Display Adv Dir

COX ENTERPRISES
PO Box 34665
Charlotte, NC 28234
Ph: 704/335-4931
Fax: 704/335-4944
Joyce Brayboy, Co-op Sls
Consultant
Kathy Fletcher, Retail Mktg
Mgr

CRAFT-N-FLOWER INC
8299 Wyatt Rd
Broadview Hts, OH 44147
Ph: 216/838-4485
David Hill, Adv Dir

**CREATIVE
DIMENSIONS**
1 Mill Reach Ln
Hamilton, HM05
Bermuda
Ph: 809/292-4891
Fax: 809/292-0473
Neil Hillier, Graphic Aris
Catherine Mahoney, Sr Acct
Exec

CREATIVE DESIGN
3905 Tyndall Rd
University Hgts, OH 44118
Ph: 216/321-6627
Virginia Levitt, Art Dir

**CRESMER
WOODWARD**
1 E. Wacker Dr, #2410
Chicago, IL 60601
Ph: 312/321-6367
Fax: 312/321-6364
Thomas Schuba, VP-Retail Sls

**CROSSROADS OF
SAN ANTONIO**
4522 Fredericksburg Rd, #124
San Antonio, TX 78201
Ph: 512/737-1230
Fax: 512/732-5205
Priscilla Gonzaba, Mktg Dir

CROWLEY'S
2301 Lafayette
Detroit, MI 48216
Ph: 313/962-2400
Fax: 313/962-2529
Stanley Siwula, Sls Prom Dir

CROWN AUTO
PO Box 1217
Minneapolis, MN 55440
Ph: 612/937-9000
Lee Bergstrom, Adv Mgr

CROWN CENTER
2405 Grand Ave, Ste 200
Kansas City, MO 64108
Ph: 816/274-3357
Fax: 816/274-4567
Marcia Butterbaugh, Adv Mgr

CUB FOODS
127 Water St
Stillwater, MN 55082
Ph: 612/779-2006
Fax: 612/779-2102
Robert Bausch, Dir-Mktg
Sarah Jewell, Creative Dir
Ph: 612/779-2061
Elizabeth Jurchisin, Media Mgr
Ph: 612/439-7200

**CUSHMAN
FURNITURE**
5711 Winnequah Rd
Monona, WI 53716
Ph: 608/244-5588
David Christensen, President
Vicki Christensen, VP

**DC PRYOR
MARKETING
CONSULTANT**
708 N First St, Ste 646
Minneapolis, MN 55401
Ph: 612/375-0463
Fax: 612/375-9877
Debra Pryor, President

D-J ASSOCIATES
77 Danbury Rd/Box 2048
Ridgefield, CT 06877
Ph: 203/431-8777
Fax: 203/431-3302
Kathy Duggan-Josephs, Pres

**DAGENS NYHETER
TIDNINGSBYRAN**
Stockholm, S-10515
Sweden
Ph: 87381355
Anders Zederman, Copy Dir

THE DAKIS CONCERN
103 Orinda Way, Box 758
Orinda, CA 94563
Ph: 415/254-6606
Fax: 415/254-8808
Frank Forker, VP-Creative Dir

**DALE BOWMAN
ASSOCIATES**
9310 Jefferson Blvd
Culver City, CA 90232-2914
Ph: 213/306-4255
Fax: 213/306-4285
Tricia Kremer, Media Dir

**DALLAS MORNING
NEWS**
Communications Center
Dallas, TX 75202
Ph: 214/977-8563
Fax: 214/977-8168
Jerry Coley, Dir Retail-Adv
Thomas Sandoz Jr, Dir-Sls
Ph: 214/977-8558

DALLAS FURNITURE
7200 Kingston Pike
Knoxville, TN 37919
Ph: 615/588-2419
Julie Matthews, President
Janice Reid, Asst Mgr

**DALLAS TIMES
HERALD**
1101 Pacific Ave
Dallas, TX 75202
Ph: 214/720-6309
Fax: 214/720-6465
Scott McKibben, Retail Adv Dir
Jim Wall, VP-Adv
Ph: 214/720-6337
Fax" 214/720-6364

DANCER'S
566 N Cedar - PO Box 100
Mason, MI 48854
Ph: 517/676-4474
Fax: 517/676-4554
Kevin Ball, Adv Dir

**DAYTON'S HUDSON'S
MARSHALL FIELD'S**
700 on the Mall
Minneapolis, MN 55402
Bill Bloedow, Supv Art Dir
Ph: 612/375-3357
Fax: 612/375-3340
Dyer Davis, Supv Copywriter
Ph: 612/375-4088
Eric Erickson, Adv Copy Chief
Ph: 612/375-3031
Michael Francis, Print Media Mgr
Ph: 612/375-4626

Kent Hensley, Supv Art Dir
Ph: 612/375-6526
Debra Herdman, Supv Art Dir
Ph: 612/375-2515
Paul Karmann, Dir-Media Plnr
Ph: 612/375-3976
Jeff Mueller, Print/Brdcst
Copywriter
Ph: 612/375-4089
Jack Mugan, Dir-Creative Ser
Ph: 612/375-3001
Vicky Rossi, Sr Copywriter
Ph: 612/375-2515
Connie Soteropulos, Exec Art Dir
Ph: 612/375-3286
Kristin Staubitz, In-Store
Media Mgr
Ph: 612/375-3997
Cheryl Watson, Senior Art Dir
Ph: 612/375-2181
Nancy Whitney, Mgr Brdcst
Ph: 612/375-3010
Stewart Widdess, Sr VP-Mktg
Ph: 612/375-3124

DAYTON DAILY NEWS
45 S Ludlow St
Dayton, OH 45458
Ph: 513/225-2082
Fax: 513/225-2088
Stephen Bernard, Adv Dir

DDB-NEEDHAM
2600 W Big Beaver Rd, #500
Troy, MI 48084
Ph: 313/643-4300
Fax: 313/649-0102
Rod Burton, VP-Mgmt Supv

**DDB NEEDHAM/
ELGIN SYFERD**
1008 Western Ave
Seattle, WA 98104
Ph: 206/223-2356
Fax: 206/223-6309
Leann Ebe, Acct Mgr

**DE FEVER
PRODUCTIONS**
157 Chambers St
New York, NY 10007
Ph: 212/233-7177
Fax: 212/277-3587
Gerard Longobardi, Artists Rep

DEB SHOPS INC
9401 Blue Grass Rd
Philadelphia, PA 19114
Ph: 215/676-6000
Jane Krate, Adv- Dir

**DECISIONBASE
RESOURCES**
36 W 44th St, Ste 1111
New York, NY 10036
Ph: 212/575-6543
Brian Beckee, Sr VP

DEJONG'S
306 Main St
Evansville, IN 47708
Ph: 812/542-3116
Jane Smith, Adv Dir

**DEKORNE
FURNITURE**
3450 28th St SE
Grand Rapids, MI 49512
Ph: 616/949-4966
Fax: 616/949-0881
Dale DeKorne, VP-Mktg

DELONG ADVERTISING
7657 Sheffield Village Ln
Lorton, VA 22079
Ph: 703/339-8567
Mike DeLong, President

DENVER POST
1560 Broadway
Denver, CO 80202
Ph: 303/820-1392
Fax: 303/820-1406
Mike Lynch, Adv Dir

**DES MOINES
REGISTER**
715 Locust St
Des Moines, IA 50309
Ph: 515/284-8060
Fax: 515/286-2530
Marilyn Tanious, Retail Adv Mgr
Christine Wilson, Major
Acct Supv
Ph: 515/284-8389

AF DESCENZA
387 Washington St
Boston, MA 02108
Diane Descenza

<u>Electronic Color Page Production</u>

Three questions to ask yourself...

Are we taking advantage of the desktop?

Are the options confusing?

Isn't it time to call Kreber Graphics?

<u>The Experts</u>

800-777-3501

KREBER GRAPHICS, INC.

COLOR SEPARATORS

DESIGNER COLOR SYSTEMS
11971 Borman Dr
St. Louis, MO 63146
Ph: 314/275-7171
Mary Ann Gibson, President
Dan Gibson, Acct Exec

DETROIT NEWSPAPER AGENCY
615 Lafayette
Detroit, MI 48226
Ph: 313/222-2464
Fax: 313/222-2433
Joseph Holt, Natl Retail Sls Mgr
Dave McDade, Display Adv Dir
Ph: 313/222-2445
Fax: 313/222-2545
Kristina Petzer, Retail Adv Dir
Ph 313/222-2437

DIAMOND ARTS STUDIO
11 E 36th St
New York, NY 10016
Ph: 212/685-6622
Debra Phillips, Freelancer

IB DIFFUSION
Apparel Center #170
Chicago, IL 60654
Ph: 312/836-6192
Fax: 312/836-6171
Dana Cohen, Adv Sls Prom
Kerri Neubek, Adv Mgr
Ph: 312/836-4477
Fax: 312/222-0039

DILL'S BEST BUILDING CENTER
1833 E Main S
Peekskill, NY 10566
Ph: 914/739-3150
Fax: 914/739-2188
Carl Dill, President
Diane Greco, Adv Mgr

DILLARD'S
1616 S Priest Dr
Tempe, AZ 85281
Ph: 602/829-5328
Fax: 602/829-5265
Bob Baker, VP-Mktg/Sls Prom
Bonnie Burton, VP-Mktg/Sls Prom
Matthew Ratkovic, Adv Creative Dir
Ph: 602/829-5308

DILLARD'S
1600 Cantrell Rd, 1st fl
Little Rock, AR 72201
Ph: 501/376-5976
Fax: 501/376-5885
Jan Bolton, VP-Sls Prom
Pat Gallia, Bus Mgr
Phyllis Lueken, Direct Mail Mgr
Mary Mitchell, Brdcst Mgr
Chris Smith, Prod Mgr
Beth Stewart, Mktg Analyst

DILLARD'S
9315 Broadway
San Antonio, TX 78217
Ph: 512/821-7611
Fax: 512/821-7776
Linda Sholtis, VP-Sls Prom

DILLARD'S
3301 Veterans Blvd
Metairie, LA 70002
Ph: 504/833-1075
Susan Peterson, Adv Admin

DIRECT MARKETING OF TECHNOLOGY
955 American Ln
Schaumburg, IL 60173
Ph: 708/517-5600
Fax: 708/517-5609
Bob Mutranowski, Acct Exec

DIRECT DIGITAL DESIGN
1100 W Cambridge Cir Dr
Kansas City, KS 66103
Ph: 913/371-4333
Fax: 913/371-6382
Herb Taylor, Gen Mgr

DISCOVER CARD SVCS
2500 Lake Cook Rd
Riverwoods, IL 60015
Ph: 708/405-3261
Fax: 708/405-4139
Susan Zingle, VP-Retail SLs

DISPLAY & DESIGN IDEAS
180 Allen Rd, Ste 300 N
Atlanta, GA 30328-4893
Ph: 404/252-8831
Fax: 404/252-4436
Karen Benning, Editor
Doug Hope, Natl Sls Mgr

DMB & B CANADA
2 Bloor St W, Ste 1400
Toronto, ON M4W 3R3
Canada
Ph: 416/922-2211
Fax: 416/922-8590
Brad Collis, Acct Exec
Michael Fung-A-Ling, Acct Exec
Craig Hannah, Acct Sup
Peter Harris, Sr VP-Group Acct Dir

DMDA INC
1621 W Crosby Rd Ste 112
Carrollton, TX 75006
Ph: 214/466-2611
Fax: 214/466-0433
Sharon Brown, VP-Mktg
Tommie Turner, President

DMW ADVERTISING
40 Holly St Ste 402
Toronto, ON M45 3C3
Canada
Ph: 416/322-7728
Fax: 416/322-7722
Suzan Mandell, Acct Dir

DOMINICK'S FINER FOODS
505 Railroad Ave
Northlake, IL 60164
Ph: 708/562-1000
Fax: 708/409-6021
Larry Nauman, VP-Adv Sls Prom

WB DONER & CO
9455 Koger Ste 200
St. Petersburg, FL 33702
Ph: 813/576-6920
Fax: 813/576-8510
Linda Angelacci, VP
Ann Bergstrom, Sr VP

WB DONER & CO
25900 Northwestern
Southfield, MI 48075
Ph: 313/827-8320
Fax: 313/827-8440
John Considine, Exec VP Plnr
Barb Craig, Acct Supv
Ph: 313/827-8439
Thomas Downey, Acct Supv
Ph: 313/827-9784
Alan Kalter, Exec VP
Ph: 313/827-8354
Jonathan Katov, VP-Acct Supv
Ph: 313/827-8359
Ross Lerner, VP
Ph: 313/827-8350
Nathan Roth, Acct Mgr
Ph: 313/827-8352
Michael Shapira, President
Ph: 313/827-8354
Monica Tysell, Acct Supv
Ph: 313/827-8351
Jill Vedder, Acct Supv
Ph: 313/827-8443
Vera Yardley, VP
313/827-8307

WB DONER & CO
9455 Koger Blvd, #200
St. Petersburg, FL 33702
Ph: 813/576-6920
Fax: 813/576-8510
Ginny Vonckx, Acct Supv

DONNELLEY MARKETING
70 Seaview Ave
Stamford, CT 06904
Ph: 203/353-7013
Fax: 203/353-7157
Sally Ann Ciarlo, Acct Mgr
Bill Hodgkinson, Asst VP
Ph: 203/353-7000
Kimberlie Leon
203/353-7036
Julie Adamson
203/353-7000
Susanne Bashkin, Exhibit Mgr
203/353-7409
Laura Bonafide, Acct Exec
203/353-7129
Adrian Dessi, Dir-Mktg
Ph: 203/353-7421
Joseph DiMauro, Natl Acct Mgr
Ph: 203/353-7094
Victoria James, VP-Sls
Ph: 203/353-7111
Thomas Kobak, Mktg Mgr
Ph: 203/353-7088
Barbara Lundy, Acct Exec
Ph: 203/353-7157

DONNELLEY MARKETING
1901 S Meyers Rd, #700
Oakbrook Terrace, IL 60181
Ph: 708/495-1211
Fax: 708/495-0613
Scott Lynn, Acct Exec
David McSweeney, Acct Exec
Leslie O'Hare, Acct Exec
Lynda Richey, Mgr-Trade Shows and Conference
Ph: 708/495-1279

DONNELLEY MARKETING
900 Dartmouth Dr
Wheaton, IL 60187
Ph: 708/495-1211
Jeff Slabaugh, VP-Sls

DONNELLEY MARKETING
2401 E Katella Ave, #600
Anaheim, CA
Ph: 714/978-1122
Fax: 714/978-2018
Cynthia Clark, Acct Exec
Beth Robertson, Acct Exec

RR DONNELLEY
2223 S King Dr
Chicago, IL 60616
Ph: 312/326-8088
Fax: 312/326-8078
Ed Davis, Prod Specialist

RR DONNELLEY
1722 Two Tandy Center
Fort Worth, TX 76102
Ph: 817/878-6205
Fax: 817/878-6240
Kenzie MacDonald, VP-Sales

RR DONNELLEY
13355 Noel Rd, #1415
Dallas, TX 75240
Ph: 214/702-7338
Fax: 214/702-7340
Richard Mullen, VP

RR DONNELLEY
11400 SE 8th St, #210
Bellevue, WA 98004
Ph: 206/455-0755
Meredith Potter, Sls Rep

RR DONNELLEY
2122 York Rd
Oak Brook, IL 60521
Ph: 708/574-3840
David Saxman, VP

RR DONNELLEY
128 S Tryon Suite 1720
Charlotte, NC 28202
Ph: 612/342-9510
Larry Tarman, VP

RR DONNELLEY
701 Fouth Ave S, 1310
Minneapolis, MN 55415
Ph: 612/342-9510
Fax: 612/342-9518
Dave Wieggel, VP-Sls

DONOHOE, O'BRIEN & CO
Curtis Center,
#700 Indep Sq W
Philadelphia, PA 19106
Ph: 215/238-6400
Fax: 215/238-6420
Laurie Wolfe, Asst VP-Dir, Corp Mktg

DONOVAN & ASSOCIATES
5065 Shore Line Rd, Ste 201
Barrington, IL 60010
Ph: 708/382-6550
Fax: 708/382-0034
Kathleen Cooper, President
Anne McCormick, VP

THE DRESS BARN
69 Jefferson St
Stamford, CT 06902
Ph: 230/352-7690
Michael Cohen, Dir Adv & Sls Prom

DRUG TRADING
1960 Eglinton Ave, E
Scarborough, ON M1L 2M5
Canada
Ph: 416/288-1700
Fax: 416/288-7951
Chris McEvenue, Retail Div Mgr

DUCKWALL-ALCO STORES
401 Cottage
Abilene, KS 67410
Ph: 913/263-3350
Fax: 913/263-7531
Dorothy Haslouer, Dir-Adv
Patricia Storm, Adv Prod Mgr

E & B MARINE
201 Meadow Rd
Edison, NJ 08818
Ph: 201/819-7400
Fax: 201/819-4771
Richard Goldberg, VP-Mktg
Thomas Ludington, Dir Retail Adv & Prom

EARLE PALMER BROWN & SPIRO
1650 Market St
Philadelphia, PA 19103
Ph: 215/851-9600
Fax: 215/851-9509
Mary Ann Sesso, VP

EAST-WEST NETWORK
2650 N Lakeview, #2204
Chicago, IL 60614
Ph: 312/472-4928
Benette Seide, Acct Mgr

T EATON CO
1 Dundas St W, 8th fl
Toronto, ON M5B 1C8
Canada
Ph: 416/343-3359
Fax: 416/343-2335
Colette Berry, Media Mgr
John Dawkins, Adv Mgr
Ph: 416/343-3424
Fax: 416/343-2385

EATON & SMALLEY
388 King St, W #102
Toronto, ON M5V 1K2
Canada
Ph: 416/977-3724
Ken Eaton, President

ECKERD DRUG CO
8333 Bryan Dairy Rd/Box 4689
Largo, FL 34647
Ph: 813/398-8339
Fax: 813/398-8409
Kenneth Banks, VP-Mktg Comm
Brian Crank, Ad Mgr-Print
Ph: 813/397-7461
Julie Gardner, Mgr Adv & Mktg
Betsi O'Neill, Dir-Adv/Sls Prom
Ph: 813/398-8371
Karen Sebourn, Creative Prod Mgr

ROLAND L ECKSTEIN & CO
157 Broad St
Red Bank, NY 07701
Ph: 201/530-1996
Roland Eckstein, Chairman

ROLAND L ECKSTEIN & CO
3915 Francis Rd
Alpharetta, GA 30201
Ph: 404/442-3644
Donald Love, Exec VP

ECLECTIC NTERNATIONAL
230 Clematis St
West Palm Beach, FL 33401
Ph: 407/655-2780
Fax: 407/655-4001
Steven Marks, President

ECONOMIC PERSPECTIVES
PO Box 1160
Delaware, OH 43015
Ph: 614/666-8822
James Newton, President

ECONOMIC DEVELOPMENT
9940-106 St, 6th fl
Edmonton, AB T5K 2P6
Canada
Ph: 403/427-3685
Holly Palmer, Bus Analyst-Mkt

ECONOMY DRY GOODS
92 Main St
So. Glens Falls, NY 12803
Ph: 518/792-1252
Joseph Didio, Dir Mktg/Sls Prom

EDGARS STORES
PO Box 178
Crown Mines, SA 2025
South Africa
Ph: 011/495-6813
Fax: 011/537-9340
Carol Grolman, Mktg Dir

EDMONTON JOURNAL
PO Box 2421
Edmonton, AB T5J 2S6
Canada
Ph: 403/429-5455
Fax: 403/498-5602
F.S.(Fred) Castle, Asst Adv Dir

EDWARD J DEBARTOLO CORP
7620 Market St
Youngstown, OH 44513
Ph: 216/758-7292
Fax: 216/758-3598
Mary Rutkoski, Dir-Mktg

WILLIAM EISNER & ASSOC
5307 S 92nd St
Hales Corner, WI 53130
Ph: 414/425-8800
Fax: 414/425-0021
Wyn Becker, Sr VP/Client Services
Bill Eisner, Pres & CEO
Michael Fratantuno, Mgr Retail Services

ELAINE MEIER ASSOCIATES
273 Commonwealth Ave
Boston, MA 02116
Ph: 617/267-6759
Elaine Meier, VP Acct Supv

ELDER-BEERMAN
3155 El-Bee Rd
Dayton, OH 45401
Ph: 513/296-2844
Fax: 513/296-4575
Diane Brown, Adv Mgr
Lee Causer, VP-Creative Art Dir
Ph: 513/296-4507
Sue Westbrook, Sr VP-Sls Prom Dir
Ph: 513/296-2844

ELECTRA
90 Remington Blvd
Ronkonkoma, NY 11779
Ph: 516/585-5659
Fax: 516/585-5843
Larry Ruderman, President

ELECTRIC CITY
PO Box 3779
Gulfport, MS 39505
Ph: 601/867-1253
Fax: 601/867-1211
Vicki Daniels, Coord-Adv Prom
Henry Earles, President
Ph: 601/867-1273
Fax: 601/867-1290

ELECTRONIC IMAGE
2055 Army Trail Rd
Addison, IL 60101
Ph: 708/932-7080
Fax: 708/932-7195
George Nielsen, President

ELGIN SYFERD ADVERTISING
1008 Western Ave, #600
Seattle, WA 98104
Ph: 206/442-9900
Fax: 206/223-6309
Patti Frey, VP

ELLE MAGAZINE
1633 Broadway
New York, NY 10019
Ph: 212/767-5851
Fax: 212/489-4210
Kathleen Foster, Retail Mgr
Richard Rabinowitz, Adv Dir/VP
Ph: 212/767-5817
Stephanie Smith, NY Mgr
Ph: 212/767-5816

ELLE MAGAZINE
625 N Michigan, 14th fl
Chicago, IL 60611
Ph: 312/280-0312
Fax: 312/280-0351
Corinne Kirby, Midwest Mgr

ELLE PUBLISHING
551 Fifth Ave, 8th Fl
New York, NY 10176
Ph: 212/808-5800
Lulu Bagnall, Dir-Special Proj
Marie Larsen, Retail Mgr
212/808-5815
Richard Rabinowitz, Adv Dir
Ph: 212/808-5817
Barbara Szpak, Retail Prom Dir

Saffer
RAC Winners

THE ELS GROUP
Thomas House, Prescot Rd
Merseyside
St Helens, England WA10 3X
UK
Ph: 074/461-2181
Fax: 074/420-585
Gordon Cox, Mng Dir
Roger Ephraims, Buying/
Mktg Dir

ELTE CARPETS
80 Ronald Ave
Toronto, ON M6E 5A2
Canada
Ph: 416/785-7885
Fax: 416/785-9157
Laurence Metrick, Dir Mktg
& Adv

EMBRY'S
755 Newtown Rd
Lexington, KY 40511
Ph: 606/252-3431
Fax: 606/254-9027
Joyce Buckley, Adv Dir

EMPORIUM
835 Market St
San Francisco, CA 94103
Ph: 415/764-3678
Fax: 415/764-3178
Div VP-Creative Services
Alice MacNaughton, Sr VP-
Sls Prom

EMW DESIGN ASSOC
107 Grand St
New York, NY 10013-2615
Ph: 212/677-2060
Walter Taurins, VP
Ellen Wandzilak, President

EMW
107 Grand St
New York, NY 10013-2615
Ph: 212/677-2060
Pam Wong, VP/Creative Dir

**ENGLISH SPORTS
SHOP**
49 Front St
Hamilton, Bermuda HM EX
Ph: 809/295-2672
Ramona Anderson, Adv Dir

EQUIFAX
8430 W Bryn Mawr, #660
Chicago, IL 60631
Ph: 312/693-0070
Fax: 312/693-1723
Scott Purlee, Sr Consultant-
Retail

EQUITY PROPERTIES
2033 Turfland Mall
Lexington, KY 40504
Ph: 606/276-4411
Steven Barg, Mktg Dir

EQUITY PROPERTIES
2 North Riverside Plaza
Chicago, IL 60606
Ph: 312/454-1800
Mark London, President
Carlene Palmquist, Regl Dir
Mktg

EQUITY PROPETIES
7601 S Cicero Ave
Chicago, IL 60652
Ph: 312/767-6400
Marlaina Recknagel, Specialty
Leasing Coord

EQUITY PROPETIES
2250 Oak Ct
Hollywood, FL 33026
305/435-8132
Chris Roberts, Regl Mktg Dir

ERNST & YOUNG
787 Seventh Ave
New York, NY 10019
Ph: 212/773-6101
Fax: 212/586-8283
Eileen Laymon, Dir-Mktg-Retail
Services

**ESQUIRE
ASSOCIATES**
1790 Broadway
New York, NY 10019
Ph: 212/459-7614
Fax: 212/245-6533
Kevin O'Malley, Retail Mktg
Mgr

ESQUIRE MAGAZINE
1790 Broadway
New York, NY 10019
Ph: 212/659-7650
Fax: 212/245-6533
W. Randall Jones, Publisher

ESTES FURNITURE
101 E Grand River Ave
Lansing, MI 48906
Ph: 517/372-8710
Fax: 517/372-1089
Julie Demers, Design Coord
Brad Foster, VP-Sls
Wayne Foster, Chairman
Al Herring, VP-Adv

ESTEY
103 Santa Rosa Ave
Sausalito, CA 94965
Ph: 415/331-9335
Melinda Estey, Brdcst Prod

ETHAN ALLEN
Ethan Allen Drive
Danbury, CT 06811
Ph: 203/743-8222
Linda Carter, Copywriter
Frank Ricchezza, Art Dir
Ph: 203/743-8221

EVANS
36 S State, #1620
Chicago, IL 60603
Ph: 312/855-2197
Fax: 312/855-3138
Roseanne Campanelli, Art Dir
Pat Kanz, Brdcst Mgr
Ph: 312/855-2275
Cheryl O'Donovan, Copy Dir
Ph: 312/855-2205
Randy Barberis, VP-Mktg
Ph: 312/855-3142
Mike Face, Creative Dir
Ph: 312/855-2207
Rob Steffen, Adv Mgr
Ph: 312/855-2127

EVANS/SLC
110 Social Hall Ave
Salt Lake City, UT 84111
Ph: 801/364-7452
Fax: 801/364-7484
Marta Smith, Media Buyer
Rob Pyper, VP

EVERETT MALL
1402 SE Everett Mallway
Everett, WA 98208
Marketing Director
Ph: 206/745-1786
Fax: 206/742-9255

EXPRESS-NEWS
Ave E & 3rd
San Antonio, TX 78297
Ph: 512/225-7411
Fax: 512/225-2553
Michael Allison, Adv Mgr

**FABRI-CENTERS OF
AMERICA**
5555 Darrow Rd
Hudson, OH 44236
Ph: 216/463-3444
Fax: 216/656-0089
Liz Geurink, VP-Sls Prom
Linda Goetz, Mktg Serv Dir
Ph: 216/463-3457
David Kelly, Bus Dir
Ph: 216/656-2600
Barb Semen, Dir-Adv-
216/463-3430

**FABRI-CENTERS OF
AMERICA**
23550 Commerce Pk Rd
Beachwood, OH 44122
Ph: 216/464-2500
Jackie Ollom, Creative Dir

FAIR CO
566 Southwest Cutoff
Worcester, MA 01607
Ph: 508/756-1506
Fax: 508/752-5669
Tim Brennan, Dir-Adv

W FAIRCHILD
7 E 12th St
New York, NY 10003
Ph: 212/741-4277
Fax: 212/741-6652
Nancy Brannigan, Mktg Dir

FAIRFIELD STORE
1499 Post Rd
Fairfield, CT 06430
Ph: 203/255-2661
Fax: 203/255-0307
Bruce Manasevit, Adv Mgr

**FAIRFIELD DAILY
REPUBLIC**
1250 Texas St
Fairfield, CA 94533
Ph: 707/425-4646
Fax: 707/425-5924
Ann Rollin

FAIRWEATHER
637 Lakeshore Blvd W
Toronto, ON M5V 1A8
Canada
Ph: 416/586-6901
Fax: 416/586-6904
Sally Edmonds, VP/Dir-Mktg
Mark Steinberg, Mktg Mgr
Ph: 416/586-7417

**FAMILY CIRCLE
MAGAZINE**
110 Fifth Ave
New York, NY 10011
Ph: 212/463-1667
Julie Baker, Prom
Carrie Chehayl, Research
Ph: 212/463-1671
Barbara Costello, Category Mgr
Ph: 212/463-1548

**FAMILY DOLLAR
STORES**
PO Box 1017
Charlotte, NC 28201-1017
Ph: 704/847-6961
Fax: 704/847-5534
Edgar Paxton, VP-Adv/Sls
Prom

FAMILY MEDIA
3 Park Ave
New York, NY 10016
Ph: 212/725-1700
Robin Whaley, Sls Rep

FAMOUS-BARR
601 Olive St
St. Louis, MO 63101
Ph: 314/444-2775
Victoria Rosenkoetter, VP-
Adv Dir

FAN FAIR CORP
12425 Knoll Rd
Elm Grove, WI 53122
Ph: 414/784-8884
Fax: 414/784-3595
Keith Harmon, VP-Mktg

FARRAR/FARRAR INC
200 Park Ave S, #1603
New York, NY 10003
Ph: 212/475-6749
Carol Estrich, Partner

FASHION BAR
401 S. Buckley Rd
Aurora, CO 80017
Ph: 303/695-7979
Jeff Phillips-Strain, VP-Mktg &
Sls Prom

**FASHION VALLEY/
R ELLIS**
352 Fashion Valley
San Diego, CA 92108
Ph: 619/297-3381
Marilee Bankert, Mktg Dir

FAWN CREEK, INC
7675 Interlachen Rd
Lakeshore, MN 56468
Ph: 218/963-4669
Sonja Larsen, President

**FEDERATED DEPT
STORES**
7 W 7th St
Cincinnati, OH 45202
Ph: 513/579-7541
Fax: 513/579-7547
Judy Evans, Dir-Corp
Purchasing

FEDERATED ALLIED
1440 Broadway
New York, NY 10018
Ph: 212/704-1574
Mimi Irwin, VP-Mktg

FILE AD SERVICE
1544 W Devon
Chicago, IL 60660
Ph: 312/743-3303
Fax: 312/465-1054
Steven Pippenger, President

FILENE'S
426 Washington St
Boston, MA 02101
Ph: 617/357-2416
Fax: 617/357-2996
Lisa Korklan, Adv Mgr
Paul Benevich, Copy Dir
Ph: 617/357-2988
Charlotte Brewer, VP-Mktg
Sls Prom
Ph: 617/357-2725
Dick Diamond, Dir-Ad Opers
Ph: 617/357-2098
Kevin Gardiner, Prod Mgr
Ph: 617/357-2413
Donna LaVita, Print Adv Mgr
Ph: 617/357-2531

FILENE'S BASEMENT
40 Walnut Dr
Wellesley, MA 02181
Sam DePhillippo, Sr VP-Mktg
Ph: 617/239-9256
Fax: 617/348-7128
Jennifer Reed, Prin-Media Mgr
Ph: 617/348-7288
Myrna Reiss, VP Visual &
Creative Adv
Ph: 617/348-7269
Johnathan Swain, Asst
Copy Dir
Ph: 617/357-2413

**FINEPRINT
PUBLICATIONS**
807 Haddon Ave Ste 212
Haddonfield, NJ 08033
Ph: 609/427-9620
Fax: 609/427-9619
Jim Lamb, Gen Mgr

FINKE
2918 W Farwell
Chicago, IL 60645
Ph: 312/704-4512
Sharon Finke

**M FINKEL &
ASSOCIATES**
1104 Crescent Ave
Atlanta, GA 30309
Ph: 404/874-5900
Fax: 404/881-3812
M Finkel, President

**FINLAY FINE
JEWELRY**
521 Fifth Ave, 3th Fl
New York, NY 10175
Ph: 212/382-7423
Fax: 212/682-4197
Patricia Veneziano, VP
Sls Prom

FINNEGAN & AGEE
100 W Franklin St
Richmond, VA 23220
Ph: 804/643-4100
Fax: 804/697-4440
Bob Whitmore, Sr VP

FISHER BIG WHEEL
102 Nesbitt Rd
New Castle, PA 16105
Ph: 412/658-3781
Fax: 412/658-7728
Cindy Gard, Div VP-Adv

**FISHER
BROADCASTING**
PO Box 2
Portland, OR 97207
Ph: 412/658-3781
Tom Oberg, Gen Sls Mgr
Katherine Gulick, Mktg Mgr
Ph: 503/231-4272
Fax: 503/236-0952

**FISHER
BROADCASTING**
100 Fourth Ave, N
Seattle, WA 98109
Ph: 206/443-4081
Fax: 206/443-3897
Phelps Fisher, VP/Dir-Mktg

**FLEET WHOLESALE
SUPPLY**
PO Box 1199
Appleton, WI 54912
Ph: 414/731-8121
Polly Bunker, Adv Mgr

FLEMING COMPANY
6301 Waterford Blvd
Oklahoma City, OK 73118
Ph: 405/841-8595
Dave Dunphy, Mgr Adv Serv

**FLORIDA MEDIA
AFFILIATION**
800 Douglas Rd Ste 500
Coral Gables, FL 33134
Ph: 305/445-4500
Graham Gloss, VP/Group
Publisher

**FLYING COLOR
GRAPHICS**
1001 W North St
Pontiac, IL 61764
Ph: 815/842-2811
Fax: 815/844-1044
Darline Ross-Pitchford, Acct Rep

FOOD LION INC
Harrison Rd
Salisbury, NC 28145
Ph: 704 633-8250
Tom Crabtree

FOOTE & DAVIES
3101 McCall Dr
Atlanta, GA 30340
Ph: 404/451-4511
Jerry Joiner, Sales Rep
Chris Liedel, Sls/Mktg Mgr
William Little, VP-Retail Sls

**FOREST CITY
ENTERPRISES**
5745 Chevrolet Blvd
Cleveland, OH 44130
Ph: 216/842-6300
Fax: 216/842-6508
Debbi Glosserman, VP-Dir
Mktg/Adv
Marie Graf, Group Mktg Dir
Ph: 216/842-6300
Margaret Krush, Grp Mktg Dir

**FORT ERIE DUTY
FREE SHOPPE**
Box 339/Peace Bridge Plz
Fort Erie, ON L2A 5N1
Canada
Ph: 416/871-5400
Fax: 416/871-6335
David Amos, Gen Mgr

**FORTINO/
MORIARITY**
10 S Fifth St, Ste 610
Minneapolis, MN 55402
Ph: 612/332-0445
Fax: 612/332-1114
Douglas Haynes, Art Dir
Suzanne Moriarity, Co-Creat Dir

**M FORTUNOFF OF
WESTBURY**
1044 Old Country Rd
Westbury, NY 11590
Ph: 516/832-9000
Beth Siegel, VP-Adv

THE FORUM
101-5th Street, N
Fargo, ND 58102
Ph: 701/241-5411
Fax: 701/241-5487
Tim Larson, Retail Sls Mgr

FOSTER GRAPHICS
21400 Mullin
Warren, MI 48089
Ph: 313/757-5300
Daryl Foster, President
Elaine Monto, Sls Mgr

RON FOTH RETAIL
8100 N High St
Columbus, OH 43235
Ph: 614/888-7771
Fax: 614/888-5933
Ronald Foth, President

G FOX
960 Main St
Hartford, CT 06115
Ph: 203/241-3698
Fax: 203/241-3617
Raina D'Amico, Div VP-
Creative Dir
Bill Gaunt, Asst Adv Dir
Ph: 203/241-3647
Karen Labout, Asst Adv Dir
Ph: 203/241-3239
Jack Mullen, Div VP-Dir
Adv/Mktg
Ph: 203/241-3204
Donna Torsiello, Print Buyer
Ph: 203/241-3205

FOX RIVER MALL
4301 W Wisconsin Ave
Appleton, WI 54915
Ph: 414/739-4100
Julie Jones, Manager

FRANKEL & COMPANY
111 E Wacker Dr
Chicago, IL 60601
Ph: 312/938-3491
Fax: 312/938-1901
Pamela Church, VP

**FRANKS NURSERY
CRAFTS INC**
6501 E Nevada
Detroit, MI 48234
Ph: 313/366-8400
Fax: 313/366-5386
Norau Morley, Exec VP Mktg

**FREDERICK'S OF
HOLLYWOOD**
6608 Hollywood Blvd
Hollywood, CA 90028
Ph: 213/466-5151
Fax: 213/962-9935
James Stanton, VP Adv

THE SHORTEST DISTANCE BETWEEN YOUR AD

AND AMERICA'S NEWSPAPERS.

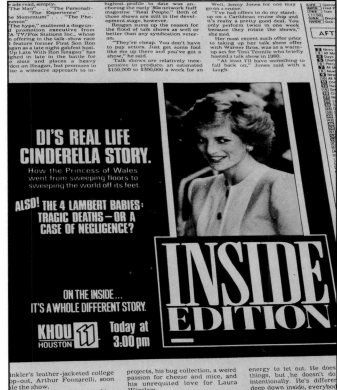

AD/SAT announces Remote Ad Entry from Anywhere, USA.

Now, at last, the power to send newspaper ads at the speed of light is available to everyone everywhere.

It's this simple. Create your ad with any program that generates PostScript® files, such as Aldus PageMaker,® QuarkXPress,® Adobe Illustrator® or MacDraw.®

Then, modem your ad to AD/SAT. We'll satellite it to any or all of our 125 Network newspapers. In minutes.

And now you can reserve space instantly with ADSPACE,

the electronic reservation system that links you 24 hours a day with America's newspapers.

AD/SAT & ADSPACE: the fastest way to go from Anywhere to Everywhere.

To put the power of AD/SAT & ADSPACE on your desktop, call Diana Moore at 1-800-777-0759.

FREIGHT LIQUIDATORS
923 Bidwell St
Pittsburgh, PA 15233
Ph: 412/323-1300
Fax: 412/323-2016
Jack McGowan, Exec VP

AI FRIEDMAN
44 W 18th St
New York, NY 10011
Ph: 212/243-9000
Jeff Goldfarb, VP-Sls

FURNITURE FAIR INC
507 Bell Fork Rd
Jacksonville, NC 28540
Ivans Popkin, President
Ph: 919/455-9595
Fax: 919/455-1481

GI JOE'S INC
9805 Boeckman Rd
Wilsonville, OR 97070
Ph: 503/682-2242
Fax: 503/682-7200
Dennis Irish, Dir-Adv

GS&B ADVERTISING
4104 Acrora St
Coral Gables, FL 33155
Ph: 305/444-4221
Fax: 305/444-6327
Evan Contorakes, Exec VP-Ptr

G&G ADVERTISING
2 Berkeley St, #300
Toronto, ON M5A 2W3
Canada
Ph: 416/863-6335
Fax: 416/863-1951
Laurie Hart, Sr VP

GALLAGHER COMPANY
2215 N Lake Dr
Milwaukee, WI 53202
Ph: 414/272-6119
Jim Biggins, VP

GALLINARO
120 S Taylor
Oak Park, IL 60302
Ph: 708/386-6076
Theresa Gallinaro

GANNETT NEWSPAPER SALES
444 N Michigan Ave, 2nd Fl
Chicago, IL 60611
Ph: 312/527-0550
Fax: 312/527-9089
Becky Bucci, Retail Acct Exec

GANNETT
535 Madison Ave
New York, NY 10022
Ph: 212/715-5430
Fax: 212/832-5123
Elliott Huron, Acct Exec
Sheldon Lyons, President
Ph: 212/715-5312
John McGuinness, Acct Exec
Ph: 212/715-5317
Bette Ann Yarus, Eastern Sls Dir
Ph: 212/715-5306

GANNETT
1100 Wilson Blvd
Arlington, VA 22234
Ph: 703/284-6791
Fax: 703/527-7167
William Nusbaum, VP-Adv Sls

GANNETT DIRECT MARKETING
3400 Robards Ct
Louisville, KY 40218
Ph: 502/454-6660
Fax: 502/456-6179
Raymond Radford, VP-Natl Sls

GANNETT WESTCHESTER
One Gannett Dr
White Plains, NY 10604
Ph: 914/694-5157
Fax: 914/694-5111
Paul Wilkinson, Dept Store Mgr

GANNETT OUTDOOR
444 N Michigan
Chicago, IL 60611
Ph: 312/527-0550
Fax: 312/527-9019
Felicia Jackson, Acct Exec

GARDELLA & COMPANY
781 Miami Cir NE
Atlanta, GA 30324
Ph: 404/231-1316
Fax: 404/231-1318
Patricia Gardella, President

GARMEZY MEDIA
703 2nd Ave S
Nashville, TN 37210
Ph: 615/242-6878
Fax: 615/242-6870
Pat Parker, VP

GAZETTE
250 St Antoine St, W
Montreal, PQ H2Y 3R7
Canada
Ph: 514/987-2345
Fax: 514/987-2380
Marcel Bilodeau, Sls Mgr

GAZETTE MARKETING SYSTEMS
2920 Seventh St
Berkeley, CA 94710
Ph: 415/540-8500
Fax: 415/540-6632
Diane Broch, Dir-Sls & Mktg
Marshall Richman, Regl Sls Mgr

GEIST & ASSOCIATES
327 Renfrew Dr
Markham, ON L3R 9S8
Canada
Ph: 416/475-1022
Fax: 416/475-2204
Rene Geist, Copy Chief
Sam Geist, President

GENERAL GROWTH CENTER COMPANIES
Smith Haven Mall
Rtes 25 & 347
Lake Grove, NY 11755
Maryellen Lovell, Mktg Dir
Ph: 516/724-1505
Fax: 516/724-5067

GENERAL GROWTH CENTER COMPANIES
400 S. Highway 169, #800
Minneapolis, MN 55426
Ph: 612/525-1200
Fax: 612/525-2602
Greg Mack, Art Dir
Randy Richardson, President/Mktg Group
Doug Kline, VP-PR

GENTRY SHOPS
2851 E Kemper Rd
Cincinnati, Ohio 45241
Ph: 513/771-1199
Fax: 513/771-2713
James Jerow, VP-Mktg
Diane Singer, Adv Services Mgr

GEORGE-GORDON PARTNERS
41 Peter St, 3rd Fl
Toronto, ON M5V 2G2
Canada
Ph: 416/971-7755
Fax: 416/599-5076
Gerald George, Chairman/Creative Dir
David Gordon, President/CEO
Danny Nanos, Art Dir
Ph: 416/971-7755

GI JOE'S
9805 Boeckman Rd
Wilsonville, OR 97070
Ph: 503/682-2242
Fax: 503/682-7200
Michael Egan, Prom Mgr

GIBSON GROUP
8515 Cedar Place Dr
Indianapolis, IN 46240
Ph: 317/257-7478
Laura Eickstein, Writer/Prod
Donald Nicholls, Creative Dir
Laura Sandin, Office Mgr

HENRY GILE ADVERTISING
1225 17th St., #2500
Denver, CO 80202
Ph: 03/830-8389
Kathy Hagan, Principal

GINTHER AGENCY
One Appletree Sq. Ste 1031
Bloomington, MN 55420
Ph: 612/854-0845
Paul Ginther, President

GLAMOUR MAGAZINE
350 Madison Ave
New York, NY 10017
Ph: 212/880-7995
Fax: 212/880-8336
William Abbott, Adv Dir
Milton Kaplan, Retail Sls Rep
Ph: 212/880-8674

PETER GLEN INC
#8 Sniffen Court
New York, NY 10016
Ph: 212/683-5520
Fax: 212/689-8067
Peter Glen, President

GLOBAL MARKETING
3924 Chesswood Dr
Downsview, ON M3J 2W6
Ph: 416/636-8900
Fax: 416/636-6404
Brad Milne, President

GLOBE
119 Wyoming Ave
Scranton, PA 18505-0978
Ph: 717/346-7271
Steven Genett, Sls Prom Dir

GLOBE-TIMES
202 W 4th St
Bethlehem, PA 18015
Ph: 215/867-5000
Fax: 215/866-1771
Ernest Reed, Adv Dir

GLOBMAN'S
P O Box 711
Martinsville, VA 24112
Ph: 703/632-3404
Fax: 703/632-3543
Randy Clay, Adv Dir
Richard Globman, President
Ph: 703/632-7816

A GOLD & SONS
2050 Bleury
Montreal, PQ H5A 2J5
Canada
Ph: 514/288-4653
Michael Gold, Mng Dir

GOLDBERG, MARCHESANO, KOHLMAN
927-15th St, NW
Washington, DC 20005
Ph: 202/789-2000
Fax: 202/289-2557
Norman Goldberg, Chairman
Carole Marchesano, President

GOLDBLATTS
1615 W Chicago Ave
Chicago, IL 60622
Ph: 312/421-5300
Fax: 312/421-1057
Marian Hayes, Dir Sls Prom & Mktg

GOLDE'S DEPT STORES
9957 Manchester Ave
Warson Woods, MO 63122
Ph: 314/968-2900
Richard Lee, VP

GOLDFARB HOFF CO
26250 NW Highway
Southfield, Mi 48076
Ph: 313/350-8200
Fax: 313/350-8213
Steve Rosen, VP Dir/Mktg

GOLUB CORP
501 Duanesburg Rd
Schenectady, NY 12306
Ph: 518/356-9345
Fax: 518/356-9272
Shawn Gonzalez, Mktg Mgr
Heidi Lorch, Adv Co-op Coord
Diane Lowe, Mgr-Adv Opers

GOOD'S FURNITURE & CARPET
707 W Main St
New Holland, PA 17557
Ph: 717/354-4461
Fax: 717/354-4390
Robert Clymer, VP-Sls & Mktg

BUDD GORE INC
Bin 676, Box 9802
Austin, TX 78766-0802
Ph: 512/847-5144
Fax: 512/223-8725
Budd Gore, President

GOTTSCHALKS
PO Box 1872
Fresno, CA 93718
Ph: 209/488-7355
Fax: 209/485-8680
Nancy Maxwell, Dir-Adv & Sls Prom

GOULD
1250 N Dearborn, Apt 9B
Chicago, Il 60610
Ph: 312/664-1404
Francesca Gould, Freelance Art Dir

GOULD PAPER CORP
3003 Carlisle St, #110
Dallas, TX 75204
Ph: 214/871-9501
Bill Crisler, VP

GOULD PAPER CORP
315 Park Ave, S
New York, NY 10010
Ph: 212/505-1000
Fax: 212/505-0812
Harry Gould, Jr, President

GQ MAGAZINE
350 Madison Ave
New York, NY 10017
Ph: 212/880-6673
Fax: 212/850-8342
Beverly Cogan, Retail Adv Mgr
Janice Orefice, Merchan Mgr
Ph: 212/880-7987
Fax: 212/880-7969

GRAFTON-FRASER
9 Sunlight Park Rd
Toronto, ON M4M 3G1
Canada
Ph: 416/461-9411
Fax: 416/461-1044
Paul Bogdon, Adv Mgr
Charles Parsons, Adv Mgr
Bonnie Shore, Dir-Adv

GRAHNQUIST
2415 Briarcliff Dr
Irving, TX 75062
Ph: 214/754-0703
Fax: 214/871-1060
Gary Grahnquist, Retail Mktg Consultant

GRANADA CANADA
60 International Blvd
Toronto, ON M9W 6J2
Canada
Ph: 416/675-7555
Fax: 416/675-0034
Meredith Dickison, Asst VP-Mktg

GRAND RAPIDS PRESS
155 Michigan NW
Grand Rapids, MI 49503
Ph: 616/459-1638
Fax 616/459-1667
Steve Davis, Major Acct Mgr
Beverly Ohlmann, Natl Sls Mgr
Ph: 616/459-1567

GRANDE GOURMET INC
434 Frandor Avenue
Lansing, MI 48912
Ph: 517/351-5522
Patricia Alexander, VP

GRANDVILLE PRINTING CO
4719 Ivanrest Ave
Grandville, MI 49418
Ph: 616/534-8647
Fax: 616/534-8293
Pat Brewer, President

GRANDVILLE PRINTING
PO Box 247
Grandville, MI 49468
Ph: 616/534-8647
Fax: 616/534-8293
Dale Ranson, VP-Sls

GRAPHIC ARTS SPECIALISTS
4727 A N Royal Atlanta Dr
Tucker, GA 30084
Ph: 404/496-9992
Fax: 404/496-1408
Douglas Gulley, VP-Client Services
Richard Watson, Pres& CEO

GRAPHIC PROMOTIONS
305 East 17th
Topeka, KS 66601
Ph: 913/234-6684
Fax: 913/234-1519
Rose Marie Hankins, VP-Sls/Customer Service

GRAPHIC TRANSPORTATION
752 Cochrane Dr
Unionville, ON L3R 8C9
Canada
Ph: 416/477-4245
Tom Milani, Dir-Opers
Bill Yarn, Dir-Mktg

GRAPHIC WEB
10481 Young St
Richmond Hill, ON L4C 3C8
Canada
Ph: 416/661-3681
James Hyslop, Dir-Sls/Mktg

GRAPHICS ATLANTA
1555 Oakbrook Dr
Norcross, GA 30093
Ph: 404/448-4091
Richard Davis, Sls Mgr

GRAPHICS PLUS
1493 Bradshire Dr
Columbus, OH 43220
Ph: 614/459-2142
William Johnson, Acct Exec

GREAT WESTERN PUBLISHING
1850 E Watkins
Phoenix, A Z 85034
Ph: 602/229-1212
Fax: 602/340-1644
Nasser Farrokh, President
Ray Qualls, VP Gen Mgr

GREAT UNIVERSAL STORES
5375 Wercote De Liesse
Montreal, ON H4P 1A2
Canada
Ph: 514/747-6581
Gilles Charlebois, Sr VP-Mktg

GREEN MOUNTAIN FURNITURE
Route 16
Ossipee, NH 03864
Ph: 603/539-2236
Marshall Kendall, President

THE GREENHUT GROUP
2020 Hamilton St
Allentown, PA 18104
Ph: 215/820-9150
Fax: 215/820-9201
Linda Heydt, President

GREENS DEPT STORE
Orange Plaza, Rte 211 E
Middletown, NY 10940
Ph: 914/342-5484
Fax: 914/343-0835
Rosemarie Rizzoto, Adv Dir
Judy Green, Gen Mgr
Donald Green, President

GREENS APPAREL INC
PO Box 2512
East Lansing, MI 48826
Ph: 517/351-9611
Stephen Flaster, VP

GREENSBORO NEWS & RECORD
200 E Market St-Box 20848
Greensboro, NC 27420
Ph: 919/373-7109
Fax: 919/373-7152
Joe Antle, Adv Mgr
Kathy Lambeth, Retail Ad Mgr

GREY PERSPECTIVES
PO Box 11553
Johannesburg, SA 2000
South Africa
Ph: 011/883-3151
Denise Stamm, Mng Dir

GREY ADVERTISING
777 Third Ave
New York, NY 10017
Ph: 212/546-1909
Fax: 212/546-1495
Nina Kessler, Acct Supv
Susan Marber, VP
Ph: 212/546-2000
Bob Ravitz, Exec VP-Mgmt Rep

GREY O'ROURUE SUSSMAN
110 Eglinton Ave W
Toronto, ON M4R 1A3
Canada
Ph: 416/485-7400
Fax: 416/485-3671
Harry Teitelbaum, Acct Dir

GREY RETAIL
1881 Yonge St
Toronto, ON M4S 3C4
Canada
Ph: 416/322-0152
Fax: 416/322-0375
Jack Steckel, Gen Mgr

CHILDREN ARE DYING FOR ATTENTION. 40,000 A DAY.

Our priorities seem to be elsewhere. Every minute 15 children in the world die for want of essential food and inexpensive vaccines, and every minute the world's military machine takes another $1,900,000 from the public treasury.

1.5 million children die each year from measles coupled with malnutrition, when a measles vaccine costs 13¢ a dose. Yet we can bail out the Savings and Loan entrepreneurs.

Of the 22 million Americans on Food Stamps, more than half are children. Children are by far the poorest Americans, and have grown poorer in the 1980s as America has grown richer. One out of five U.S. children (20.6%) live in poverty. If another country were doing this to our children, we'd be at war.

The End Hunger Network works with the entertainment and advertising community to help create public awareness about hunger and motivate people to do something about it. We produced the educational spots during the Live Aid concert and organized last year's Prime Time to End Hunger campaign, when the three major TV networks cooperated for the first time to broadcast special episodes of top primetime television programs about hunger, homelessness and volunteerism.

The End Hunger Network was founded by Hollywood celebrities and entertainment industry professionals. We're looking for corporate partnership for high-visibility entertainment and educational events, cause-related tie-ins with advertising campaigns, and media space/time contributions. We can help you design promotional events and suggest ways to work with local community groups. Interested? Give us a call at (213) 273-3179.

Maybe together we can put in a good word for the kids. **The End Hunger Network.**

GRIFFIN & LAPHEN
885 Don Mills Rd, #121
Toronto, ON M3C 1V9
Canada
Ph: 416/444-8852
Fax: 416/444-1797
Roger Griffin, Exec VP
Douglas Laphen, President

HERB GROSS & CO
18 Harvard St
Rochester, NY 14607
Herb Gross, President
716/244-3711
716/244-5279

GROUP 243
3490 Piedmont Rd NE
Atlanta, GA 30305
Ph: 404/231-4320
Fax: 404/233-0145
Lee McComb, Acct Exec

GROUP III MARKETING
PO Box 348
Wayzata, MN 55391
Ph: 612/475-3269
Bart Foreman, President

GROUPE HUGRON & ASSOC
3556 Boul, St-Lawrent
Montreal, PQ H2X 2V1
Canada
Ph: 514/849-4133
Fax: 514/849-9500
Sylvie Chagnon, VP-Client
Services

GRUMBACHER & SON
PO Box 2821
York, PA 17405
Ph: 717/757-7660
Richard Schwab, Sr VP Sls
Prom Mktg

GRUPIAS, INC
699 Madison Ave
New York, NY 10021
Ph: 212/888-0611
Fax: 212/371-1242
Richard Grubman, President

GS&B ADVERTISNG
4104 Aurora St
Coral Gables, FL 33146
Ph: 305/444-4221
Fax: 305/444-6327
Evan Contoraces, Exec VP/Dir-
Acct Services
Bruce Fitzgerald, Creative Dir

GUCCI AMERICA
50 Hartz Way
Secaucus, NJ 07094
Celia Gramkow, Mktg Mgr
Ph: 201/867-8800
Fax: 201/867-7412

**GULL GROUP
ADVERTISING**
706 Route 101A
Merrimack, NH 03054
Ph: 603/595-8497
Dennis DiPaolo, President

**GUMPERTZ, BENTLEY,
FRIED**
5900 Wilshire Blvd Ste 2400
Los Angeles, CA 90036
Ph: 213/931-6301
Fax: 213/932-2683
Richard Fried, President

**GUTSELL &
ASSOCIATES**
6141 N Elston
Chicago, IL 60646-4722
Ph: 312/792-2480
Philip Gutsell, President

HP & ASSOCIATES
110 Berkeley St
Toronto, ON M5A 2W7
Canada
Ph: 416/362-0011
Fax: 416/360-6272
Howard Petrook, President

**HABERSHAM
PLANTATION**
171404/886-9142 Collier Rd,
Toccoa, GA 30577
Ph: 404/886-1476
Matthew Eddy, VP

**THE HADLEY
COMPANIES**
11001 Hampshire Ave
S Bloomington, MN 55438
Ph: 612/943-8474
Joan Lee, Dir-Mktg & Comms

202

**HAGGAR APPAREL
COMPANY**
6113 Lemmon Ave
Dallas, TX 75209
Ph: 214/956-0214
Fax: 214/956-0216
Peter Mitchell, VP-Adv

**BRAD HAHN
PHOTOGRAPHY**
530 Molino St Ste 814
Los Angeles, CA 9001-2226
Ph: 213/621-2041
Brad Hahn, Freelance

HAHN SHOES
7600 Jefferson Ave
Landover, MD 20785
Ph: 301/322-4550
Fax: 301/772-0312
Mina Ponchick, Dir-Mktg

**HALIFAX BUILDING
SOCIETY**
Trinity Rd, Box 60
Halifax, England, HX1 2RG
UK
Ph: 004/226-5777
Richard Spelman, Gen Mgr-
Mktg

**HALL OLSON
MARKETING**
PO Box 8268
Newport Beach, CA 92660
Tracey Hall, President
714/752-2007
714/955-3668
Tracey Olson, Exec VP

**HALL DICKLER
LAWLER**
460 Park Ave
New York, NY 10022
Ph: 212/838-4600
Fax: 212/751-5022
Douglas Wood, Partner

NAN S HALLOCK
401 N. Michigan Ave
Chicago, IL 60611
Ph: 312/644-6610
Nan Hallock, Dir-Mktg

**HALLS
MERCHANDISING**
200 E 25th St
Kansas City, MO 64108
Ph: 816/274-8277
Fax: 816/545-6801
Sue Adams, Spec Events Mgr
David Bryant, Art Dir
Ph: 816/274-4531
Allen Kleinbeck, Copywriter
Carnie Kline, Sls Prom Dir
Ken McCormack, VP-Stores
Joann Neuhauser, Art Dir
Doug Rooks, Asst. Art Dir

**HAMILTON
SPECTATOR**
44 Frid St
Hamilton, ON L8N 3G3
Canada
Ph: 416/526-3399
Fax: 416/522-1696
W Bill Bratt, Natl Adv Mgr

**HANDY ANDY HOME
IMPROVEMENT
CENTERS**
905 Golf Rd
Schaumburg, IL 60173
Ph: 708/517-4020
Fax: 708/605-1628
Rose Woodley, Adv Dir

HANYANG STORES
14B Aupkuyung-Dong,
Kangnam-
Seoul, Korea
Ph: 82-2-511-3103
Fax: 82-2-542-9102
Thomas Lange, Dir Visual
Merch-Admins

**HARMELIN &
ASSOCIATES**
525 Righters Ferry Rd
Villanova, PA 19085
Ph: 215/668-7900
Fax: 215/668-9257
Joanne Harmelin, President

HARPER'S BAZAAR
1700 Broadway
New York, NY 10019
Ph: 212/903-5412
Fax: 212/265-8579
Marilyn Bauer, Mktg Dir
Jeannette Chang, Assc Publr
Ph: 212/903-5385
Martin Schrader, Publisher
Ph: 212/903-5382

**HARRIS CONTROLS &
COMPOSITION**
PO Box 430
Melbourne, FL 32902-0430
Ph: 407/242-5370
H.W. Coates, Dir-N Amer Sls

HARRIS ADVERTISING
1900 N Amidon
Wichita, KS 67203
Ph: 316/832-0405
Fax: 318/832-9784
Max Harris, President

HARRIS
786 Hampton Ridge Dr
Akron, OH 44333
Ph: 216/864-1726
Betty Harris

HARRISON SERVICE
8 West 38th St
New York, NY 10018
Ph: 212/302-1999
Fax: 212/921-5691
David Brown, Exec VP/
Creative Dir
James Nebenzahl, President

**HARTE HANKS DIR
MARKETING**
100 Alco Place
Baltimore, MD 21227
Ph: 301/247-6433
Fax: 301/536-0214
Charles Dall'Acqua, Sr VP

HARTE-HANKS
1329 Arlington St
Cincinnati, OH 45225
David Geiser, VP-Sales
513/835-7710
513/853-7644

**HARTE HANKS
DATA TECH**
25 Linell Cir
Billerica, MA 01810
Ph: 508/663-9955
Spencer Joyner, VP

**HARTE-HANKS
MARKETING SERVICES**
65 Route 4 E
River Edge, NJ 07660
Ph: 201/342-6400
Fax: 201/342-1709
Harry Seymour, VP-Media
Group

HARTMARX
101 N Wacker Dr, 20th fl
Chicago, IL 60606
Ph: 312/372-6300
Thomas Rice, Creative Dir

**HARTMARX
SPECIALTY STORES**
101 N Wacker Dr, 20th fl
Chicago, IL 60606
Ph: 312/372-6300
James Round, VP-Adv

**SUSAN J HARVEY
MARKETING**
732 Kenington Dr
Westbury, NY 11590
Ph: 516/333-9232
Fax: 516/338-7511
Susan Harvey, Database
Consultant

**THE HAWORTH
GROUP INC**
6117 Blue Cir Dr
Minnetonka, MN 55343
Ph: 612/935-4454
Fax: 612/935-2403
Dale Haworth, Chairman
Tom Siqveland, VP-Mgr-Plng
Claude Stevens, President
Brenda Swanson, VP-Mgr
Brdcst

HECHINGER
1616 McCormick Dr
Landover, MD 20775
Ph: 301/925-3090
Fax: 301/925-3912
Ann McClenahan, VP-Sls Prom
& Adv

**HECHT'S DEPT
STORES**
685 N Glebe Rd
Arlington, VA 22203-2199
Ph: 703/558-1749
Fax: 703/558-1467
Joyce Perl, VP-Adv Dir

**CAP HEDGES &
ASSOC**
1825 Northwest Marshall
Portland, OR 97209
Ph: 503/227-2497
Fax: 503/227-2513
Cap Hedges, President

HEINZ
2550 Pasadena Blvd
Wauwatosa, WI 53226
Ph: 414/476-4504
Robert Heinz, Consultant

HELZBERG DIAMONDS
1600 Baltimore
Kansas City, MO 64108
Ph: 816/842-7780
Fax: 816/842-7780
Laura Mayer, Dir-Adv

HENNEGAN
1001 Plum St
Cincinnati, OH 45202
Ph: 513/621-7300
Louis Callegari, Exec VP/Sls

MARK HENRI
500 Law Building
Cedar Rapids, IA 52401
Ph: 319/364-0178
Fax: 319/364-7461
Nicki Hart, CEO
Sarah Poole, Mktg Dir
Ph: 319/398-1638

HENRY'S
119 Church St
Toronto, ON M5C 2G5
Canada
Ph: 416/868-0872
Fax: 416/868-0243
Anne McIntosh, Purchasing/
Adv Mgr
Andrew Stein, President

HERBERGER'S
PO Box H-120
St. Cloud, MN 56302
Ph: 612/654-2208
Fax: 612/654-2200
Wayne Engstrand, Adv Dir
Steve Lindgren, Sls Prom Dir
Ph: 612/654-2211
Barbara Thiessen, Creat Dir

HESS'S
Hamilton Mall @ 9th
St Allentown, PA 18101
Ph: 215/821-5238
Fax: 215/821-5270
Adolf Klova, VP-Adv

HIGBEE COMPANY
100 Public Sq
Cleveland, OH 44113
Ph: 216/579-3662
Fax: 216/579-3648
Ross Fredrichs, Adv Dir
Jerry Hoegner, VP-Comms
Ph: 216/579-3653

HILDT & ASSOCIATES
303 E Army Trail Rd, Ste 111
Bloomingdale, IL 60108
Ph: 708/893-6111
Fax: 708/893-7636
Joanne Hildt, Principal

HOECHST CELANESE
1211 Ave of the Americas
New York, NY 10036
Ph: 212/719-8827
Fax: 212/719-7881
Jacqueline DeGraff, Mdse Mgr

**HOLLADAY-TYLER
PRINTING**
7100 Holladay-Tyler Rd
GlennDale, MD 20769
Ph: 301/464-9100
Fax: 301/464-6069
Graden Laycook, Dir- Mktg

**HOLLAENDER
MARKETING**
29 Bala Ave, #103
Bala Cynwyd, PA 19004
Ph: 215/667-2142
Fax: 215/667-4806
Judy Daniels, President

DH HOLMES
3301 Veterans Blvd
Metairie, LA 70002
Ph: 504/561-6697
Ray Knight, Brdct Mgr
Toni Newton, Asst Mgr
Print Adv

HOLT RENFREW
50 Bloor St, W
Toronto, ON M4W 1A1
Canada
Ph: 416/960-2977
Fax: 416/922-3240
Diana Edmiston, Copy Writer
Isabel Keirstead, Media &
Mktg Mgr
Ph: 416/922-2333
Beth Park, VP-Sls Prom &
Mktg
Ph: 416/960-2925

**HOMART
DEVELOPMENT CO**
55 W Monroe, #3100
Chicago, IL 60603
Ph: 312/875-8437
Fax: 312/875-8244
F Bachelor, Corp Mktg/Coord
Melinda Batchelor, Dir-
Shopping Center Mktg

HOME DEPOT
2727 Paces Ferry Rd
Atlanta, GA 30339
Ph: 404/433-8211
Fax: 404/431-2708
Dick Hammill, VP-Adv Mktg

HOME EXPRESS
26534 Danti Ct
Hayward, CA 94545
Ph: 415/732-9600
Colleen Buckley, Dir-Adv

HOME NEWS CO
123 How Ln, Box 551
New Brunswick, NJ 08903
Ph: 201/246-5633
William Boyd, President

**HOME NEWS
PUBLISHING CO**
123 Tennyson Rd
Plainsboro, NJ 08536
Ph: 609/799-8526
Jim Enright, Exec VP/Gen Mgr

JMS HOMEMAKERS
1013 Butterfield Rd
Downers Grove, IL 60515
Ph: 708/960-4100
Fax: 708/960-3578
Frank Czopek, EDP Dir
Susan Gawron, Mdse Mgr
Arthur Landen, President
Herbert Laufman, Agency
Coord
Gloria Meyers, Adv Mgr
Robert Smyth, Adv Dir

**HOMETOWN RADIO
NETWORK**
1375 Euclid Ave, #300
Cleveland, OH 44115
Ph: 216/781-0030
Fax: 216/781-7508
Alex Kelemen, VP

HOOK DRUGS
PO Box 26285
Indianapolis, IN 46219
Ph: 317 353-1451
Fax: 317/351-3037
Peg Rogers, VP

HOST/RACINE
PO Box 1648
1405 16th St
Racine, WI 53401
Ph: 414/637-4491
Fax: 414/637-2446
Denise Lange, Adv Mgr

HOUSE BEAUTIFUL
1700 Broadway
New York, NY 10019
Ph: 212/903-5114
Fax: 212/586-3439
Tony Hoyt, Publisher
Marjorie Rubin Cohen, Mktg Dir
Ph: 212/903-5104

**HOUSTON, EFFLER&
PARTNERS**
360 Newbury St
Boston, MA 02115
Ph: 617/267-5050
Fax: 617/267-6472
Donald Effler, President

HOUSTON CHRONICLE
801 Texas Ave
Houston, TX 77002
Ph: 713/787-3013
Fax: 713/220-7868
Ralph Harrington, Display
Adv Mgr
Cathy Crosby, Display Adv Mgr
Ph: 713/220-7326
Vickie McClain, Printing
Projs Mgr
Ph: 713/220-7644
James Pollard, Display Adv Dir
Ph: 713/220-6483

HOUSTON ADVERTISING
535 Bolyton St
Boston, MA 02116
Ph: 617/267-5050
Fax: 617/267-6472
James Blinn, President
Dawn Jacobs, Dir-Mktg Serv

HOUSTON METROPOLITAN MAG
3988 N Central Expressway
Dallas, TX 75204
Ph: 214/827-5000
Fax: 214/827-8844
Ann Brumleve, Natl Mktg Mgr

HUFFMAN KOOS
Rte 4 at Main St
River Edge, NJ 07661
Ph: 201/343-4300
Fax: 201/343-8148
Pat Bruno, Adv Dir

HUGHES-RUCH
12660 W North Ave, Bldg D
Brookfield, WI 53005
Ph: 414/796-1300
Fax: 414/796-0659
JoAnn Cekanor, Acct Exec
Carrie Powell, Writer, Prodr
Isabel Rocha, Acct Exec

HULT FRITZ MATUSZAK
245 NE Perry
Peoria, IL 61603
Ph: 309/673-8191
Fax: 309/674-5330
Adam Sloan, Exec VP
Bernice Sullivan, Media Buyer

HUNTER TAVERNOR LACOMA DIRECT
2107 Elliot Ave, #302
Seattle, WA 98121
Reilly Jensen

DON HURT & ASSOCIATE
P O Box 5550
Winter Park, FL 32793
Ph: 407/679-8718
Donald Hurt, Dir

IC SYSTEM
444 E Highway 96
St. Paul, MN 55164-0226
Ph: 612/483-0585
Fax: 612/481-6363
Susan Jablonski, Regl Sls Mgr
Dieter Pape, Dir Natl Sls
Ph: 612/481-6325

IDEAS INC
4377 Carolina
Richmond, VA 23222
Ph: 804/228-5751
Robert Taylor, Gen Mgr

IMPACT RESOURCES
25 Dillmont Dr
Columbus, OH 43235
Ph: 614/888-5900
Fax: 614/888-8825
Duane Palmo, Gen Mgr
Scott Sandberg, Sr VP-Opers

IN THE EVENT INC
1440 St Charles St
Milwaukee, WI 53213
Ph: 414/778-1760
Fax: 414/332-5304
Peggy Menos, Mktg Dir

INDIANAPOLIS STAR NEWS
307 N Pennsylvania
Indianapolis, IN 46206
Ph: 317/633-1132
Alan Judkins, Adv Dir

INFINITEE COMMUNICATIONS
333 Peachtree Rd, Ste 630
Atlanta, GA 30326
Ph: 404/231-3481
Fax: 404/262-1277
Barbara McGraw, President
Kelly Cobb, Acct Exec
Jocelyn Smith, President

INFOBASE SERVICES
301 Industrial Blvd
Conway, AR 72032
Ph: 501/329-6836
Fax: 501/450-4500
Tim Prunk, President

INNERVISION PRODUCTIONS
11783 Borman Dr
St. Louis, MO 63146
Ph: 314/569-2500
DeLancey Smith, VP-Sls & Mktg

INSIDE PRINT MAGAZINE
274 Madison Ave #601
New York, NY 10016-0701
Ph: 212/972-6300
William Holiber, Publisher

INSTITUTE OF OUTDOOR ADV
342 Madison Ave
New York, NY 10173
Ph: 212/986-5920
Don Byer, President

INSTITUTE FOR INNOVATION
21 Benedict Place
Greenwich, CT 06830
Ph: 203/629-2868
William Foster, President

INTELIMAIL
14601 W 99th St
Lenexa, KS 66215
Ph: 913/888-0050
Fax: 913/888-1356
John Schulte, VP& Gen Mgr

INTERBEAUTE
1500 Atwater
Montreal, PQ H3Z 1X5
Canada
Ph: 514/989-2030
Andree Favre, Mgr
Florent Paquet, Supv

INTEREP RADIO STORE
205 N Michigan
Chicago, IL 60601
Ph: 312/819-0702
Kevin Simkowski, Acct Exec

INTERFACE GROUP
1230 31st St NW
Washington, DC 20007
Ph: 202/342-7200
S Hope Johnson, Sr Assoc

INTL COUNCIL OF SHOPPING CENTERS
665 Fifth Ave
New York, NY 10022
Ph: 212/421-8181
Hance Jeannie,
Dir-Publications

ITALIA & ASSOCIATES
6135 Wilshire Blvd, 2nd fl
Los Angeles, CA 90048
Ph: 213/937-4400
Fax: 213/937-0675
Alicia Dunn, Acct Supv
Carmen Italia, President
Jerry Wessels, VP

IVEY'S
PO Box 34799
Charlotte, NC 28234
Ph: 704/372-3511
Fax: 704/331-2839
Gayle Ireland, Mktg Coord
Cheryl O'Connor, Direct Mail
Supv

IVEY'S
308 Regal Dr
Lawrenceville, GA 30245
Ph: 704/372-3511
Ed Holt, Direct Mail Mgr

JACK WAHL AB
Box 5332
Stockholm,
Sweden
Ph: 08/7830505
Jack Wahl, Dir

JACOBSON STORES
3333 Sargeant Rd
Jackson, MI 49201
Ph: 517/764-6400
James Batterson, Dir Adv

JACOBSON STORES
245 Diggs Dr
Winter Park, FL 32792
Ph: 407/677-0700
Fax: 407/679-1722
Joseph Fisher, VP-Gen
Mdse Mgr
Sue Tihansky, Sls Prom Dir

JBYRONS
15600 NW 15th Ave
Miami, FL 33169
Ph: 305/620-3341
Fax: 305/625-2750
Roger Busby, Adv Dir
Shelia Moffitt, VP-Sls Prom

JC PENNEY
Two Lincoln Centre, 5420 LBJ
Dallas, TX 75240
Ph: 214/591-4139
Fax: 214/591-9543
Edward Hayward, Mgr-Adv
Gary Patz, Natl Ad Proj Mgr
Ph: 214/591-4140
Toby Aurilia, Creative Dir
Ph: 214/591-4228

JCPENNEY
5430 LBJ Freeway LC2 17th fl
Dallas, TX 75240
Ph: 214/591-4209
Fax: 214/591-9543
Jeanne Brennan, Creative
Proj Mgr
Shapiro Harry, Creative
Proj Mgr
Ph: 214/591-4227
Rusty Ryan, Art Supv
214/591-4990

JCPENNEY
PO Box 659000,1006
Dallas, TX 75265
Ph: 214/591-3708
Fax: 214/591-9549
Mary Joe Church, Div Adv Mgr
Robert Fogarty, Div Adv Mgr
Ph: 214/591-3760
Stephen Foy, Div Adv Mg
Ph: 214/591-3717
Kathleen Holliday, Sr Adv Mgr
Ph: 214/591-3712
Herb Geminder, Div Adv Mgr
Ph: 214/591-3369

JCPENNEY BUSINESS
PO Box 100
Dallas, TX 75221-0100
Ph: 214/960-5100
Fax: 214/960-5275
Pat Bielefeld, Natl Acct Mgr
Karen Wald, Acct Mgr
Ph: 214/960-5287

JEFFERSON-PILOT RETAIL SERVICES
1 Julian Price Place
Charlotte, NC 28208
Ph: 704/374-3632
Fax: 704/374-3889
Dan Phillippi, Gen Mgr

JET STORES
PO Box 122
Johannesburg S Africa,
R.S.A.
Ph: 011/495-7481
Fax: 011/837-3304
A.H. Barnes, Mktg Mgr

JK COMMUNICATIONS
799 W Roosevelt Rd, Bldg 6
Glen Ellyn, IL 60137
Ph: 708/790-4844
Fax: 708/790-4852
Joan King, President

JLC MEDIA MARKETING
1 East 42nd St
Ph: 212/682-3184
Fax: 212/949-8267
New York, NY 10017
Judith Casper, President

JMB PROPERTIES CO
900 N Michigan Ave, 14th fl
Chicago, IL 60611
Charlene Slack, Regl Mktg Mgr
Ph: 312/915-2488
Fax: 312/915-2453
James Zielinski, VP/Dir
Retail Mktg
Ph: 312/915-2511

JOHN RYAN CO
3033 Excelsior Blvd
Minneapolis, MN 55416
Ph: 612/924-7716
Fax: 612/924-7700
Jeannie Kant, Acct Supv
Nancy Radermecher, Exec VP
Ph: 612/924-7700

JOHNSON & CLARK
770 N Halsted St, Ste 207
Chicago, IL 60622
Ph: 312/733-7677
Fax: 312/733-5725
Gregory Clark, Principal
Sharon Johnson, Principal

JOHNSON PUBLISHING
820 S Michigan Ave
Chicago, IL 60605
Norman Davis, Midwest
Adv Mgr
Ph: 312/322-9245
Fax: 312/322-9375

SOL JOHNSON DESIGN
230 Lyon St
Valley Stream, NY 11580
Ph: 516/285-9593
Fax: 212/475-2149
Sol Johnson, President

JOHNSTON & MURPHY
Genesco Park
Nashville, TN 37202
Ph: 615/367-7145
Bret Moore, Dir

JORDAN MARSH CO
450 Washington St
Boston, MA 02205
Ph: 617/357-3888
Fax: 617/357-4391
Joel Benjamin, Creative Dir
Joan Buckley, Dir- Creat Serv
Ph: 617/357-3160
Susan Cappadonia Love, Copy
Writer
Ph: 617/357-3155
Paul Devine, Sr Art Dir
Ph: 617/357-3707
Robert Gottlieb, Sr VP-
Dir- Mktg
Ph: 617/357-3235
Ken Green, Art Dir/
Spec Projects
Ph: 617/357-3147
Kathleen Holland, VP Mktg
Ph: 617/357-3161
Mike Kelly, VP Adv
Ph: 617/357-3130
Dan Lynch, Copywriter
Ph: 617/357-3139
Jean Publicover, Brdcst Dir
Ph: 617/357-3161
Jennifer Ray, Copy Dir
Ph: 617/357-3161
Ann Scheffler, Print Media Dir
Ph: 617/357-3564
Jill Stah, Direct Mail Mgr
Ph: 617/357-3151
Larry Damato, Sr Art Dir
Ph: 617/357-3484

JOSEPH HORNE CO
501 Penn Ave
Pittsburgh, PA 15222
Ph: 412/553-8066
Fax: 412/553-8758
Marie Alexander, Adv Dir

JOURNAL REGISTER
50 W State St
Trenton, NJ 08608
Ph: 609/396-2200
Fax: 609/396-2292
David Bonfield
David Larson, Research Dir

JOURNAL/SENTINEL
333 W State St, Box 661
Milwaukee, WI 53201
Howard Hoerl, Ss Devpmt Mgr
Ph: 414/224-2085
Fax: 414/224-2485
Ken Nogalski, Sls Mgr
Ph: 414/224-2294
Tom Schmanski, Sls Mgr
Ph: 414/224-2520
Scott Stollberg, Sls Mgr
Carlyn Ziarek, Sls Mgr
Ph: 414/224-2423

JS AUTOMOTIVE
123 N Wacker Dr Ste 1190
Chicago, IL 60606
Ph: 312/701-3047
Fax: 312/701-3039
Jack Sayer, President

KALB TV
PO Box 951
Alexandria, LA 71301
Ph: 318/445-2456
Fax: 318/442-7427
Wayne Bettoney, Local Sls Mgr
Carol Christensen, Sls Coord

KAROLL'S
1408 S Clinton
Chicago, IL 60607
Ph: 312/738-0548
Fax: 312/738-4006
Linda Wright, Adv Mgr

KATV TV
PO Box 77
Little Rock, AR 72203
Ph: 501/372-7777
Charlotte Whitt, Mktg Mgr

KDBC TV
2201 Wyoming
El Paso, TX 79903
Ph: 915/532-6551
Margie LaFleur, Sls Mgr

KENSINGTON GROUP
4579 Laclede Ave, Ste 332
St. Louis, MO 63108
Ph: 314/367-2676
David Sarama, Chairman

KEPPELL PRINTING
8 Davis Rd Wetherill Park
NSW, 2166
Australia
Ph: 02/6040888
Fax: 02/6096948
John Austin, Mgr Dir

KERBS PHOTOGRAPHIC
615 W Van Buren St
Chicago, IL 60607
Ph: 312/648-4020
Tom Cheng, Sls Mgr

KEROFF & ROSENBERG ADV
444 N Wabash
Chicago, IL 60611
Ph: 312/321-9000
Fax: 312/321-1735
Deborah Karabin, Acct Supv

KERR DRUG STORES
8380 N Blvd
Raleigh, NC 27661
Ph: 919/872-5710
Fax: 919/872-3442
Krista Knight, Adv Dir

KERRISONS DEPT STORE
260 King St
Charleston, SC 29401
Ph: 803/722-4011
Gene Poulnot, VP-Adv

KERT ADVERTISING
600-2200 Yonge St
Toronto, ON M4S 1S5
Canada
Ph: 416/481-6422
Fax: 416/481-9293
Erick Baillie, VP-Gen Mgr
Mary Lou Gossage, VP-Client
Strategy
Ph: 416/481-6422
Debra Lewis, Acct Supv
Jerome Shore, President

KETV
27th & Douglas St
Omaha, NE 68131
Ph: 402/978-8947
Fax: 402/978-8922
Tam Falvo, Dir-Retail Dev

KFVS TV
PO Box 100
Cape Girardeau, MO 63701
Ph: 314/335-1212
Gary Seaberg, Local Sls Mgr

KGW TV
1501 SW Jefferson
Portland, OR 97201
Ph: 503/226-5129
Fax: 503/226-4998
Robert Rector, Dir/Client Dev
Miyon Yonemoto, Mktg &
Research Dir
Ph: 503/226-5180
Caroline Albertson, Local
'Sls Mgr
Ph: 503/226-5172

KIDS "R" US
461 From Rd
Paramus, NJ 07652
Ph: 201/599-7175
Fax: 201/262-7581
Corey Romao, Dir- Adv

KIMIST INC
5750 Larchmont Dr
Erie, PA 16509
Ph: 814/868-9766
Kim Kalvelage, President

NANCY KING HODGE
3219 N Summit Ave
Milwaukee, WI 53211
Nancy King Hodge, Student
Ph: 414/962-1560

KIRBY GRAPHICS
1782 Monterey Ct
Hoffman Estates, IL 60194
Ph: 708/991-5535
Kenneth Kirby, Pres/Owner

THE VISUAL REFERENCE LIBRARY
BY RETAIL REPORTING CORP.

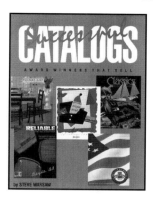
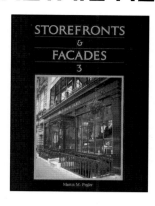
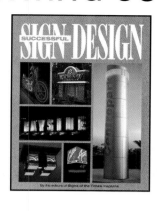
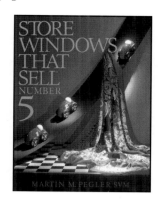

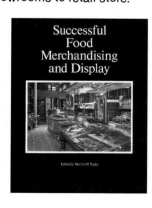

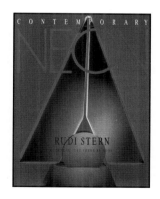

KITTLE'S
8600 Allisonville
Indianapolis, IN 46250
Ph: 317/849-5300
Fax: 317/849-6572
Kathy Devereux, Mktg Dir
Karen Gartland, AdvAsst
Elizabeth Joyal, Asst Mtkg Dir

KLINE'S
515 W Lincoln Hwy
Chicago Heights, IL 60411
Mitch Kline, Executive VP
708/481-4200
708/748-8788

KLINE BROTHERS
3830 Kelley Ave
Cleveland, OH 44114-4534
Ph: 216/881-5300
Fax: 216/881-1419
Nancy Stone, Dir-Adv

K MART
3100 W Big Beaver
Troy, MI 48084
Ph: 313/643-5043
Fax: 313/643-3207
Betty DiBartolomeo, Dir/Corp &
Brand Identity
Jerry Habeck, Sr Dir Adv
Ph: 313/643-1423
Fax: 313/643-1279
Tim White, Adv Dir
Ph: 313/643-1867
Marianita Howard, Dir/
Creative Prod
Ph: 313/643-1423

KNORR MARKETING
13709 W Bayshore Dr
Traverse City, MI 49684
Ph: 616/947-9707
Fax: 616/947-3608
Douglas Knorr, President
Bill Vandervelt

KNOX LUMBER
801 Transfer Rd
St. Paul, MN 55114
Ph: 612/641-8632
Lori Swanson, Adv Mgr

KOBACKER CO
6606 Tussing Rd
Columbus, OH 43216-6751
Ph: 614/863-7281
Fax: 614/575-7285
David Weiss, Media Dir

KOHL
N54 W13600 Woodale Dr
Menomonee Falls, WI 53051
Ph: 414/783-1301
Fax: 414/783-6501
Glen Guszkowski, VP-Adv
R Don Oscarson, Sr VP-Mktg
Ph: 414/783-1300
Vikki Stevens, Adv Copy Mgr
Ph: 414/783-1308
Kirsten Karraker, Brdcst/
Special Events
Ph: 414/783-5800

KOIN TV
222 SW Columbia St
Portland, OR 97201
Ph: 503/464-0638
Fax: 503/464-0717
Dean Gustafson, Mktg-
Research Mgr

KOKESH ATHLETIC
7106 Shady Oak Rd
Eden Prairie, MN 55344
Susan Layton, Adv Mgr

KPRC TV
8181 SW Freeway
Houston, TX 77074
Jon Campbell, Mktg Mgr
Ph: 713/778-4782
Fax: 713/995-4712

KRAMER'S
2227 Ala Moana Center
Honolulu, HI 96814
Ph: 808/946-2883
Melvin Yawata, Adv Dir

**KRANZ-KRANZ &
ASSOC**
1967 Cedar Dr, Box 142
Grafton, WI 53024
Ph: 414/375-0101
Fax: 414/375-0073
Terry Kranz, Partner

KRON TV
1001 Van Ness Ave
San Francisco, CA 94119
Ph: 415/561-8127
Fax: 415/561-8759
Jack Schwartz, Retail Sls Mgr
Jay Sondheim, Dir- New Bus
Develop
Ph: 415/561-8126

KRUEGER RINGIER
One Pierce Plaza
Itasca, IL 60143
Ph: 312/941-6611
Andy Sulskis, Sr Acct Exec

KSBW TV
238 John St
Salinas, CA 93901
Cindy Lindsay, Gen Sls Mgr
Ph: 408/758-8888

KSEE TV
5035 E McKinley
Fresno, CA 93727
Ph: 209/454-2424
Fax: 209/454-2487
Connie Batti, Mktg
Specialist

KSTP TV
3415 University Ave
St. Paul, MN 55114
Ph: 612/646-5555
Lisa Meier, Acct Exec

KTVU TV
#2 Jack London Sq
Oakland, CA 94623
Ph: 415/874-0228
Fax: 415/272-9957
Richard Hartwig, Retail
Mktg Dir

KTVX TV
1760 Fremont Dr
Salt Lake City, UT 84104
Ph: 301/972-1776
Fax: 301/972-9341
Jan Bournstein, Mktg Mgr

KTXA-TV
1712 E Randol Mill Rd
Arlington, TX 76011
Sandra Cooke, Retail Sls Mgr
Ph: 817/265-2100

**KUNZELMANN-
ESSER**
710 W Mitchell St
Milwaukee, WI 53204
Ph: 414/671-6600
Fax: 414/671-2740
Roger Clark, Adv/Sls Mgr

KUWAIT FOOD CO
PO Box 5087
Safat, Kuwait
Eorhan El Kilany, Dir-Mktg
Ph: 965/481-5900

KWGN TV
6160 S Wabash
Way Englewood, CO 80209
Debbee Cde Baca, Retail Mktg
Mgr

**LA GAVERIE
DU MEUBLE**
18 Courcelette
Quebec City, PQ G1N 3C1
Canada
Ph: 418/681-0171
Gilles Vaillancourt, President

LA OPINION
411 W 5th St, 9th Fl
Los Angeles, CA 90013
Ph: 213/896-2082
Fax: 213/896-2080
Claudette LaCour, Dir-Adv
Susanna Whitmore, Majors Acct
Exec
Ph: 213/896-2094

LA PRESSE LTEE
7 Rue St Jacques
Montreal, PQ H2Y 1K9
Canada
Ph: 514/285-7240
Fax: 514/845-5830
Denis Belanger, Retail Adv Dir

LAURA ASHLEY
1300 MacArthur Blvd
Mahwah, NJ 07430
Ph: 201/934-3195
James Terminiello, Adv Mgr

**LA-Z-BOY
ADVERTISING**
1284 N Telegraph Rd
Monroe, MI 48161
Ph: 313/241-2831
Fax: 313/241-4422
Michael Hauser, Creative
Services Mgr
Catherine McBride, Creative
Services Coord
Ph: 313/241-2974

LA-Z-BOY SHOWCASE
601 Conkey St
Hammond, IN 46320
Ph: 219/937-3360
Fax: 219/937-6315
Mike Carlson, President
Chuck Forcey, President
Bob Kaspar, Adv Dir

**LAMAR ADVERTISING
OF DAYTON**
P O Box 580
Dayton, OH 45402
Ph: 513/228-9143
Rod Morris, Sls Mgr

LAMONTS
3650 131st Ave SE
Bellevue, WA 98006
Ph: 206/644-5783
Fax: 206/746-3185
Mary Ann Arnone, Copy Dir
Brent Frerichs, VP
Ph: 206/644-5780
Laura Schlicker, Prod Dir
Ph: 206/644-5782
Mary Seto, PR Dir
Ph: 206/644-5758

**LANCASTER
NEWSPAPERS**
8 W King, Box 1328
Lancaster, PA 17603
Ph: 717/291-8821
Fax: 717/291-8728
Monica Benedict, Retail Adv
Mgr

LANDSMAN ASSOC
PO Box 66
Oxford, OH 45056
Ph: 513/523-2644
Fax: 513/523-1376
John Landsman, Mktg Cons

**LASALLE
PARTNERS LTD**
Union Station 40 Mass Ave
Washington, DC 20002
Ph: 202/289-1908
Fax: 202/289-4945
Andrew Gallima, Dir-Mktg

**LAWNER REINGOLD
BRITTON & PARTNERS**
101 Arch St
Boston, MA 02110
Ph: 617/737-6401
Fax: 617/737-6658
Ann Gary, VP-Acct Supv

**LAWRANCE
ADVERTISING**
8380 Arjons Dr
San Diego, CA 92126
Ph: 619/586-7666
Fax: 619/566-1759
Ann Maloney-Rhee, Adv Dir

**LE CHATEAU
OF CANADA**
5695 Ferrier St
Montreal, PQ H4P 1N1
Canada
Ph: 514/738-7000
Fax: 514/342-0851
Mario Chiofolo, Adv Coord

**LEADING NATIONAL
ADVERTISING**
136 Madison Ave
New York, NY 10003
Ph: 212/725-2700
Jim Farrell, VP-Sls Mktg

LEAR'S
655 Madison Ave
New York, NY 10021
Ph: 212/888-0007
Fax: 212/888-0087
Diane Dunst, Dir-Prom Serv

LECHMERE
275 Wildwood St
Woburn, MA 01801
Ph: 617/935-8340
Howard Benidt, Sr VP-
Adv/Sls Prom
Bob Comora, Creative Services
Mgr
Deborah Jackson, Adv Mgr

LEE ENTERPRISE
215 Maine Putnam Bldg
Davenport, IA 52801
Ph: 319/383-2126
Fax: 319/323-9608
Mike Kment, Regl Sls Mgr
Bruce Whittenberg, Mgr-
Adv/Sls

LEEWARDS
1200 St Charles St
Elgin, IL 60120
Ph: 708/888-5753
Fax: 708/888-5719
Lori Crane, Media Plnr
Kimberly Lee, Dir-Mktg
Ph: 708/888-5939
Barry Schwaab, Adv Dir

**LEGEND
PHARMACUTICAL**
North Shore Atrium ll
Syosset, NY 11791
Ph: 516/921-8787
Richard Scoza, Exec Dir Mktg

LEGGETT STORES
3415 Candlers Mountain Rd
Lynchburg, VA 24502
Ph: 804/237-6601
Fax: 804/237-6604
Kerry Giles, Special Events
Coord
Marcia Hallmann, Adv Coord
Mary Ann Newton, Regl
Adv Mgr
Ph: 804/237-6055

LEHIGH PRESS
51 Haddonfield Rd
Cherry Hill, NJ 08002
Ph: 609/665-5200
Denise Draper-Villena,
VP-Natl Sls

LEHNDORFF GROUP
2841 Greenbriar Pkwy, SW
Atlanta, GA 30331
Ph: 404/344-6611
Fax: 404/344-6631
Nancy Blocker, Mktg Dir

LEHNDORFF GROUP
2501 Cedar Springs, #340
Dallas, TX 75201
Ph: 214/855-5800
Charlotte Ellis, Dir-Mktg
Patricia Gleason, Mktg Dir
Susan Handley, Mktg Dir
Brenda Lowery, Asst Dir-Mktg
Ph: 214/855-5635

LEHNDORFF GROUP
3121 N Third Ave
Phoenix, AZ 85013
Ph: 602/264-5575
Fax: 602/274-9946
Nina Pruitt, Mktg Dir

LEHNDORFF GROUP
1961 Chain Brdge Rd, Ste 105
McLean, VA 22102
Ph: 703/893-7720
Fax: 703/847-3089
Debbie Withers, Mktg Dir

LEHNDORFF GROUP
50 S Main, #75
Salt Lake City, UT 84144
Ph: 801/363-1558
Fax: 801/532-4345
David Zukowski, Mktg Dir

LEIGH STOWELL
2025 1st Ave
Seattle, WA 98121
Ph: 206/726-5550
Fax: 206/621-0454
Anthony Schlee, VP
Psychographics & Schlee

LEON'S CASUALS
PO Box 1016
Selma, AL 36702
Ph: 205/872-7401
Jim Malone, Exec VP

LERNER
460 W 33rd St
New York, NY 10001
Ph: 212/629-2755
Fax: 212/629-2719
Susan Frankenberg, Mktg Dir

LERNER
2001 International Blvd
McLean, VA 22102
Ph: 703/827-7700
Clarke Green, Mktg Dir

LESLIE ADVERTISING
874 S Pleasantburg Dr
Greenville, SC 29607
Ph: 703/827-7700
William White, Group VP

LICHTER FURNITURE
818 Third Ave N
Birmingham, AL 35203
Ph: 205/323-1674
Fax: 205/226-0399
Steve Lichter, VP

**LILLIAN VERNON
CORP**
510 S Fulton Ave
Mount Vernon, NY 10550
Ph: 914/699-4131
Fax: 914/699-7698
Mary-Leslie Ullman, Mgr
Wholesale/Retail

LINCOLN MALL
208 Lincoln Mall
Matteson, IL 60443
Ph: 708/747-5600
Fax: 708/747-5629
Stephanie Hall, Mktg Dir

**LINDENMEYR
CENTRAL**
100 Park Ave, 12th fl
New York, NY 10017
Ph: 212/818-9199
Robert McBride, VP

**LIPTONS
INTERNATIONAL**
29 Connell Ct, #2
Toronto, ON M8Z 3T7
Canada
Ph: 416/251-3121
Fax: 416/251-8583
Stephen Goodman, VP-Mktg

LITHO PLUS
390 Consumers Rd
Willowdale, ON M2J 4H1
Canada
Ph: 416/495-8293
Fax: 416/495-8582
Ivan Morton, Acct Mgr

**LITTLE FOLK SHOP/
KIDS MART**
801 Sentous
City of Industry, CA 91748
Ph: 818/965-4022
Fax: 818/854-3127
Frank Hirsch, Adv Dir

**LIVING ROOM
GALLERY**
PO Box 220
Liverpool, NY 13088
Ph: 315/453-2543
Michael Goldberg, VP

LIVING ROOM
4485 S Hamilton Rd
Groveport, OH 43125
Ph: 614/294-6464
Towny Quinn, President

LMD ASSOCIATES
7430 Baltusrol Ln
Charlotte, NC 28210
Ph: 704/552-0716
Lee Dubow, President

LOEB LTD
Spitalgasse 47-51 3000
Berne, Switzerland
Ph: 31/21-7299
Fax: 31/21-7236
Martin Buehler, Mktg Dir
P Christener, Mgng Dir
Ph: 31/21-7111
Francois Loeb, Mgng Dir

LOEHMANN'S
2500 Halsey St
Bronx, NY 10461
Ph: 212/960-1806
Fax: 212/863-3249
Hy Leder, VP-Adv & PR

**LONDON FREE
PRESS**
PO Box 2280
London, ON N6A 4G1   Canada
Ph: 519/679-1111
Fax: 519/667-4523
Ron Kipp, Major Retail Sls Mgr

**LONG ISLAND
MONTHLY**
600 Community Dr
Manhasset Long Island, NY
11030
Ph: 516/562-5832
Florence Forman, Sls Mgr

**LONGMEADOW
FURNITURE**
62 W Longmeadow Rd
Hagerstown, MD 21740
Ph: 301/739-9491
Mary Wilfong, VP

OCTOBER 18, 1991

JANUARY 29 – FEBRUARY 1, 1992

IF YOU ARE IN RETAIL MARKETING OR ADVERTISING, THESE DATES ARE IMPORTANT TO YOU!

October 18, 1991

Deadline day for entries in the annual RAC Awards Competition, the most prestigious awards program in retail advertising. Honoring the best in both broadcast and print. Enter your best work for an opportunity to take your place among the stars of retail advertising.

January 29– February 1, 1992

The 40th annual Retail Advertising Conference, the largest and most important annual gathering of retail marketing and advertising executives anywhere. The famous RAC attracts top level professionals from all over the world. If you are in any way involved in retail marketing and advertising, you owe it to yourself and your company to attend.

For full information on the RAC Awards Competition and the annual Retail Advertising Conference in Chicago, please write, fax or call: Retail Advertising & Marketing Association, 500 N. Michigan Ave., Suite 600, Chicago, IL 60611. Phone: 312/245-9011; Fax: 312/245-9015.

LORD & TAYLOR
424 Fifth Ave
New York, NY 10018
Ph: 212 391 3344
Fax: 212/391-3443
Patricia Doyle-Burgevin, VP-Mktg
Julie Furr, VP-Adv
Ph: 212/391-3482
Russell Hardin, VP-Creat Dir
Rita Lennick, Sr VP-Adv
James Nolan, Bus Mgr
Ph: 212/382-7399

LOREL MARKETING GROUP
500 N Gulph Rd, Ste 307
King of Prussia, PA 19406
Ph: 215/337-2343
Fax: 215/768-9511
Beverly Rosen, Dir-Comm
Lorna Rudnick, President

LORTZ DIRECT MARKETING
11316 "P" Street
Omaha, NE 68137
Ph: 402/331-5740
Fax: 402/331-5769
Scott Lortz, VP/Media Dir

LOS ANGELES TIMES
Times Mirror Square
Los Angeles, CA 90053
Ph: 213/237-3016
Fax: 213/237-3152
Len Pomerantz, Retail Adv Mgr

LOTUS COMMUNICATIONS
6777 Hollywood Blvd, #401
Hollywood, CA 90028
Hal Rosenberg, Exec VP
Ph: 213/461-8225

GEORGE W LOVE ASSOC
200 E Delaware
Chicago, IL 60611
Ph: 312/943-1423
Fax: 312/245-9015
George Love, President

LOWE'S COMPANY
PO Box 1111
North Wilkesboro, NC 28656
Ph: 919/651-4351
Ralph Buchan, Jr-VP-Adv

JUDY LOYD & PARTNERS
28400 Hughes
St. Clair Shores, MI 48081
Ph: 313/259-6037
Judy Loyd, President
Tobye Wietzke, Sr VP-Mktg

LYON & CO
2080 Park Run Dr Ste D
Columbus, OH 43220
Jennifer Lyon, President

MACHESNEY PARK MALL
8750 N 2nd St
Rockford, IL 61111
Ph: 815/654-9880
Greg Stevenson, Mktg Dir

MACLAREN: LINTAS RETAIL
20 Dundas St W
Toronto, ON M5G 2H1
Canada
Ph: 416/977-2244
Fax: 416/977-8062
Biz Stormsk, Acct Dir
Terry Morgan, Sr VP-Gen Mgr

MACLEAN HUNTER COMMERCIAL
360 Consumers Rd
Willowdale, ON M2J 1P8
Canada
Ph: 416/495-8868
Fax: 416/495-0611
Mark Fainmel, Retail Sls Mgr
Richard Fisher, Gen Mgr/Sls & Mktg

MACY'S NORTHEAST
151 W 34th St
New York, NY 10001
Ph: 212/560-4413
Fax: 212/629-6814
Howard Adler, VP-Adv Dir
Rosanne Cooper, Sr VP-Sls Prom
Ph: 212/560-4415
Nan Cooper, VP-Creative Dir-Sls Prom
Ph: 212/560-4415
Robin Hal, VP-Creative Dir
Ph: 212/560-4282
Audrey Nizen, Brdcst Dir
Ph: 212/560-4428

MACY'S SOUTH/BULLOCK'S
180 Peachtree St, NW
Atlanta, GA 30303
Ph: 404/222-2151
Fax: 404/221-3853
Nancy Fraleigh, Art Dir
Joseph Garbarino, Sr VP-Sls Prom
Ph: 404/222-2121
Jane Hanshumaker, Copy Dir
Ph: 404/222-2154

MADDEN CORP
70 W Madison, #1370
Chicago, IL 60602
Ph: 312/372-5583
Peter Littley, Sr Sls Rep

MADEMOISELLE
350 Madison Ave
New York, NY 10017
Ph: 212/880-8361
Fax: 212/880-8165
Wendy Blair, Beauty/Retail Adv Mgr

MADIGANS
7440 Central Ave
River Forest, IL 60305
Ph: 312/771-7400
Patricia Claire, Graphic Design
Jeanne Radysh, Adv Mgr

MADISON DIRECT MARKETING
500 W Putnam Ave
Greenwich, CT 06830
Ph: 203/869-8008
Fax: 203/869-3988
Bruce Gold, VP

MADISON'S STORES
72 N. High St
Columbus, OH 43215
Cindy Hetrick, Mktg Mgr
614/221-4325
614/221-0769

MAILING LIST SYSTEMS
711 Directors Dr
Arlington, TX 76011
Ph: 817/640-7007
James Johnson, Dir

MAISON BLANCHE
1500 Main St
Baton Rouge, LA 70821
Ph: 504/389-7280
Fax: 504/336-5098
Karon Love, Copy Dir
Sally Ann Lowry, Sr VP
Ph: 504/389-7282
Amy Pritchett, ROP Art Dir
Ph: 504/389-7265

MAITHEWS BELK
PO Box 2088 E
Gastonia, NC 28053
Ph: 704/867-3671
Fax: 704/853-1326
Gloria Gaddy, Adv Mgr

MALCY/PEARLSTEIN ADV
10500 Barkley
Overland Park, KS 66212
Ph: 913/642-7177
Fax: 913/642-7260
Bruce Pearlstein, VP/Partner

MALEY GRAPHIS LTD
71 Prospect St
Freeport, NY 11520
Ph: 516/623-5257
Alvin Maley

MALL COMPANY
987 E Ash St
Piqua, OH 45356
Sally Hanson, Mktg Dir
Ph: 513/773-1225
Fax: 513/773-1013

MALL COMPANY
1234 N Main St
Bowling Green, OH 43402
Ph: 419/354-4447
Fax: 419/353-6383
Beth Isaacs, Mktg Dir
Linda Peters, Gen Mgr

MANDEE SHOPS
12 Vreeland Ave
Totowa, NJ 07512
Ph: 201/890-0021
Rosemary Linder, Day Adv Dir

TH MANDY
2930 Prosperity Ave/Box 1685
Merrifield, VA 22116
Ph: 703/698-8909
Suzanne Yorkuna, Adv Mgr

MANOR HOUSE FURNITURE
240 Curry Hollow Rd
Pittsburgh, PA 15236
Ph: 412/653-7000
Fax: 412/653-6266
Patricia Weitz, Dir-Adv

MARC ADVERTISING
4 Station Sq. #500
Pittsburgh, PA 15219
Ph: 412/562-2000
Fax: 412/562-2022
Anthony Bucci, President
Michele Fabrizi, Sr VP/Dir-Client Services
William Wietecha, VP-Mgmt
Cindy Zeth, Exec VP-Creative-Mktg Services

MARINE CORPS
P O Box 5010
El Toro, CA 92709
Ph: 714/726-3340
Lilee Ma, Visual Mdse Mgr

ROBERT MARK ENT
1 Westchester Tower
Mt Vernon, NY 10550
Ph: 914/667-5290
Fax: 914/667-5465
David Arwood, Acct Exec
Robert Brown, Sls Mgr
Gene Carson, Sls Mgr
Roger Cruz, President

MARKE COMMUNICATIONS
105 Madison Ave
New York, NY 10016
Ph: 212/684-5600
Fax: 212/2213-1090
Sandra Cooper, VP-Creat Serv
Diane Elkan, VP
Allen Rosenberg, VP
Amy Schwartz, Acct Exec

MARKE/SROGE COMMUNICATIONS
233 E Wacker Dr
Chicago, IL 60601
Ph: 312/819-1890
Fax: 312/819-0411
Maxwell Sroge, President

MARKETING & COMMUNICATIONS
492 W Willow Ct
Milwaukee, WI 53217
Ph: 414/351-3392
Roy Boutillier, President

MARKETING DEVELOPMENTS
231 W 4th St, #603
Cincinnati, OH 45202
Ph: 513/651-5557
Fax: 513/651-5590
Stan Eichelbaum, President

MARKETING CONCEPTS
Cottage Club Rd
Howes, VT 05672
Ph: 802/253-7281
Laura Riordan, President

MARKETPLACE 2000
2333 Ponce de Leon Blvd,
#1104
Coral Gables, FL 33134
Ph: 212/492-2601
Cynthia Turk, President

MARKS ADVERTISING
2970 Maria Ave, Suite 206
Northbrook, IL 60062
Ph: 708/205-0636
Fax: 708/205-0949
Bernie Marks, President

MARLOWE INTERIORS
140 S Dearborn, #1717
Chicago, IL 60603
Ph: 312/407-0300
Becky Marlowe, Assoc IDS

MARSHALL MARKETING
1699 Washington Rd, Ste 500
Pittsburgh, PA 15228-1629
Ph: 412/854-4500
Fax: 412/884-5030
Kay Marikop, Dir Client Serv

MARSHALL GROUP
808 Greensboro Rd
High Point, NC 27260
Ph: 919/454-3056
Fax: 301/381-9438
Marshall Sudderth

MARSHALLS
200 Brickstone Sq
Andover, MA 01810
Ph: 508/474-7136
Fax: 508/474-7252
Patricia King, Adv Mgr
Virginia Meyer, Dir-Sls Prom

MARTINO & COMPANY
7 West 18th St
New York, NY 10011
Ph: 212/645-9200
Fax: 212/645-9425
Richard Martino, President

MARX FAIRMAN ADVERTISING
5225 N Ironwood Rd, #201
Glendale, WI 53217
Ph: 414/963-1100
Fax: 414/963-1876
Paul Kelly, VP-Agency Dir
David Mar, Mgng Sr Partner

MASIN FURNITURE
220 2nd Ave S
Seattle, WA 98104
Ph: 206/622-5606
Fax: 206/625-1088
Robert Masin, President

MATTHEWS BELK
PO Box 2088,
Eastridge Mall
Gastonia, NC 28053
Ph: 704/867-3671
Fax: 704/853-1326
Mickey Ramsey, Adv Dir
Gene Matthews, VP-Sls Prom

HMD MATTINGLY
21-31 Goodwood St
Victoria, AU 3121
Australia
Ph: 03/426-1111
Fax: 03/426-1588
David Mattingly, Chairman

MATTRESS DISCOUNTERS
631 S Pickett St
Alexandria, VA 22304
Ph: 703/823-8351
Karin Edgett, Dir-Adv

MAXWELL COMMUNICATION
35 E Wacker Drive, Ste 1390
Chicago, IL 60601
Ph: 312/368-1111
Fax: 312/368-1912
Bill Adams, VP/Sls

MAXWELL COMMUNICATION
1999 Shepard Rd
St. Paul, MN 55116
Ph: 612/690-7598
Judy Dorff, Mkt Planner

TJ MAXX
770 Cochituate Rd
Framingham, MA 01701
Ph: 508/390-3570
Fax: 508/390-2366
John Arruda, VP Mktg
Karen Claunch, Mgr-Adv
Ph: 508/390-3430
Sandy Keating, PR Mgr
Ph: 508/390-3628

MAY D&F
16th at Tremont Place
Denver, CO 80439
Ph: 303/620-7578
Fax: 303/620-7990
Jan Ladnier, Sr VP-Mktg
Judith Zook, VP-Creative Dir
Ph: 303/620-7582

MAY COMPANY
6160 Laurel Canyon Blvd
North Hollywood, CA 91606
Ph: 818/348-3425
Christopher Delaney, Co-op Adv Mgr

MBS MULTIMODE
7 Norden Ln
Huntington Station, NY 11746
Ph: 516/673-5600
Fax: 516/673-5626
Roger Abelson, President
Stanley Braunstein
Robert Riley, Sr VP-Strategic Mktg

MBS MULTIMODE
509 Madison Ave, Ste 1400
New York, NY 10022
Ph: 212/750-9170
Joyce Kole, VP Mktg

MCCORMACK CO
7151 Woodrow Dr
Oakland, CA 94611
Ph: 415/339-1134
Richard McCormack, Owner

MCCURDY & CO
285 E Main St
Rochester, NY 14645
Ph: 716/232-1000
Fax: 716/546-0136
Ann Cordy, Div VP-Sales Prom

MCDONALD DAVIS & ASSOC
250 W Coventry Ct
Milwaukee, WI 53217
Ph: 414/228-1990
Fax: 414/228-1990
Dick McDonald, Pres & CEO
Carrie Nygren, Sr Producer/Sr Art Dir
Larry Stuart, VP-Mgmt Supv

MCFARLAND & DRIER
99 SE Fifth St
Miami, FL 33131
Ph: 305/358-0108
Fax: 305/358-8430
Martha Falcon, Acct Supv

MCGILL/JENSEN
655 N Fairview Ave
St. Paul, MN 55104
Ph: 612/645-0751
Ron Kehoe, Asst Sls Mgr

MCGRAW-HILL BROADCASTING
1221 Ave of the Americas
New York, NY 10020
Ph: 212/512-4572
Fax: 212/512-2282
Cheryl Zeranti, Mgr-Mktg Serv

MCKIM ADVERTISING
100 Osbourne St
Winnipeg, MB R3L 1Y5
Canada
Ph: 204/284-2221
RM Telpner, VP-Mgr

WILLIAM MCKINLEY STUDIOS
113 N May St
Chicago, IL 60607
Ph: 312/666-5400
Mike Wade, VP

MCKINNEY GRAPHICS
933 W Washington
Chicago, IL 60607
Jerry McKinney, President
Ph: 312/243-4600

MCMAHAN'S FURNITURE
PO Box 1251
Santa Monica, CA 90406
Ph: 213/473-8411
Fax: 213/312-1765
WJ "Bill" Taylor, Mktg Dir

MCNAMARA
2048 N Cleveland, #309
Chicago, IL 60614
Ph: 312/477-0357
Mary McNamara

MCNITT MARKETING
2000 N Racine, #2150
Chicago, IL 60614
Ph: 312/404-1286
Fax: 312/348-8473
Ruth McNitt, President

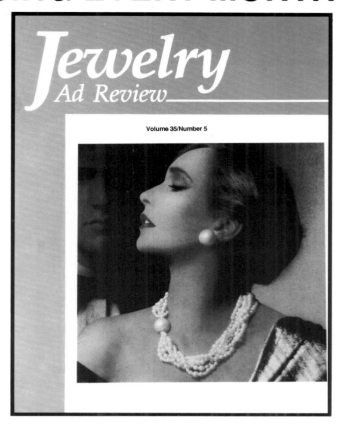
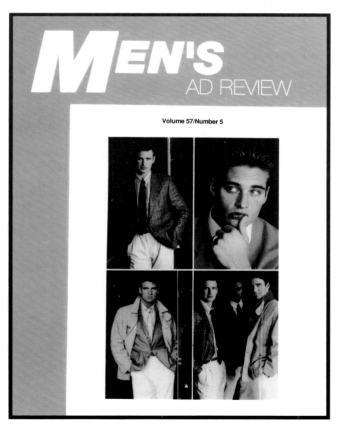
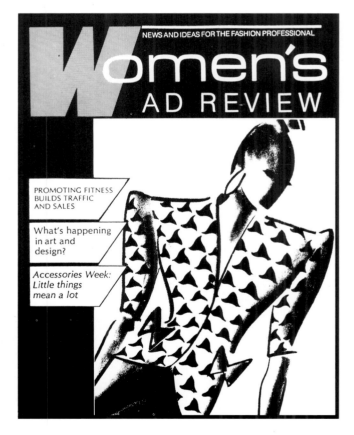

MCRAE'S
PO Box 20080
Jackson, MS 39209
Ph: 601/968-4204
Fax: 601/968-5320
Bubba Carter, Adv Dir
Ed Ebert, Creative Dir
Oscar Hancock, Sr VP-
Sls Prom
Vaughan McRae, CEO

MCS-MARKETING COMMUNICATIONS SYSTEM
1044 Polinski Rd
Ivyland, PA 1974
Ph:215/675-2000
Barbara Reid, Mgr-Sls/Mktg

MEDIA IMPRESSION
150 Holiday Inn Dr
Cambridge, ON N3C 1Z5
Canada
Ph: 519/654-2022
Fax: 519/658-9502
Charlotte Strawn, VP & PR
Wayne Straw, VP-Mktg
Virginia Thomas, Mktg
Consultant

MEDIA BUYING SERVICES LIMITED
150 Bloor St, W
Toronto, ON M5S 2X9
Canada
Ph: 416/961-1255
Fax: 416/961-4441
Richard Peirce, Group VP

MEDIA GROUP
1823 Ranch View Dr #200
Naperville, IL 60565
Ph: 708/416-9933
John Witherspoon, Natl
Mktg Dir

MEDIA TEXAS
PO Box 1073
Abilene, TX 79604
Ph: 915/673-8341
Fax: 915/677-3776
Steve Krazer, President

MEIER & FRANK
621 SW 5th Ave
Portland, OR 97204
Nancy Altman, Dir-Adv
Ph: 503/241-5327
Fax: 503/241-5343
David Miller, VP-Adv
Ph: 503/241-5326
Betty Pope, Creative Dir
Ph: 503/241-5335
Susan Stebner, Brdcst
Adv Mgr
Ph: 503/241-5331

MEIER ADVERTISING
907 Broadway
New York, NY 10010
Ph: 212/460-5655
Fax: 212/460-5957
Diane Meier, President

MEIER
2929 Walker Ave, NW
Grand Rapids, MI 49504
Ph: 616/791-3370
Fax: 616/791-2572
Gordon Ondersma,VP-Adv
Tom Vilella, Media Dir
Ph: 616/791-3505

MENDIOLA
10720 Stateline Rd
Chicago, IL 60617
Kim Mendiola

MERCHANTS ASSOCIATION
The Fashion Center
Paramus, NJ 07652
Ph: 201/447-0255
Fax: 201/592-6249
Margaret Kupilik, Mktg Dir

MEREDITH/BURDA
100 Park Ave, 3rd fl
New York, NY 10017
Ph: 212/351-3771
Fax: 212/351-3750
Michael Lesch, VP/Regl Mgr

MERIDIAN MALL
1982 Grand River Ave
Okemos, MI 48864
Ph: 517/349-4800
Fax: 517/349-7737
Sherry Laidler, Mktg Dir

MERVYN'S
25001 Industrial Blvd
Hayward, CA 94545
Ph: 415/786-7739
Fax: 415/786-7343
Michael Foote, Sls Prom Mgr
Walter Hern, Sls Prom
Prod Mgr
Ph: 415/786-4795
Fax: 415/786-7338
Pat Holt, Dir Creative Adv
Ph: 415/785-8800
Judi Jones, Mgr Mktg
Research
Ph: 415/786-4747
Ruth Lindley, Dir- Plng/Media
Ph: 415/786-8903
Steven Proffitt, Creative
Mgr-Brdcst
Ph: 415/786-8919
Susan Sprunk,VP-Sls Prom
Ph: 415/786-8907
Tali Temple, Mgr/Media
Research
Ph: 415/786-4067

MESBLA
R. do Passeio 56/90
Rio de Janeiro, BZ 20021
Brazil
Ph: 021/297-7720
Miguel Barros, Dir

MESSENGER-INQUIRER
1401 Frederica St
Owensboro, KY 42301
Ph: 502/926-0123
Fax: 502/685-3446
Tim Thompson, Retail Ad Mgr

METIER MARKETING
3505 Sims Rd
Snellville, GA 30278
Ph: 404/979-2570
Fax: 404/979-5853
William McDonald, President

METRO-RICHELIEU
11011 Blvd Maurice duplessis
Montreal, PQ H1C 1Z6
Canada
Ph: 514/643-1000
Diane Heon, VP-Strategic Plng
Richard Lapointe, Publicity/
Prom Mgr

METROLAND PRINTING
10 Tempo Ave
Willowdale, ON M2H 2N8
Canada
Ph: 416/493-1300
Fax: 416/756-2252
Ted Lynes, Dir- Sls
Michael Ziegler, Acct Mgr

METROMAIL
360 E 22nd St
Lombard, IL 60148
Ph: 312/932-2723
Susan Henderson, Acct Mgr

METROMAIL
529 Fifth Ave
New York, NY 10017
Ph: 212/599-2616
Elyssa London, Acct Mgr

METROMAIL
901 West Bond
Lincoln, NE 68521
Ph: 402/473-9750
Fax: 402/473-9753
Leanne Myers, Mktg
Research Rep

FRED MEYER
5100 SW Macadam
Portland, OR 97201
Ph: 503/721-3466
Dan Albaum, Strategic Plnr
Scott Thompson, Mktg
Dept Mgr
Ph: 503/721-3427
Lori Jones, Copywriter Mgr
Ph: 503/721-3440

FRED MEYER
210 SW Morrison Ste 300
Portland, OR 97201
Ph: 503/221-3901
Fax: 503/222-0155
Scott Bradley, VP-Sls
Prom Mgr

FRED MEYER
3800 SE 22nd Ave
Portland, OR 97242
Ph: 503/233-4591
Fax: 503/233-4530
Gary Cox, Creative Dir
Norman Myhr, Sr VP

FRED MEYER
P O Box 42121
Portland, OR 97242
Ph: 503/232-8844
Fax: 503/239-7807
Chris Doeneka, VP-Merchan
Particia Knowlton, Adv Coord
John Lesser, VP-Ladies Div
Mary Manning, VP-Intimate
Apparel
Mary Sammons, Sr VP Dir/
Gen Merchan
Jim Sundem, Adv Creative
Plnr
Darrell Webb, VP
Ted Williams, Divisional VP
D. Gordon Wilson, VP-
Domestics/Crafts

SAM MEYERS INC
3400 Bashford Ave Ct
Louisville, KY 40218
Ph: 502/459-4885
Sam Corbett, VP

MIAMI HERALD
One Herald Plaza
Miami, FL 33132
James Currow, VP-Adv
Ph: 305/376-2858
Fax: 305/376-2677
Linda Prange, Retail Adv Mgr
Ph: 305/376-2861
Fax: 305/376-4596

MIAMI VALLEY PUBLISHING
P O Box 1679
Fairborn, OH 45324
Ph: 513/879-5678
Fax: 513/878-5283
Chuck Bonkofsky, Sr VP-Sls/
Gen Mgr

MICHAEL J'S
320 S. Linn Street
Iowa City, IA 52240
Ph: 319/338-7921
Fax: 319/354-6491
Heidi Held, Merchan Mgr
Kathy McCue, VP
Lisa Wise, Dir-Operations
Ph: 319/354-4406

MICHIGAN BC
7325 Oak Ridge Highway
Knoxville, TN 37931
Ph: 615/690-9988
Fax: 615/691-3960
Thomas Campbell, Mktg Dir
Iaim MacFarlane

MICRO MEDIA
7 Dumont Pl
Morristown, NJ 07960
Ph: 201/644-5503
Fax: 201/984-5497
John Carnahan, Corp Mktg Dir

MIDT MARKETING
Thrigesved 5
7430 Ikast,
Denmark, Holland
Ph: 45/97155222
Fax: 45/99156888
Thomas Schacht, Asst Dir

MILLER & RHOADS
517 E Broad St
Richmond, VA 23219
Ph: 804/771-5485
Bob Hardy, VP-Sls Prom

MILLER MARKETING
156 Fifth Ave Ste 619
New York, NY 10010
Ph: 212/989-4600
Fax: 212/989-7659
Judy Miller, President

MILLER FURNITURE
500 W. Basin Rd
New Castle, DE 19720
Ph: 302/322-5451
Andrew Miller, President

MILLER & ASSOC
135 S. Sampson
Tremont, IL 61568
Ph: 309/925-5505
Carol Miller, President/Owner

MILLER/ZELL
4750 Frederick Dr 5W
Atlanta, GA 30336
Harmon Miller, III

MILLS BROTHERS LTD
5486 Spring Garden Rd
Halifax, NS B3J 1G4
Canada
Ph: 902/429-6111
Fax: 902/429-7711
Heather MacLellan, Mktg Mgr

MILWAUKEE JOURNAL
333 W State St Box 661
Milwaukee, WI 53201
Ph: 414/224-2423
Fax: 414/224-2485
Dick Lutz, Sls Mgr

MINNEAPOLIS ST. PAUL MAGAZINE
12 S 6th St #400
Minneapolis, MN 55402
Ph: 612/339-7571
Pat Mathews, VP-Mktg

MINNEAPOLIS STAR TRIBUNE
425 Portland Ave
Minneapolis, MN 55488
Ph: 612/372-3975
Fax: 612/372-4070
Tom Bach, Major Acct Rep
Andrea Fox Jensen, Mktg
Plng Mgr
Ph: 612/372-4109
Virginia Spaniolo, Adv Acct Rep
Ph: 612/372-3813

MINNESOTA SUBURBAN
7831 E Bush Lake Rd
Bloomington, MN 55435
Ph: 612/896-4767
Fax: 612/896-8818
Bruce Boe, Major Acct Mgr

MIRABELLA
10 E 53rd St
New York, NY 10022
Ph: 212/527-2477
Fax: 212/527-3897
Kate Myers, Adv Sls

MIRABELLA
200 Madison Ave
New York, NY 10016
Ph: 212/447-4573
Fax: 212/447-4762
Peggy Pollack, Fashion/
Retail Mgr

MMT SALES INC
150 East 52nd St
New York, NY 10022
Ph: 212/319-8008
Ken Better, VP-Mktg Bus Dev

MOBIUM
131 Steuart St
San Francisco, CA 94105
Ph: 415/957-0940
Fax: 415/227-0652
Marsha Williams, Acct Exec

MODERN WOMAN
1850 Colonial Village Ln
Lancaster, PA 17601
Ph: 717/396-9000
Fax: 717/394-5235
Denise Tarantino, Sls
Prom Mgr

MODUS OPERANDI: GRAPHICS INC
5357 N 13th St
Milwaukee, WI 53209
Ph: 414/352-2998
Fax: 414/288-7295
Christine Schmid, President

MOFFAT COMMUNICATIONS
Cky Blds Polo Park
Winnipeg, Manitoba R36 0L7
Canada
Ph: 204/788-3439
Fax: 204/956-2710
Jim McLaughlin, VP-Radio

MOFFAT COMMUNICATIONS
1000 Yonge St
Toronto, ON M4W 2K2
Canada
Ph: 416/922-4662
Brian Minton, VP-Radio Mktg

MOKRYNSKI & ASSOC
401 Hackensack Ave
Hackensack, NJ 07601
Ph: 201/488-5656
Fax: 201/488-9225
Florence Kohn, VP

MONTALDO'S
52-40 39th Dr
Woodside, NY 11377
Ph: 212/840-1616
Fax: 212/921-9807
Elaine Argiro, Dir-Adv/
Sls Prom

MONTGOMERY ADVERTISING
21675 Coolidge Hwy
Oak Park, MI 48237
Ph: 313/399-5430
Al Haberstroh, VP-Mktg

MONTGOMERY WARD
619 W Chicago Ave
Chicago, IL 60610
Ph: 312/467-3124
Fax: 312/467-7927
James Neustadt, Dir-
Creative Specialty

MONTGOMERY WARD
Montgomery Ward Plaza
Chicago, IL 60671
Ph: 312/467-3348
Fax: 312/467-2393
Dale Pond, Sr VP-Mktg

MOORS ENTERPRISES INT'L
2429 Medinah Dr
Evergreen, CO 80439
Ph: 303/674-5712
Fax: 303/674-5343
Michael Moors, President

THE MORNING CALL
P O Box 1260
Allentown, PA 18105
Ph: 215/820-6173
Fax: 215/820-6617
Rocky DeLeo, Retail Sls Mgr
Matthew Miller, Major Acct
Sls Mgr
Ph: 215/820-6173

MORRIS STUDIOS & ASSOC
236 Lesmill Rd
Don Mills, ON M3B 2T5
Canada
Ph: 416/449-9333
Fax: 416/449-1782
Neil Morris, VP

MORRISON INC
P O Box 160266
Mobile, AL 36625
Ph: 205/344-3000
Fax: 205/344-3066
Mike Feeney, Regl Dir

MP & COMPANY
R. Sen. Simonsen 12-106
Rio De Janeiro, RJ 22461
Brazil
Ph: 021/246-0931
Fax: 021/246-5347
Fernando Castro, Art Dir

MP & COMPANY
19300 Detroit Rd
Rocky River, OH 44116
Ph: 216/333-6670
Norman Rosenthal, Dir-
Mktg/Adv

MUNCIE NEWSPAPERS
125 S High St, Box 2400
Muncie, IN 47307-9985
Ph: 317/747-5742
Fax: 317/747-5782
Richard Morrow, Retail
Adv Mgr

MYERS MARKETING & RESEARCH
322 Route 46 West
Parsippany, NJ 07054
Ph: 201/808-7333
Fax: 201/882-3651
Jack Myers, President

SAM MYERS
3400 Bashford Ave Ct
Louisville, KY40218
Ph: 502/459-4885
Sam Corbett, VP

MYSTROM ADVERTISING
808 E St
Anchorage, AK 99501
Ph: 907/274-9553
Fax: 907/274-9990
Rick Nerland

NASHLAND ASSOC-RIVERGATE
1000 Two Mile Park Way, Ste 1
Goodlettsville, TN 37072
Ph: 615/859-2035
Fax: 615/851-9656
Vicki Popular, Mktg Dir

ABSOLUTE RETAIL

THE COMPLETE AND QUINTESSENTIAL PUBLICATION ON RETAIL ADVERTISING!

For a complimentary issue contact:

RETAIL REPORTING BUREAU
302 Fifth Avenue, New York, NY 10001 • 800-251-4545 • Fax 212-279-7014

NATHANS FURNITURE
Box 335, Velmont Pkwy
Hazelton, PA 18201
Ph: 717/455-9288
Ian Lipton, President

NHD STORES, INC
365 Washington St
Stoughton, MA 02072
Ph: 617/341-1810
Fax: 617/341-2291
Anita Lofchie, VP-Adv

NATIONAL COLORITE CORP
61229 W Ryerson Rd
New Berlin, WI 53151
Ph: 414/784-8980
Earl Leiske, Sls Rep

NATIONAL HOME FURNISHINGS ASSOC
305 W High St
High Point, NC 27260
Ph: 919/883-1650
Fax: 919/883-1195
Rhonda Harvey, Dir-Educ

NATIONAL RETAIL FEDERATION
100 W 31st St
New York, NY 10001
Ph: 212/244-8780
Fax: 212/594-0487
Judith Owens, VP-Mktg

NATURES GALLARY
509 Laurel Ave
Vanesville, WI 53545
Ph: 312/951-8432
Lara Hedberg, Gallary Mgr

NAUSSAU BROADCASTING CO
221 Witherspoon St
Princeton, NJ 08540
Ph: 609/924-3600
John Morris, President

NBBJ/RETAIL CONCEPTS
111 S Jackson St
Seattle, WA 98104
Ph: 206/223-5193
Fax: 206/621-2301
Scott David Fedje

NBC TV
30 Rockefeller Plaza
New York, NY 10112
Ph: 212/664-7152
Fax: 212/489-7471
Ann Reed, Dir-Affiliating Mktg

NCL GRAPHICS
1970 Estes Ave
Elk Grove Village, IL 60007
Ph: 708/593-2610
Fax: 708/593-0129
Vinnie Connor, Sls Rep
Larry McDermott, Sls Rep

NEIMAN MARCUS
1618 Main St
Dallas, TX 75201
Ph: 214/573-5828
Fax: 214/573-5992
Donna Edding, Sr Prod Mgr
Rosanne Kosanda, Dir-Adv Prod/Media
Ph: 214/573-5822
Mark Olsen, Dir
Ph: 214/573-5970
Fax: 214/573-6136
Daria Retian, VP-Creat Services
Ph: 214/573-5766

NERLAND'S HOME FURNISHINGS
501 E Dimond Blvd
Anchorage, AK 99515
Ph: 907/349-1572
Fax: 907/349-8031
Kate Horn, Adv Dir

NETWORK MUSIC
16935 W Bernardo D #100
San Diego, CA 92127
Ph: 619/451-6400
Michael Anderson, Sr Acct Exec

THE NEW YORK TIMES
229 W 43rd St
New York, NY 10036
Ph: 212/556-7028
Stu Getz, Group Mgr

NEW ENGLAND DEVELOPMENT
One Wells Ave
Newton, MA 02159
Ph: 617/243-7050
Fax: 617/243-7059
Adrienne Davis-Brody,VP/Dir-Mktg
Donna LaVita-Tefft, Dir-Adv
Ph: 617/243-7051

NEW WOMAN MAGAZINE
215 Lexington Ave
New York, NY 10016
Ph: 212/685-4790
Paula Hains, Retail Mgr

NEW YORK DAILY NEWS
220 E 42nd St
New York, NY 10017
Ph: 212/210-2063
Fax: 212/210-1942
John Ancona
Les Goodstein, Adv Mgr
Robert Harrod, Adv Mgr
Ph: 212/210-2092
Jerry McCann, Sls Mgr

NEW YORK MAGAZINE
755 Second Ave
New York, NY 10017
Ph: 212/880-0716
Fax: 212/972-2185
Beth Fuchs Brenner, Sls Dev Mgr
Frances Orner, Retail Sls Mgr
Ph: 212/880-0727

NEW YORK POST
210 South St
New York, NY 10002
Ph: 212/815-8543
Fax: 212/815-8374
Patrick Judge, Retail Adv Dir
Ellen Mullins, Publisher Asst
Ph: 212/815-8147
Robert Scott, VP-Adv
Ph: 212/815-8423

NEW YORK TIMES
229 W 43rd St
New York, NY 10036
Ph: 212/556-4104
Fax: 212/302-5975
Alexis Buryk, Retail Adv Dir
Paul Corvino, Adv Mgr
Ph: 212/556-1786
Chris Garrity, Sls Rep
Ph: 212/556-1210
Claire LaRosa, Adv Group Dir
Ph: 212/556-1625
Erich Linker, Jr, Sr VP-Adv
Ph: 212/556-7557
Raymond Mariash, Dept Store Group Mgr
Ph: 212/556-1210
Kevin Martinez, Group Mgr-Chain Stores
Ph: 212/556-1612

NEW YORK TIMES
701 W Chester Ave
White Plains, NY 10604
Ph: 212/428-2699
Fax: 214/428-2428
Donald Casey, Retail Adv Mgr

NEW YORK WOMEN MAGAZINE
541 N Fairbank Ste 2030
Chicago, IL 60025
Ph: 312/644-0952
Fax: 312/661-0791
Paula Johnson, Assoc Mgr

NEWCITY COMMUNCATIONS
Bridgewater Pl
Syracuse, NY 13204
Ph: 315/472-9797
Candy Burke, Dir-Special Program

NEWHOUSE NEWSPAPERS
485 Lexington Ave
New York, NY 10017
Ph: 212/697-8020
Fax: 212/972-3146
Robert Schoenbacher

NEWMAN, JORDAN & ASSOC
307 W 200 S
Salt Lake City, UT 84101
Ph: 801/364-5505
Susan Newman, Owner

NEWS & OBSERVER
215 S McDowell St
Raleigh, NC 27601
Ph: 919/829-4658
Fax: 919/829-4808
Tim Allen, Retail Adv Mgr
Jim McClure, Retail Adv Mgr
Ph: 919/829-4617
Kathy Baker, Group Sls Mgr
Ph: 919/829-4618
Jeff Glance, Adv Sls Rep
Ph: 919/829-4643

NEWS & OBSERVER
6200 Falls of Neuse
Raleigh, NC 27609
Ph: 919/878-8032
Fax: 919/872-3756
Judy Wilson, Sls Mgr

NEWS TRIBUNE
1 Hoover Way
Woodbridge, NJ 07095
Ph: 201/324-7120
Fax: 201/442-8705
Peter Stocker, Retail Adv Mgr
Jonathan Theophilakos, Dir-Adv
Ph: 201/324-7101

NEWSDAY INC
235 Pinelawn Rd
Melville, NY 11747
Ph: 516/454-2635
Fax: 516/694-4709
Richard Beekman, Retail Adv Mgr
Douglas Fox, VP-Mktg
Ph: 516/454-2610
Fax: 516/454-0321
Lou Gazitano, Adv Dir
Ph: 516/756-3420
Fax: 516/454-0312
Ray McCutcheon, Mgr-Major Acct Dept
Ph: 516/454-2515
Fax: 516/694-4709
John McKeon, Retail Sls Mgr
Ph: 516/454-3643
Jim Roberti, Mgr-Major Acct Dept
Ph: 516/454-2610

NEWSPAPER ADV BUREAU
1180 Aveune of the Americas
New York, NY 10036
Ph: 212/704-4538
Fax: 212/704-4616
Ann Hunt, VP-Partner
Alfred Eisenpreis, Senior VP
Ph: 212/704-4535
Patricia Thavenot, Retail Vice President

NEWSPAPER ADV BUREAU
4532 N Wildwood Ave
Milwaukee, WI 53211
Ph: 414/332-4788
Del Wakley, Mgr-Retail Sls Develop

NEWSPAPER ADV BUREAU
400 N Michigan Ave
Chicago, IL 60611
Ph: 312/644-1290
Fax: 312/644-2879
Jeffrey Greene, Retail VP

NEWSPAPER FIRST
711 Third Ave
New York, NY 10017
Ph: 212/692-7100
Fax: 212/286-9004
John Murphy, Sr VP
Roz Namacher, NE Retail Sls Mgr

NEWSPAPER FIRST
444 N Michigan Ave
Chicago, IL 60611
Ph: 312/822-8666
Fax: 312/822-9835
Donald Simmons, Acct Exec
Ronald Tossey, VP
Gary Voss, Retail Sls Exec

NEWSPAPER FIRST
20 N Wacker Dr
Chicago, IL 60606
Ph: 312/263-6270
Fax: 312/263-2013
Gary Voss, Retail Sls

NIKE
3700 W Murray Blvd
Beaverton, OR 97005
Ph: 503/641-6453
Fax: 503/641-0731
Ron Dumas, Graphic Designer

NOBART INC
1133 S Wabash
Ph: 312/427-9800
Fax: 312/427-4603
Chicago, IL 60605
Phil Denofrio
Warren Yamakoshi, President

NOLL PRINTING CO
625 N Michigan Ave, Ste 500
Chicago, IL 60611
Ph: 312/751-3463
Fax: 312/751-2731
Deborah San Gabino, Sls Rep

NOLL PRINTING CO
100 Noll Plaza
Huntington, IN 46750
Ph: 219/356-2020
Fax: 219/356-4584
Mead Twitchell, VP

NORDSTROM
1501 Fifth Ave
Seattle, WA 98101
Ph: 206/628-1924
Fax: 206/628-1901
Barbara Bryce, Direct Mail Mgr
Linda Finn, Adv Dir
Ph: 206/628-1989
Alice Gannett, Art Dir
Ph: 206/628-1964
Randy Mecham, Copy Dir
Ph: 206/628-1984
Fax: 206/622-1632
Cheryl Zahniser, Creative Dir
Ph: 206/628-1964

NORLING STUDIOS
221 Swathmore Ave, Box 7167
High Point, NC 27264
Ph: 919/434-3151
John Pardy, Acct Exec

NORTH FACE
999 Harrison St
Berkeley, CA 94710
Ph: 415/527-9700
Fax: 415/527-5769
Tom Applegate, VP

NORTH HILLS INC
4217 Six Forks Rd
Raleigh, NC 27609
Ph: 919/787-9042
LuAnn Slawinski, Mktg Dir

NORTH SHORE NEWS
1139 Lonsdale Ave
Vancouver, BC V7M 2H4
Ph: 604/980-0511
Fax: 604/985-1435
Linda Stewart, Display Adv Dir

DC NORTHAM/ ST MARYS
1 Westbrook Corp Ctr #820
Westchester, IL 60154
Ph: 708/562-5500
Fax: 708/562-5574
John Gillen, Sls Rep
Jeffrey Hill, Sls/Mkg
Rada Subotic, Sls Rep

NORTHWEST HERALD
One Herald Sq, Box 250
Crystal Lake, IL 60014
Ph: 815/459-4040
Fax: 815/477-4960
JoAnn Nelson, Ad Sls Supv
Jim Ringness, Acct Exec

NY MARKET RADIO BROADCASTERS ASSOC
675 Third Ave #1700
New York, NY 10017
Ph: 212/490-6950
Fax: 212/370-4957
Sandy Josephson, VP-Mktg

JOHN J. O'BRIEN
7815 Zenith Dr
Citrus Heights, CA 95621
Ph: 916/723-0134
John O'Brien, Freelance

OCTOBER ART LTD
120 Park Ave
New York, NY 10017
Ph: 212/986-3680
Delores Abelson, President

JO ODIO
15572 SW 54 Terrace
Miami, FL 33185
Ph: 305/223-4287
Jo Odio, Consultant

OFFSET SEPARATIONS
30 E 33rd St
New York, NY 10016
Ph: 212/545-0466
Fax: 212/545-0478
Mark Groff, Sls Rep
Clark McKnight, VP-Sls

OGILVY & MATHER
309 W 49th St
New York, NY 10019
Ph: 212/237-7603
Fax: 212/237-5393
Linda Ladick, Acct Mgr
Mary Ann Zeman, Assoc Creative Dir
Ph: 212/237-5901

OGILVY & MATHER
676 N St Clair
Chicago, IL 60611
Ph: 312/988-2600
Bill McCarthy, Sr VP-Group Dir
Austin McGmie, Client Service Dir

OGILVY & MATHER RIGHTFORDS
P O Box 784427
Sandton 2146, SA 2000
South Africa
Ph: 011/783-4417
Mike Welsford, Client Service Dir

OK&D ADVERTISING
70 Ferguson Ave N
Hamilton, ON L8R1L4
Ph: 416/525-8437
Fax: 416/525-2336
Joseph Duda, VP/Creative Dir

OMNI/GRAFX
775 W Jackson
Chicago, IL 60611
Ph: 312/715-0990
Fax: 312/715-1020
Bunny Cline, Dir-Sls

OREGONIAN
1320 SW Broadway
Portland, OR 97201
Ph: 503/221-8329
Fax: 503/294-4199
Glenn Breniman, Retail Adv Mgr
Elizabeth Ryan Wolf, Sr Acct Exec
Ph: 503/221-8093

ORENT GRAPHIC ARTS
4805 "G" St
Omaha, NE 68117
Ph: 402/733-6400
Fax: 402/733-2083
Bob Wieck, President

OTTAWA CITIZEN
1101 Baxter Rd
Ottawa, ON K2C 3N4
Canada
Ph: 613/596-3585
James Orban, Retail Adv Mgr

HELENA OWENS GRAPHICS
4322 Murfield Dr East
Bradenton, FL 34203
Ph: 813/758-0398
Fax: 813/755-6079
Tom Owens, Owner/Freelancer
Helena Owens, Owner/Freelancer

P R ASSOCIATES EXEC SEARCH
12740 Hillcrest #203
Dallas, TX 75230
Ph: 214/960-2911
Fax: 214/960-8636
Nancy Porter, President

P S PARTNERS INC
305 E 45th St
New York, NY 10017
Michael Potter, President
Ph: 212/826-4012

PACE
3350 Peoria
Aurora, CO 80010
Ph: 303/367-3657
Steven Ross, Adv Mgr

PACE MEMBERSHIP WAREHOUSE
5680 Greenwood Plaza Blvd
Englewood, CO 80111
Ph: 303/843-8558
Fax: 303/843-8051
Mary Crowley, Adv Mgr
Patrick Smid, VP-Mktg

PACIFIC PRESS
2250 Granville St
Vancouver, BC V6H 3G2
Canada
Ph: 604/732-2441
Fax: 604/732-2497
Peter Jensen, Retail Adv Mgr

PACIFIC PROPERTY SERVICE
Four Embarcadero Ct #2600
San Francisco, CA 94111
Ph: 415/772-0550
Fax: 415/982-1780
Terri Lagrisola, Mktg Mgr
Christin Lopez, Mktg Asst

PADULO ADVERTISING
1670 Bayview Ave
Toronto, ON M4G 3C2
Canada
Ph: 416/483-4000
Fax: 416/483-4012
Lewis Cattapan, Acct Dir
Don Freedman, VP-Client Services
Rick Padulo, President/CEO
Gord Steventon, VP/Acct Dir

PAGANETTI
152 E 94th St
New York, NY 10128
Ph: 212/860-3165
Jo An Paganetti, Mktg Consultant

PALMER JARVIS ADV
1600-1176 W Georgia St
Vancouver, B.C. V7G1Y4
Canada
Ph: 604/687-7911
Fax: 604/684-8683
Roy Crowe, Acct Dir
Frank Palmer, CEO
Fax: 604/662-8610
Rick Truman, VP

PAPER TRADE INC
P O Box 996
Wheeling, IL 60090
Ph: 708/381-0532
Fax: 708/381-0542
Walter Ruggles, President

PAPPAS
1735 Wagner Rd
Glenview, IL 60025
Ph: 708/341-3843
Evan Pappas

PARISIAN
750 Lakeshore Pkwy
Birmingham, AL 35211
Ph: 205/940-4810
Fax: 205/940-4987
Patty Bystrom, Sls Prom Dir
Dan Copus, Creative Dir
Ph: 205/940-4815
Diane Vogel, Copy Director
Ph: 205/940-4000

PARISIAN
200 Research Parkway
Birmingham, AL 35211
Ph: 205/940-4819
Fax: 205/940-4987
Kim Sisty, Direct Mktg Mgr

PARKSON CORPORATION
G26, Subang Parade
47500 Petaling Jaya,
Selangor Darul Ehsa
Malaysia
Ph: 60/03-241-2155
Fax: 60/03-242-2710
Tony H M Tam, Adv/Prom Mgr

PATRIOT LEDGER
400 Crown Colony Dr
Quincy, MA 02169
Ph: 617/786-7175
Fax: 617/786-7298
George White, Regl/Natl Adv Dir

PATSY'S BRIDAL
4321 Lincoln
Groves, TX 77619
Ph: 409/962-5871
Patsy McDonald, Owner

PATY
P O Box 250
Piney Flats, TN 37686-0250
Ph: 615/538-8101
Fax: 615/538-8101 Ext226
John Seward Jr, President

PAYLESS CASHWAYS
P O Box 419466
Kansas City, MO 64141
Ph: 816/234-6328
Fax: 816/234-6070
Brenda Bryan, Mgr-Mkt Research

PEARLMAN'S
P O Box 19228
Asheville, NC 28815
Ph: 704/253-4873
Fax: 704/252-3243
Skip Pearlman, President

PEEBLES INC
One Peebles St
South Hill, VA 23970-5001
Ph: 804/447-5200
James Jonas, Adv Mgr

PEMBROOK MANAGEMENT
305 E 47th St
New York, NY 10017
Ph: 212/715-2287
Susan Nocella, Creative Dir

PENN-DANIELS
505 N 24th St
Quincy, IL 62301
Ph: 217/224-1525
Fax: 217/224-6621
Joe DeAngelo, Dir-Adv
James Halwig, Creative Dir

JCPENNEY
P O Box 659000
Dallas, TX 75265
Ph: 214/591-3329
Fax: 214/591-9570
Bob Bowler, Adv Mgr
John Hoerres, Div Adv Mgr
Ph: 214/591-3339
Bill Kelly, VP-Dir Catalog Adv
Ph: 214/591-3767
Fax: 214/591-9549
Jose Ortiz-Marrero, Adv Proj Mgr
Ph: 214/591-4231
Fax: 214/591-9543

PEOPLES JEWELLERS LIMITED
1440 Don Mills Rd
Don Mills, Ontario M3B3M1
Ph: 416/441-1515
Fax: 416/441-3287
Susan Burns, VP Mktg

PERLMUTER PRINTING
4437 E 49th St
Cleveland, OH 44125
Ph: 216/271-5300
Fax: 216/271-7650
Mary Huff, Sls Rep

TOM PETERSON INC
4322 NW Yeon Ave
Portland, OR 97210-1423
Ph: 503/777-3300
Fax: 503/777-1075
Tom Peterson, President
Retail Adv-Mktg Mgr
Ph: 503/774-8022

PETTERSON ASSOC
950 Linden Ave
S. San Francisco, CA 94080
Ph: 415/873-8787
Fax: 415/873-8786
Michael Foote, Studio Dir

PFALTZGRAFF
140 E Market St
York, PA 17401
Ph: 717/852-2517
Fax: 717/771-1442
Shirley Kehr, Retail Adv Mgr

PHAR MOR INC
6507 Wilhims Ave
Pittsburgh, PA 15217
Ph: 412/362-8700
Fax: 412/362-8519
Carol Robinson, Adv Mgr

PHILADELPHIA NEWSPAPERS
400 N Broad St
Philadelphia, PA 19101
Ph: 215/854-5550
Fax: 215/854-5671
Bill Burgess, Retail Adv Mgr
John Kramer, Adv Dir
Raymond Simon, Dir-Mktg/Retail Adv
Ph: 215/854-5153

PHOENIX FURNITURE
2700 N Broadway
Los Angeles, CA 90031
Ph: 213/225-5935
Ruben Jaime, VP-Merch/Adv

PHOTO-MECHANICAL SERVICES
333 W 78th St
Minneapolis, MN 55420
Ph: 612/881-3200
Fax: 612/881-5076
John Love, Dir-Sls
Len Sands, Dir-Mktg

PHOTO-MECHANICAL SERVICES
6509 Cecilia Circle
Bloomington, MN 55435
Ph: 612/942-9900
Robert Revere, Dir-Sls/Mktg

PICINI KRAMER & THOMAS INC
1313 Slocum Rd #106
Dallas, TX 75207
Ph: 214/761-9377
Fax: 214/745-1411
Susan Puckett, Sls Rep

PICINI KRAMER & THOMAS INC
76 Ninth Ave, W Penthouse
New York, NY 10011
Ph: 212/627-8660
Fax: 212/633-9078
Ted Thomas, VP-Mktg

PICTURES & TYPE
388 King St W
Toronto, ON M5V 1K2
Canada
Ph: 416/977-1986
Mike Machida, Copywriter
Jacqueline Mahovlich, Layout Artists

PICWAY SHOES
6606 Tussing Rd
Columbus, OH 43216-6751
Ph: 614/575-7219
Fax: 614/575-7285
Anthony Matteo, President

PIER 1 IMPORTS
301 Commerce St #600
Ft. Worth, TX 76161-0020
Ph: 817/878-8345
Fax: 817/332-5727
Joy Purcell, PR Coord
Phil Schneider, VP-Adv
Ph: 817/878-8340
Loretta Terrill, Dir Adv Prod
Ph: 817/878-8352

PIERCING PAGODA
3910 Adler Plaza
Bethlehem, PA 18016-1024
Ph: 215/691-0437
Brooke McDermott, Natl Mktg Mgr

PIM INC
123 N Third St
Minneapolis, MN 55401
Ph: 612/340-0365
Mary Shellum, President

PIONEER UNITED MALL VISION
1700 66th St N #207
St. Petersburgh, FL 33710
Ph:813/347-3055
Fax: 813/347-0984
Lisa East, Asst Regl Dir
Randall Richards, Sr VP-Mktg/Sls
Judy Stem, Regl Dir-Mktg/Sls

PITTSBURGH PRESS
34 Boulevard of the Allies
Pittsburgh, PA 15222
Ph: 412/263-1547
Fax: 412/263-0147
Louis Naples, Retail Sls Mgr

PIZZA HUT
13635 Genito Rd
Midlothian, VA 23112
Ph: 804/744-6355
Linda Bender, Mktg Dir

PM PLACE'S
P O Box 555
Bethany, MO 64424
Ph: 816/425-6301
Roger Reece, Mktg/Adv Dir

PLAIN DEALER
1801 Superior Ave
Cleveland, OH 44114
Ph: 216/344-4350
Fax: 216/344-4210
Robert Hagley, Retail Adv Mgr

PLAZA MERCHANTS ASSOC
4625 Wornall Rd
Kansas City, MO 64112
Ph: 816/753-0100
Fax: 816/753-4625
Brenda Tally, Prom Dir

POLLARD BANKNOTE
1499 Buffalo Pl
Winnipeg, MB R3T 1L7
Canada
Ph: 204/474-2323
Fax: 204/453-1375
Ben Lowery, VP-Sls/Mktg
Guy Perrault, Mgr-Games/Prom

THE POPULAR
P O Box 1890
El Paso, TX 79999
Ph: 915/532-7755
Fax: 915/533-7671
Diane Fortenberry, Sls Prom Dir
Glen Utter, Adv Dir

POWELL
2120 Hassell Rd #202
Hoffman Estates, IL 60195
Ph: 708/835-0827
Richard Powell

PRANGE WAY INC
2800 S Ashland Ave
Green Bay, WI 54304-5389
Ph: 414/496-5540
Fax: 414/496-5548
Robert Gmeiner, Adv Dir
Mary Ann McLain, Creative Adv Mgr
Ph: 414/496-5541

PRANGE'S DEPT STORES
301 N Washington St
Green Bay, WI 54307
Ph: 414/436-5029
Fax: 414/436-5066
Kathy Lemke, Admin Adv Mgr
Sue Toepel, Adv Dir
Ph: 414/435-6611
Richard Unger, President
Ph: 414/436-5025

LYNN M PREGONT
260 E Chestnut #3205
Chicago, IL 60611
Ph: 312/266-9375
Fax: 312/266-9340
Lynn Pregont, President

PRICE COMMUNICATIONS
695 Delaware Ave
Bufflao, NY 14209
Ph: 716/884-5101
Fax: 716/882-2048
Ken Casseri, Gen Sls Mgr

PRICE MANAGEMENT INC
35 Century Pkwy
Salt Lake City, UT 84092
Ph: 801/486-3911
Fax: 801/486-7653
Jeffrey Price, Dir Enclosed Malls

PRICE/MCNABB ADVERTISING
4600 Marriott Dr Ste 510
Raliegh, NC 27612
Ph: 919/782-9393
Fax: 919/782-8329
Chris Starin, VP-Acct Supv

PRICE & PIERCE INTL
P O Box 971
Stamford, CT 06904
Ph: 203/328-2022
Fax: 203/358-8633
Chris Lawlor, VP

PRINGLE & BOOTH STUDIOS
1133 Leslie St
Don Mills, ON M3C 2J6
Canada
Ph: 416/447-5121
Gerry Morris, President

PRINTCOM
2071 Ceaman Circle
Chamblee, GA 30341
Ph: 404/452-1491
W C Lamparter, President

PRINTED MEDIA SERVICES
815 Zane Ave N
Golden Valley, MN 55422
Ph: 612/593-0921
Fax: 612/593-5066
Jon Gowan, VP-Sls
Patrick Stahel, President

PRO DISTRIBUTION SERVICES
1145 Sutton Dr
Burlington, ON L7L 5Z8
Canada
Ph: 416/332-8000
Fax: 416/332-5419
Ray Colasimone, VP-Oper
Clement Messere, VP

PRO HARDWARE
9137 E Mineral Circle
Englewood, CO 80155
Ph: 303/792-3000
Fax: 303/792-5589
Maureen Egilchrist, Adv Dir
John McGraw, VP-Prom Program

PRODIGY SERVICES INC
445 Hamilton
White Plains, NY 10031
Ph: 914/993-2578
James Beran, Program Mgr

PROFFITT'S
P O Box 388
Alcoa, TN 37701
Ph: 615/983-7000
Fax: 615/982-0690
Thomas Waltz, Sls Prom Mgr

PROJECT EARTH
921 SW Davenport
Portland, OR 97201
Ph: 503/228-6077
Lynn Stull

PROVA MARKETING GROUP
500 Wayzata Blvd
Minneapolis, MN 55416
Ph: 612/591-6565
Fax: 612/591-6577
James Little

PROVAREJO
Rua General Bruce, 551
Rio de Janeiro, BZ 20921
Brazil
Ph: 021/580-3363
Fax: 021/580-9227
Jose Luis Bartolo, Dir
Paulo Oncken, Plng/Systems Dir

PROVIDENCE JOURNAL
75 Fountain St
Providence, RI 02902
Ph: 401/277-7057
Fax: 401/277-7802
Robert Cardosa, Retail Adv Mgr
Joel Gurian, Asst Natl Retail Mgr

PUBLICITE GRAY O'ROURKE SUSSMAN
1831 Dorchester W
Montreal, PQ H3H 1R4
Canada
Ph: 514/933-4235
Max Schwartz, Exec VP

WALTER PYES WOMENS SHOP
438 Meyerland Plaza
Houston, TX 77096
Ph: 713/664-5501
Bubba Silberstein, President

PYRAMID MANAGEMENT
4 Clinton Square
Syracuse, NY 13202-1078
Ph: 315/422-7000
Fax: 315/422-3887
Renee' Frontale, Dir-Mktg

A J QUAILS INC
116 Corporate Blvd
So. Plainfield, NJ 07080
Ph: 201/755-9400
Peter Jacobson, President

QUALITY STORES INC
1460 Whitehall Rd
No Muskegon, MI 49445
Ph: 616/744-2491
Fax: 616/744-2136
Bob Hebeler, Dir-Adv Mkt
Linda Jazdzyk, Adv Creative/Prod Mgr

QUEBECOR PRINTING INC
1999 Shepard Rd
St. Paul, MN 55116
Ph: 612/690-7598
Fax: 612/690-7520
Judy Dorff, Mgr-Mktg Services
Dennis Meyer, VP-Mktg
Ph: 612/690-7210

QUICK SILVER MARKETING
1793 Bloomingdale Rd
Glendale Hts, IL 60139
Ph: 708/653-280¹
Fax: 708/653-3063
Earlene Carlson, VP-Adv

W T QUINN INC
285 Davidson Ave
Somerset, NJ 08873
Ph: 201/563-6900
Fax: 201/563-6933
William Quinn, President

R & A MARKETING INC
1459 Twin Branches Circle
Marietta, GA 30067
Ph: 404/952-5768
S. Arthur Rogers Jr, President

RADIO MARKETING BUREAU
146 Yorkville Ave
Toronto, ON M5R 1C2
Canada
Ph: 416/922-5757
Fax: 416/922-6542
Jim Harnden, VP/Retail Sls
Brian Jones, President/CEO
Linda Saint, Dir-Comm

RADIO ADVERTISING BUREAU
304 Park Ave S, 7th Fl
New York, NY 10010
Ph: 212/254-4800
Fax: 212/254-8908
Laurence Norjean, Sr VP-Mktg
Warren Potash, President/CEO
Fax: 212/254-8713

RADIO BUSINESS REPORT
P O Box 782
Springfield, VA 22150
Ph: 703/866-9300
Fax: 703/866-9306
Jim Carnegie

RADIO NEW ZEALAND
P O Box 2092
Wellington, NZ
New Zealand
Ph: 474-1555
Wendy Billingsley, Mktg Exec

RADIO SHACK
279 Bayview Dr
Barrie, ON L4M 4W5
Canada
Ph: 705/728-6242
Fax: 705/728-2012
Shigeshi Aoki, Creative Dir
Bob Kemp, Prod Mgr

RADIO SHACK
300 One Tandy Center
Ft. Worth, TX 76102
Ph:317/390-2821
Fax: 817/390-2103
Frederick Roeben, Admin
Adv Mgr

RAINBOW ADVERTISING
111 Crossways Park Dr
Woodbury, NY 11797
Ph: 516/496-1794
Fax: 516/364-5519
Bob Camporeale, Dir-Local
Adv Sls
Robert Sullivan, Sls Mgr
Ph: 516/496-1540

RAINBOW ADVERTISING
855 Boylston St
Boston, MA 02116
Ph: 617/266-7711
David Adams, Sls Rep
Kelly Boshoven, Sls Mgr
W Terry Gray, Ad Sls Mgr
Frank Mancini, Sls Rep
Jeff Smith, Sales Rep
Bill Wayland, Sls Rep

RAINBOW ADVERTISING
820 Madison St
Oak Park, IL 60302
Ph: 708/524-9330
Fax: 708/383-9625
Kenn Geer, Sls Mgr

RALEY'S
P O Box 15618
Sacramento, CA 95852
Ph: 916/373-6574
Fax: 916/444-3733
Dick Schrudder, Adv Dir

RAPID PRESS INC
155 Ida St
Omaha, NE 68110-2821
Ph: 402/453-1402
Fax: 402/453-2641
Mel Hynek, Acct Exec
Art Villani, Acct Exec
Shari Otterson, Mktg Services Mgr
Eldon Vanness, Dir-Sls/Mktg

HOWARD RAPP ENT
1 Dag Hammarskjold Plaza
New York, NY 10017
Ph: 212/207-9878
Fax: 212/207-9888
Howard Rapp, President

RATTAN SHOPPES
601 Conkey St
Hammond, IN 46320
Ph: 219/937-3360
Daniel Welch, VP

RBC
146 Yorkville Ave
Toronto, ON M5R 1C2
Canada
Ph: 416/922-5757
Linda Pratt, Acct Exec

THE RECORD
150 River St
Hackensack, NJ 07601
Ph: 201/646-4259
Fax: 201/646-4405
John Kimball, VP-Adv
Lou Stancampiano, Retail
Adv Mgr

REDWOOD & ROSS
1904 Karen Ct #6
Champaign, IL 61821
Ph: 217/352-7285
Scott Chantos, Mgr

REGIONAL REPS CORP
1375 Euclid Ave #300
Cleveland, OH 44115
Ph: 216/781-0030
Fax: 216/781-7508
Alex Keleman, VP

REITERS
2460 W George
Chicago, IL 60618
Ph: 312/267-8849
Fax: 312/267-5838
Abby Ceppos, Adv Dir

MARY REMINGTON DESIGN
1458 Mars Ave
Lakewood, OH 44107
Ph: 216/221-3507
Mary Remington, Designer

RENBERGS
311 S Main
Tulsa, OK 74120
Ph: 918/585-5601
Fax: 918/585-5335
Robyn Ely, VP

RENT-A-CENTER
P O Box 789951
Wichita, KS 67212
Ph: 316/636-7513
Fax: 316/636-7347
Gary Stewart, VP-Mktg
Alan Wright, Dir Adv/Prom
Ph: 316/636-7378

REPUBLIC & GAZETTE
120 E Van Buren
Phoenix, AZ 85004
Ph: 602/271-8556
Fax: 602/271-8500
Jeffrey Haag, Retail Ad Mgr

RESPONSE CATALOG NETWORK
13 S Cayuga Rd
Williamsville, NY 14226
Ph: 716/626-4179
Fax: 716/626-9348
Gary Held, VP-Printing Service
Ron Thomas, VP-Creative Services
Ph: 716/648-0874

RESULTS DIRECT
1621 18th St
Denver, CO 80202
Ph: 303/292-5000
Fax: 303/294-9628
Peggy Steinemann, Acct Exec
Lisa Chewning, Acct Sup

RETAIL ADV/MKTG CONSULTANT
72 Silo Hill Circle
Riverside, CT 06878
Ph: 203/637-8332
Wallace Westphal

RETAIL COMMUNICATIONS
350 Fifth Ave Ste 5414
New York, NY
Ph: 212/564-2727
Fax: 212/465-8135
Michael Berman, President
Martin Danielson
Ben Doroff, Vice Chairman
Albert Pearl, Chairman
Don Reese, Sr VP
Barbara Zimmerman, VP-Sls

RETAIL CONCEPTS
4004 Westhollow Pkwy
Houston, TX 77082
Ph: 713/497-7811
Fax: 713/870-8947
Alexander Calicchia, Dir-Adv

RETAIL GRAPHICS
8000 Ambassordor Row
Dallas, TX 75247
Ph: 214/630-9900
Tom Hansen, VP-Sls
Jim Petrini, Sls Exec

RETAIL MARKETING ADVERTISING
10 Twin Dolphin Dr, Ste 360
Redwood City, CA 94065
Ph: 415/595-4111
Fax: 415/595-2583
Rebecca Fisher, VP
Gary Rosenberg, President

RETAIL PLANNING ASSOC
645 South Grant Ave
Columbus, OH 43206
Ph: 614/461-1820
Fax: 614/461-7195
Terry Riley

RETAIL REPORTING BUREAU
302 Fifth Ave
New York, NY 10001
Ph: 212/255-9595
Larry Fuersich, Publisher

RETAIL SOLUTIONS
998 W Lost, Dutchman Pl
Tucson, AZ 85737
Ph: 602/797-0941
Ruben Arizpe, Sr President

RETAIL TARGET MKTG SYSTEMS
607-1 Fullerton Pkwy
Chicago, IL 60614
Ph: 312/281-0434
Fax: 312/281-5252
Donna Burke, VP

RETAIL TARGET MKTG SYSTEMS
6110 N Flint Rd
Glendale, WI 53209
Ph: 414/352-8611
Fax: 414/352-7422
Tim Keane, President

CRAIG M REUMUND
R R 1 Box 256
Readsboro, VT 05350
Ph: 802/423-5222
Craig Reumund, Exec VP

REVCO
1925 Enterprise Pkwy
Twinsburg, OH 44087
Ph: 216/425-9811
Fax: 216/487-1485
George Money, Dir-Adv
Bob Newmark, VP

REVEALATIONS MARKETING
620 Alden Rd, #106
Markham, ON L3R 9R7
Canada
Ph: 416/477-0801
Fax: 416/477-4473
Paul Gaynor, President
Raye McCullough, VP-Acct
Management

REYNOLDS
2453 N Mozart
Chicago, IL 60647
Ph: 312/772-5349
John Reynolds

REYNOLDS GROUP
3305 Kashiwa St
Torrance, CA 90505
Ph: 213/534-1630
Fax: 213/539-8818
Thomas Reynolds, President

RHK ASSOCIATES
2405 S 130th Circle
Omaha, NE 68144
Ph: 402/334-6900
Fax: 402/334-7517
Lynn Hinderaker, Sr VP/Dir-
Client Services

RICH'S DEPT STORE
45 Broad St
Atlanta, GA 30303
Ph: 404/586-2167
Fax: 404/586-2160
Sandra Jackson, Creative
Services Dir

RICHARDS GROUP
10000 N Central Expwy
Dallas, TX 75231
Ph: 214/891-5726
Fax: 214/891-5844
Scott Crockett, Principal
Beverly Leibee, Media Dir/Plng
Ph: 214/891-5732

RICHMAN GORDMAN STORES
12100 W Center Rd
Omaha, NE 68144
Ph: 402/691-4219
Fax: 402/691-4269
Geri Gorman, Creative Dir
Robert Hafner, VP-Sls Prom
Ph: 402/691-4325
Linda Ringling, Prod Mgr
Ph: 402/691-4320

RICHMOND NEWSPAPERS INC
P O Box C-32333
Richmond, VA 23293
Ph: 804/649-6220
Fax: 804/775-8019
Charles Rutledge, Retail
Adv Mgr

RINGIER AMERICA INC
485 Fifth Ave
New York, NY 10017
Larry Celey, VP-Commercial Sls

RIVER PLACE GRAPHICS
329 W 18th St
Chicago, IL 60616
Ph: 312/829-0176
Fax: 312/738-7449
Rebecca Bertelle, VP-Client Dev

JAMES RIVER CORP
300 Lakeside Dr
Oakland, CA 94612-3592
Ph: 415/874-3463
Fax: 415/874-3496
Mary Plimpton, Mktg Mgr

RIVERSIDE FURNITURE
P O Box 1427
Ft. Smith, AR 72901
Ph: 501/785-8165
Fax: 501/785-8102
Michael Charlton, Dir-Mktg
Services

RIVERWALK MARKETPLACE
#1 Poydras St
New Orleans, LA 70130
Ph: 504/522-1818
Jeffrey Cohn, Mktg Mgr

RMA
501 S Rancho, Ste I-60
Las Vegas, NV 89106
Ph: 702/384-6173
Fax: 702/385-7598
Nancy Moore, Acct Exec

ROANOKE TIMES & WORLD-NEWS
P O Box 2491
Roanoke, VA 24010
Ph: 703/981-3377
Fax: 703/981-3204
Judith Perfater, VP/Adv Dir

ROBBINS FURNITURE
1231 W Main St
Owosso, MI 48867
Ph: 517/725-2138
Janet Washburn, Mktg Dir

ROBINS SHARPE ASSOC
157 Princess St
Toronto, ON M4A 2M4
Canada
Ph: 416/360-5886
Fax: 416/362-3090
Bradley Robins, Chairman

WILLIAM A ROBINSON INC
35 E Wacker
Chicago, IL 60611
William Robinson, President

JW ROBINSON'S
600 W 7th St
Los Angeles, CA 90017
Ph: 213/488-7914
Fax: 213/488-7853
Marcia Cotner, VP-Creat Dir
Judy Farris, Sr. VP-Sls Prom/
Mktg
Ph: 213/488-7900
Maureen Wright, VP-PR/
Special Events
Ph: 213/488-6003

ROBINSON'S
1160 Blair Rd
Burlington, ON L7M 2A5
Canada
Ph: 416/336-3130
Fax: 416/332-5358
Celia Saltarelli, Sls Prom Mgr
Keitha Windsor, Adv Prod Mgr
Fax: 416/336-1140

ROCKWELL INTERNATIONAL
700 Oakmont Ln
Westmont, IL 60559-5546
Ph: 708/850-5600
Fax: 708/850-6042
Barbara Gora, Mktg Mgr

ROEBLING MANAGEMENT
1402 SE Everett MallWay
Everett, WA 98208
Ph: 206/743-2722
Fax: 206/742-9255
Maria Anderson, Mktg Dir

ROGERS DEPT STORE
1001 28th St, SW
Wyoming, MI 49509
Ph: 616/538-6000
Fax: 616/538-0613
Raymond Heidenga, Mktg Dir

RON FOTH ADVERTISING
8100 N High St
Columbus, OH 43235
Ph: 614/888-7771
Jim Nardecchia, Dir-Acct
Services

HARRY ROSEN
11 Adelaide St W Ste 200
Toronto, ON M5H 3x9
Canada
Ph: 416/981-9023
Fax: 416/867-1991
Mary Pompili, Adv/Sales Prom/
Comm Mgr

ROSES STORES, INC
P O Drawer 947
Henderson, NC 27536
Ph: 919/430 2600
Fax: 919/438-5242
G.H. Crouse, Sls Prom Mgr
J.D. Fuqua, Adv Mgr
Joel Ledford, Asst. Adv Mgr
Ph: 919/430-2659

ROTMANS
725 S Bridge St
Worcester, MA 01610
Ph: 508/755-5276
Fax: 508/752-2458
Bernie Rotman, VP-Mktg

ROUSE COMPANY
10275 Little Patuxent Pkwy
Columbia, MD 21044-3456
Ph: 301/992-6243
Fax: 301/992-6363
Marlys East, VP-Dir Corp Mktg
Robin Higgins, Group Dir-Sls/
Mktg
Ph: 301/992-6261
Karen Kozemchak, Mgr Mktg
Services
Ph: 301/992-6564
Bob Rubenkonig Jr, Mgr-Corp
Mktg
Ph: 301/992-6560

ROUSE COMPANY
P O Box 14326
Austin, TX 78761
Ph: 512/454-7671
Fax: 512/452-1463
Martha Maynard, Group Mgr
Sls/Mktg

ROUSE COMPANY
1200 Mondawmin Concourse
Baltimore, MD 21215
Ph: 301/523-0862
Ann Walters, Mktg Mgr

ROUSE
1400 Willowbrook Mall
Wayne, NJ 07470
Ph: 201/785-1616
Fax: 201/785-8632
Gary Yanosick, Group Mgr-
Sls/Mktg

ROUSE/RANDHURST
999 Elmhurst Rd
Mt. Prospect, IL 60056
Ph: 708/392-2701
Fax: 708/259-0228
Barbara Nicklas, Group Mgr-
Sls/Mktg

**ROSS ROY
ADVERTISING**
100 Bloomfield Hills Pkwy
Bloomfield Hills, MI 48304
Ph: 313/433-6883
Fax: 313/433-6116
Larry Haddock, Sr VP-Mgmt

ROYAL CROWN COLA
6917 Collins Ave
Miami Beach, FL 33141
Ph: 305/866-3281
Terry Griffin, VP-Mktg

RTO RENTS
1101 Lake Cook Rd
Deerfield, IL 60015
Ph: 708/405-9300
Pamela Rosev, Dir-Mktg

RUBENSTEIN'S
2855 Prairie Rd
Eugene, OR 97402
Ph: 503/484-7677
Fax: 503/341-3760
Stephanie Riess, Adv Dir
Bob Rubenstein, Gen Mgr

**RICHARD I
RUBIN & CO**
2500 Moreland Rd
Willow Grove, PA 19090
Ph: 215/657-6000
Fax: 215/657-8898
Cheryl Dougherty, Regl
Mktg Dir

**RICHARD I
RUBIN & CO**
715 Christiana Mall
Newark, DE 19702
Ph: 302/731-9815
Fax: 302/737-8519
Todd Land, Mktg Dir

**RICHARD I.
RUBIN & CO**
200 S Broad St, 3rd Fl
Philadelphia, PA 19102
Ph: 215/875-0700
Fax: 215/546-7311
Susan Valentine, Dir-Mktg

JAY B RUDOLPH
200 S Hoover St, Bldg 205
Tampa, FL 33609
Ph: 813/286-8888
Fax: 813/286-7062
Mark Mandel, VP-Adv/
Sls Prom

**CHUCK RUHR
ADVERTISING**
1221 Nicollet Mall
Minneapolis, MN 55403
Ph: 612/332-4565
Fax: 612/332-0842
Barbara Fraley, Acct Mgr
John Murtfeldt, Sr VP/
Dir Acct Services

RUHR/PARAGON
1221 Nicollet Mall, #600
Minneapolis, MN 55403
Ph: 612/332-4565
Chuck Ruhr, Board Chairman
Ron Sackett, VP-Creative Dir
Louise Scroggins, VP-Mgmt Dir

**RUSSELL REYNOLDS -
EXEC RECRUITING**
333 S Grand Ave # 4200
Los Angeles, CA 90017
Ph: 213/489-1520
Lisa Maibach, Managing Dir

RUSSELL GROUP
221 E 78th St
New York, NY 10021
Ph: 212/988-8793
Fax: 212/988-9740
Marybeth Russell, President

RWA, INC
3055 N Beachwood Dr
Los Angeles, CA 90069
Ph: 213/465-7505
Rick Wanetik, President

**JOHN RYAN
& COMPANY**
3033 Excelsior Blvd
Minneapolis, MN 55416
Ph: 612/924-7700
Fax: 612/939-4344
Annie Bussiere, Design Dir
Marilyn Gayda, VP-Mktg
James Henke, Assoc
Creative Dir
John Ryan, Chairman/CEO
Karen Wallerius, Acct Exec
Bob Weatherall, VP-Design Dept

**JOHN RYAN
& COMPANY**
12400 Whitewater Dr
Minneapolis, MN 55343
Ph: 612/924-7700
Fax: 612/939-4344
Carl Dearing, Architectural
Design
Karen London, Acct Exec

**S B & G
ADVERTISING**
11 Mill St S, Box 719
Waterdown, ON L0R 2H0
Canada
Ph: 416/689-7986
Fax: 416/689-0120
George Bakker, President

SYLC
160 West St
Cromwell, CT 06416
Ph: 203/635-6543
Fax: 203/635-0477
Terri Kabachnick, President/
CEO

**SAFFER
ADVERTISING INC**
180 Lesmill Rd
Toronto, ON M3B 2T5
Canada
Ph: 416/449-7961
Fax: 416/449-7313
Mack Capel, Creative
Group Head
Don Curtis, Sr VP/Dir
Client Services
Allen Hatcher, Creative
Group Head
Cam Levack, Creative
Group Head
Gerald McDonnell, Sr VP /
Dir-Client Serv.
Joe Nunnaro, Prod Mgr
Jim Reid, President
Morris Saffer, Chairman
Anita Saliss, VP/Client
Service Dir
John Uriemma, VP/Producer
Mark Wicken, VP-Client
Services

SAGE-ALLEN
900 Main S
Hartford, CT 06103
Ph: 203/278-2570
Fax: 203/520-5820
Susan Scherer, VP-Sls Prom

SAKS FIFTH AVENUE
611 Fifth Ave
New York, NY 10022
Ph: 212/940-4923
Fax: 212/940-4905
Susan Alai, Copy Chief
William Berta, Sr VP-
Sls Prom Dir
Ph: 212/940-4902
Elizabeth Chabot, Adv Dir
Ph: 212/940-4911

SAKS FIFTH AVENUE
12 E 49 St
New York, NY 10017
Ph: 212/940-4195
Fax: 212/940-4103
Suzanne McMillar, Sr VP-Sls
Prom/Mktg/PA

SAKS FIFTH AVENUE
611 Fifth Ave
New York, NY 10022
Ph: 212/940-4926
Fax: 212/940-4905
Rebecca Wong-Young,
Creative Dir

**SALES HOUSE
(PTY) LTD**
P O Box 155, Crown Mines
Johannesburg, SA 2125
South Africa
Ph: 011/495-6112
Fax: 011/837-1478
Penny Lloyd, Gen Mgr-Mktg

**SALLES INTER/
AMERICANA**
Rua Borges Lagoa, 1328
Sao Paulo, BZ 04038
Brazil
Ph: 11/575-0655
Alberto Arditti, Acct Dir

**SAMCO BAZAAR
NB LTD**
P O Box 3064, Station A
Moncton, NB E1C 9C2
Canada
Ph: 506/853-8193
Fax: 506/853-6005
Darrell O'Pray, Mgr-Adv/Prom

**SAN DIEGO
UNION TRIBUNE**
350 Camino de la Reina
San Diego, CA 92108
Ph: 619/293-1424
Fax: 619/293-1769
Richard Applegate, Major
Acct Mgr
Dexter LaPierre, Mgr
Display Adv
Ph: 619/293-1561

**SAN FRANCISCO
NEWSPAPER**
925 Mission St
San Francisco, CA 94103
Ph: 415/777-7267
Fax: 415/896-6410
Harry Sage, Sls Mgr

**SANDERS
FLOOR COVERING**
2908 University Ave
Morgantown, WV 26505
Ph: 304/599-4500
Fax: 304/599-4648
Marsha Brand, VP

SARA LEE
470 Hanes Hill Rd
Winston-Salem, NC 27105
Ph: 919/744-3182
Kym Leonard, Media Analysis-
Plnr

**SAWYER
FERGUSON WALKER**
405 Lexington Ave
New York, NY 10171
Ph: 212/661-6262
Fax: 212/808-5434
Michael DeRobertis, VP/Dir
Retail Mktg

**SAWYER
FERGUSON WALKER**
500 N Michigan Ave
Chicago, IL 60611
Ph: 312/329-1780
Fax: 312/329-1787
Herb Russel, Retail Coord

SAXON PAINT
3840 W Fullerton Ave
Chicago, IL 60647
Ph: 312/252-8100
Fax: 312/252-5850
Micheal Green, Dir Sls Prom

**SCALI
MCCABE SLOVES**
800 Third Ave
New York, NY 10022
Ph: 212/735-8389
Keith Green, EVP/Dir-Mktg
Alan Jurmain, SVP-Media Dir
Ph: 212/735-8242

**SCHNUCK
MARKETS INC**
11420 Lackland Rd
St. Louis, MO 63146
Ph: 314/994-4499
Fax: 314/994-4658
Genia Weinstein, VP-Mktg

SCHUBERT IND
621 Shepherd Dr
Cincinnati, OH 45215
Ph: 513/733-4315
Fax: 513/733-1528
Les McNair, Sls Mgr

**PAUL SCHULTZ
COMPANIES**
501 E Broadway
Louisville, KY 40202
Ph: 502/587-8700
Fax: 502/589-3583
Linda Clark, VP-Creative
Services
Michael McNerney, Acct Mgr
John Rigor, Assoc Creative Dir

**ARTHUR F
SCHULTZ CO**
939 W 26th St
Erie, PA 16508
Ph: 814/454-8171
Robert Schultz Jr, VP-
Mktg Mgr

SCHUTTE & CO
1207 Delaware Ave
Buffalo, NY 14209
Ph: 716/884-2120
Fax: 716/884-7894
Barb Harmel, Acct Mgr
Susan Schutte, Acct Mgr
Alden Schutte, President
Ph: 716/884-2124

**SCHWARTZ'S
APPAREL**
1260 Monroe St
New Philadelphia, OH 44663
Ph: 216/343-6687
Ken Eschbacher, President
Judy Eschbacher, Adv Dir
John Hudson, Corporate VP

SEARS
7447 Skokie Blvd
Skokie, IL 60077
Ph: 708/291-5240
Fax: 708/291-5265
C. Bartholow, Mktg Dir

SEARS
Sears Tower
Chicago, IL 60684
Ph: 312/875-6563
Fax: 312/875-6499
Judy Biasetti, Creative Dir-
Retail Adv
Dale Buchtel, Natl Media Mgr
Ph: 312/875-0711
Fax: 312/875-2444
Al Malony, Strategic Mktg Dir
Ph: 312/875-8885
Fax: 312/906-0678

SEARS CANADA INC
222 Jarvis St
Toronto, ON M5B 2B8
Canada
Ph: 416/941-4079
Fax: 416/941-3653
Cathie Crockett, Copy Dir
Chris Smith, Mgr/Print Buying
Ph: 416/941-3605
Joy Thorne-Enright, Dir-
Creative Services
Ph: 416/941-3644
Douglas Utter, Natl Mgr/
Retail Adv
Ph: 416/941-3600

**SEARS PAYMENT
SYSTEMS**
2500 Lake Cook Rd
Riverwoods, IL 60015
Ph: 708/405-3859
Fax: 708/405-3854
Eric Gehm, Credit Mktg
Consultant
Martha Meyer, Credit Mktg
Specialist
Ph: 708/405-3913

SEATTLE TIMES
P O Box 70
Seattle, WA 98111
Ph: 206/464-2960
Greg Bennett, Major Accts
Adv Mgr

SEIFERT'S
500 Law Building
Cedar Rapids, IA 52401
Ph: 319/364-0178
Fax: 319/364-7461
Gary Baker, VP
C Dudley Brown, President/
CEO

Ph: 319/398-1638
Rae Kaiser, Adv Dir
Ph: 319/368-6517
Deb Stockman, Mktg Dir
John Whitney, Visual Dir

**SEKLEMIAN
& NEWELL**
27 Antigua Court
Coronado, CA 92118
Ph: 619/423-2050
Fax: 619/435-7044
Frederick Newell Jr, CEO

SELBER BROTHERS
P O Box 21830
Shreveport, LA 71120-1830
Ph: 318/221-2561
Truston Jacobs, Adv Mgr

SELECT MEDIA INC
1111 3rd Ave Ste 112
Minneapolis, MN 55404
Ph: 612/339-3844
Fax: 612/339-4346
Doug Denny, President

SELF MAGAZINE
350 Madison Ave
New York, NY 10117
Ph: 212/880-8309
Fax: 212/880-8982
Candia Herman, Acct Exec
Debra Pickrel, Merchandising
Dir
Ph: 212/880-7967

**SERVICE
MERCHANDISE**
1600 Vaden Blvd
Brentwood, TN 37027
Ph: 615/377-7826
Fax: 615/377-7637
Stephen Handy, Mktg Mgr

SERVISTAR CORP
P O Box 1510
Butler, PA 16003-1510
Ph: 412/283-4567
Fax: 412/284-6595
Frederick Graff, Adv Mgr
Jerry Juszak, Oper Officer
Ph: 412/284-6281
Jerry Juszak, Media/Publicity
Mgr
Fax: 412/284-6320
Sandy Mellinger, Adv Prod Mgr
Ph: 412/284-1417

SHAW CONCEPTS
77-686 Calle Las Brisas N
Palm Desert, CA 92260
Ph: 619/360-0642
Doris Shaw, President

**SHEA
COMMUNICATIONS**
643 S 6th St
Louisville, KY 40202
Ph: 502/582-4457
Fax: 502/582-4917
Jim Mitchell, Sr VP-Sls Mktg

DAVID SHEARON
R R #1 Plank Rd
Sycamore, IL 60178
Ph: 815/895-9672
David Shearon, Creative
Consultant

SHEPLERS
6501 W Kellogg
Wichita, KS 67209
Ph: 316/946-3607
Fax: 316/946-3632
Sondra Nickell, Adv Mgr
John Wilcox, VP-Sls Prom
Ph: 316/946-3706
Fax: 316/946-3730

SHERIDAN COLLEGE
Trafagar Rd
Oakville, ON L6A 2L1
Canada
Ph: 416/845-9430
F J Lefebvre, Coordinator

SHERWIN-WILLIAMS
101 Prospect Ave NW
Cleveland, OH 44115
Ph: 216/566-2309
Fax: 216/566-1832
Andrea Eminger, Natl Print
Prod Mgr
Neil Guliano, Dir- Adv
Ph: 216/566-2340
Ted Krevzer, Sr VP-Mktg
Ph: 216/566-2312
Gary Saiter, VP-Merchan
Ph: 216/566-2499

SHERYL LAVINE ASSOC
50 Rosehill Ave, #611
Toronto, ON M4T 1G6
Canada
Ph: 416/964-2261
Fax: 416/924-7003
Sheryl Lavine, Consultant

SUZY SHIER
4307 Village Centre Court
Mississauga, ON L4Z 1S2
Canada
Ph: 514/684-3651
Sue Morrison, Dir-Mktg

SHIRMAX
3901 East Rue Jarry
Montreal, PQ
Canada
Ph: 514/729-3333
Fax: 514/593-9758
Jeannette Plamondon, Mktg Dir

SHOE-TOWN
994 Riverview Dr
Totowa, NJ 07512
Ph: 201/785-1900
Fax: 201/785-8238
Eleanor Kaufman, VP-Adv

SHOPKO STORES
700 Pilgrim Way
Green Bay, WI 54307-9060
Ph: 414/496-4158
Fax: 414/496-4165
Gene Bankers, VP-Adv/
Public Affairs
William Drake, VP-Mktg
Ph: 414/496-7099
Fax: 414/496-7180
Jan Freele, Broadcast Mgr
Ph: 414/496-4242
Kathie Mickle, Print Mgr
Ph: 414/496-4301

SHOPPERS DRUG MART
225 Yorkland Blvd
Willowdale, ON M2J 4Y7
Canada
Ph: 416/490-2664
Fax: 416/492-3795
Sue MacPhail, Dir-Adv

SIBLEY'S CO
228 E Main St
Rochester, NY 14604
Ph: 781/642-3662
Paul Lurz, Asst Adv Mgr

SIGNATURE CORPORATION
2501 W Peterson Ave
Chicago, IL 60659
Ph: 312/784-0800
Fax: 312/784-6094
Gershon Bassman, Chairman

SILK GREENHOUSE INC
10117 Princess Palm Ave
Tampa, FL 33610
Ph: 813/622-7886
Fax: 813/628-6392
Vicent Osborne, Dir-Adv

SILO
6900 Lindbergh Blvd
Philadelphia, PA 19142
Ph: 215/492-7055
Fax: 215/492-7769
Joani Dittrich, Assoc Adv Dir
Chuck Jacoby, Dir-Adv
Ph: 215/492-7056
Jennifer Meyer, Creative Dir
Ph: 215/492-7058

SILVA-CONE STUDIOS
260 W 36th St #7
New York, NY 10036
Ph: 212/279-0900
Fax: 212/868-1449
Deborah Cahill, Acct Exec
Paul Cohen, President
Eliott Saltzman, VP-Gen Mgr

SILVA-CONE STUDIOS
341 Michelle Pl
Carlstadt, NJ 07072
Ph: 201/896-0110
Fax: 201/896-9043
Marc Cohen, Acct Exec

SILVERSTEIN'S
543 N St
New Bedford, MA 02740
Ph: 508/997-7436
Fax: 508/999-4823
Ruth Quarnstrom, Adv Dir

216

MELVIN SIMON & ASSOC
P O Box 7033
Indianapolis, IN 46207
Ph: 317/636-1600
Fax: 317/263-7925
Marsha Cale, Copywriter
Deb Coons, Dir-Corp Mktg
Ph: 317/263-7014
Doug David, Creative Dir
Cathy Iunghuhn, Sr Writer
Kent Iunghuhn, Producer Corp
Comm
Alison Johnsen, Acct Supv
Ph: 317/263-7941
Fax: 317/685-7220
Elizabeth Kraft, Sr VP-Mktg
Ph: 317/263-7138
Rosemary Rice McCormick, Proj
Mktg Dir
Ph: 317/685-7207
Fax: 317/685-7208
Teri Moore, Special Projects
Writer
Ph: 317/636-1600
Fax: 317/263-7150
Leslie Mueller, Dir-Retail Mktg
Ph: 317/263-7941
Jeff Nance, Gen Adv Mgr
Ph: 317/263-7015
Kevin O'Keefe, Mktg Dir
Ph: 317/236-1946
Marny Marshall Reed, Prom
Proj Mgr
Ph: 317/636-1600
Victor Ruthig, Dir-Consumer
Mktg
Ph: 317/263-7021
Billie Scott, Dir-PR
Ph: 317/263-7148

MELVIN SIMON
2051 Killebrew Dr, #500
Bloomington, MN 55425
Ph: 612/851-3555
Fax: 612/851-3553
Maureen Hooley, Dir-Adv

SIMON ADVERTISING WRITING
P O Box 756
Avon, CT 06001
Ph: 203/674-9061
Marilyn Simon Rothstein,
Creative Dir

SIMPKINS
1515 E 85th Pl
Chicago, IL 60619
Ph: 312/731-5066
Sharon Simpkins

SIMPLIFY YOUR LIFE CONCEPT
Cromwell West, 160 W St
Cromwell, CT 06416
Ph: 203/635-6543
David Archambault, Adv Dir
Sheila Babnis, Dir-Oper
Harriet Kabel, Natl Sls Mgr

SIMPSON FURNITURE CO
515 Main/P O 765
Cedar Falls, 50613
Ph: 319/266-3535
David Olson, VP

SLEEP SHOP
547 N Carrollton
Baton Rouge, LA 70806
Ph: 504/926-1287
Robert Ward, CEO

SLUMBERLAND
3060 Centerville Rd
Little Canada, MN 55117
Ph: 612/487-2081
John Newstrand, Adv Dir

SMATT FLORENCE
155 Spring St
New York, NY 10012
Ph: 212/219-8887
Fax: 212/431-9518
Don Florence, VP/Creative Dir
Karin Smatt, President/
Creative Dir

H A & E SMITH LTD
P O Box HM470
Hamilton, HM BX
Bermuda
Ph: 809/295-2288
Fax: 809/292-6330
Maureen Callanan, Adv Co-ord

SMITTY'S FINE FURNITURE
170 3rd St
Hanover, ON N4N 1B2
Canada
Ph: 519/364-3800
Fax: 519/364-5304
Lloyd Schmidt, President/CEO

SMITTY'S SUPER VALU
2626 S 7th St
Phoenix, AZ 85034
Ph: 602/262-1993
Patricia Ingram, Dir-Adv

SMULEKOFF'S
97 Third Ave SE
Cedar Rapids, IA 52401
Ph: 319/362-2181
Florence Robertson, Adv Mgr

SNYDER'S
3109 Water Plant Rd
Knoxville, TN 37914
Sandra Keeling, Dir-Sls Prom
Martha Reid-Snider, Prod Mgr
Ross Wooley, Adv Mgr

SODEMA
801 Sherbrooke # 300
Montreal, Quebec H2L-1K7
Canada
Ph: 514/527-8781
Manon Jutras, Sls Rep

SOFT WAREHOUSE
15160 Marsh Ln
Addisson, TX 75234-2699
Ph: 214/406-4746
Fax: 214/243-1406
Steve Brownrigg, Creative Mgr
Chuck Kremers, VP-Sls Prom
Ph: 214/406-4724
Dina Santschi, Adv Mgr
Ph: 214/406-4744

SOFT WAREHOUSE
7011 N Central Ave
Skokie, IL 60077
Ph: 708/933-4700
Fax: 708/933-4777
Paul Williams

SOMERSET PUBLISHING
320 Campus Dr
Somerset, NJ 08873
Ph: 201/469-0400
Fax: 201/469-9247
William Garrity, Gen Mgr

SOS PRODUCTIONS
753 Harmon Ave
Columbus, OH 43223
Ph: 614/221-0966
Fax: 614/221-3836
Jeffrey Scheiman

SOUND ADVICE
303 5th St
Eureka, CA 95501
Ph: 707/442-4462
Fax: 707/442-5609
John Graves, Adv Mgr

SOUTHAM NEWSPAPER
20 York Mills Rd, Ste 401
Toronto, ON M2P 2C2
Canada
Ph: 416/222-8000
Fax: 416/222-3400
Shannon Lee Baillie, Sls Exec
Donald Fisher, Asst Gen Mgr
Fax: 416/222-3633
Jodi Hill, Retail Sls Exec
J.A. Muir, Gen Mgr
Debra Rother, Retail Sls Exec
Cathy Whitehead, Retail
Sls Exec

SOUTHERN INDIANA GRAPHICS
333 Second St
Aurora, IN 47001
Ph: 513/651-0182
Fax: 812/926-3494
Monica Boh, Sls Person
John Lehan, Exec VP

SOUTHLAND MALL
One Southland Mall
Hayward, CA 94545
Ph: 415/782-5050
Sue Newman, Mktg Mgr

SPAINHOUR'S
P O Box 609
Hickory, NC 28603
Ph: 04/322-5380
Bobbie Johnson, Adv Dir
Mandi Shuford, VP-Adv

SPAINHOUR'S
P O Box 500
Elkin, NC 28621
Ph: 919/835-2022
Vicky Spainhour, Special
Events Dir
Al Spainhour Jr, VP-Mktg

SPEARS FURNITURE
2710 Avenue Q
Lubbock, TX 79405
Ph: 806/747-3401
Harrell Spears, President

SPENCER PRESS INC
90 Industrial Park Rd
Hingham, MA 02043
Ph: 617/749-5000
Fax: 617/749-5555
Stephen Spenlinhauer, Sr
VP-Sls

SPEIGEL INC
1515 W 22nd St
Oak Brook, IL 60522
Ph: 708/986-7500
Fax: 708/571-7496
Mario Avila
Bertha DePriest, Art Dir-Home
Neil Ptashkin, Art Dir
Ph: 708/986-7685
Fax: 708/218-7829
Robert Fiddler, Adv Plng Mgr
Ph: 708/986-8800
Darryl Giambalvo, Div Adv Mgr
Michelle Hujar, Assoc Copy
Dir-Home
Brad Matson, Gen Mgr-Adv Plng
Megan Novy, Copy Dir
Ann O'Malley, Creative Dir
Patricia Parker, Exec Art
Dir-Home
Lenora Ranp, Copy Dir
Joy Miller, Div Adv Mgr
Ph: 708/215-7507
Fax: 708/218-7600
Richard Rosen, Group Adv Mgr
Ph: 708/218-7776
Sheila Sarovich, VP Adv
Ph: 708/986-7500
Lenora Rand
Winston Simmonds, Adv
Plng Mgr
Ph: 708/218-7988
Bernard Thurmond, Copy
Chief
Karen Zaworski, Grp Plng Mgr
Ph: 708/986-8800

HARRY SPITZER NETWORK
15916 Dickens St
Encino, CA 91436
Ph: 818/784-5204
Fax: 818/789-2928
Harry Spitzer, President

SPORTWEAR INTERNATIONAL
66 E. 34th St, 3rd Fl
New York, NY 10016
Ph: 212/779-5929
Julie Mandel, Assoc Publisher

SPRINGFIELD NEWSPAPERS
1860 Main St
Springfield, MA 01108
Ph: 413/788-1065
Fax: 413/788-1199
Rita Martin, Preprint Adv Mgr

SPURGEON MERCANTILE
822 W Washington
Chicago, IL 60607
Ph: 312/738-5414
Fax: 312/738-5437
Vincent Giacomin, Asst VP

SR SUPER STORE
6901 W 70th St
Shreveport, LA 71129
Ph: 318/688-5900
Iris Reinscheld, Adv Dir

ST JOSEPH PRINTING LTD
3 Benton Rd
Toronto, On M6M 3G2
Canada
Ph: 416/248-0721
Fax: 416/248-9860
Ray D'Antonio, Sls Mgr
Frank Gagliano, VP-Mktg

ST PAUL PIONEER PRESS
345 Cedar St
St. Paul, MN 55101
Ph: 612/228-5302
Fax: 612/228-5308
Mary Altuvilla, Retail Adv Mgr

ST PETERSBURG TIMES
490 First Ave S
St. Petersburg, FL 33701
Ph: 813/893-8524
Fax: 813/893-8117
Richard Reeves, Retail Adv Mgr

STAFCO INC
547 River St
Troy, MI 12180
Ph: 518/2701122
Fax: 518/270-1150
David Stillman, President

BUD STAHL
4767 Shaunee Creek Dr
Dayton, OH 45415
Ph: 513/276-4620
Fax: 513/233-5231
Bud Stahl, Consultant

STAMFORD ADVOCATE
75 Tresser Blvd
Stamford, CT 06901
Ph: 203/964-2200
Jeanette Ryan, Retail Adv Mgr

STANDARD GRAVURE
643 S 6th St
Louisville, KY 40202
Ph: 502/582-4457
Pat Flynn, VP/Dir-Sls

STAR FURNITURE
P O Box 219169
Houston, TX 77218
Ph: 713/492-6661
Melvyn Wolff, President
Neda Yousef, Dir-Adv

STAR TRIBUNE
425 Portland Ave
Minneapolis, MN 55488
Ph: 612/673-4832
Fax: 612/673-7788
Charlie Hoag, Group Sls Dir
Bill Nittler, Adv Acct Rep
Ph: 612/673-4825

STATE-TIMES & MORNING ADVOCATE
P O Box 588
Baton Rouge, LA 70821-0588
Ph: 504/388-0158
Fax: 504/388-0348
Philip Stout, Dir-Sls/Mktg

STAUFFERS OF KISSEL HILL
P O Box 1500
Lititz, PA 17543-7025
Ph: 717/626-4771
Fax: 717/626-0499
Debi Drescher, Adv Mgr
Paul Stauffer, Adv Dir
Ph: 717/626-4661

STEIGER'S
1477 Main St
Springfield, MA 01103
Ph: 413/785-4722
Fax: 413/739-1122
Richard Lavallee, Adv Dir
John Oakland, Gen Merchan
Mgr
Ph: 413/785-4734
Robert Steiger, VP-Mktg/Sls
Ph: 413/785-4720
Albert Steiger III, VP/
Dir-Fashion
Ph: 413/785-4710

STEIN MART
1200 Gulf Life Dr
Jacksonville, FL 32207
Ph: 904/346-1517
Deanie Collier, VP-Adv/Mktg

STEINBACH
535 Old Tarrytown Rd
White Plains, NY 10603
Ph: 914/683-1360
Fax: 914/428-3147
Edward Pestovic, Adv Dir

STEINHAFELS FURNITURE
16250 W Rogers Dr
New Berlin, WI 53151
Ph: 414/784-0500
Fax: 414/784-9174
Dennis Brown, Adv Mgr
John Steinhafel
Mark Steinhafel, Merchan Mgr

STEKETEE'S
86 Monroe Center
Grand Rapids, MI 49501
Ph: 616/456-6588
Fax: 616/456-1013
Tom Vituj, Sls Pro/Creative Dir

STERLING INC
375 Ghent Rd
Akron, OH 44313
Ph: 216/668-5340
Fax: 216/668-5187
Ian Deutsch, Adv Prod Mgr
Harry Hubbard, Distribution
Mgr

Ph: 216/668-5362
Joni Lantz, Adv Mgr
Ph: 216/668-5403
Fax: 216/668-5188
George Seitzinger, VP-
Mktg/Adv
Ph: 216/668-5591
Marge Williamson, Adv Mgr
Ph: 216/668-5000

STERLING OPTICAL
357 Crossways Park Dr
Woodbury, NY 11797
Ph: 516/364-2600
Robin Bugbee, VP-Mktg

STERLING OPTICAL
255 Rte 17 South
Hackensack, NY 07601
Ph: 201/342-6008
Laura Matthes, Adv Mgr

**STERN
ADVERTISING INC**
29125 Chagrin Blvd, #300
Pepper Pike, OH 44122
Ph: 216/464-4850
William Stern, President

STEVE'S SHOES
13550 W 108 St
Shawnee Mission, KS 66215
Ph: 913/469-5535
Fax: 913/469-7518
John Plantenberg, Dir-Adv

**STOP-N-SHOP
SUPER MARKETS**
22801 Aurora Rd
Cleveland, OH 44146
Ph: 216/663-5500
Harry Graham, Exec Dir

STOR
17621 E Gale Ave
City of Industry, CA 91748
Ph: 818/912-8788
Fax: 818/913-3834
Terri Munselle, Dir-Sls Prom

STOREHOUSE
2403-D Johnson Ferry Rd
Atlanta, GA 30341
Ph: 404/457-1176
Judy Ford, Dir-Adv

**STRAWBRIDGE
& CLOTHIER**
801 Market St
Philadelphia, PA 19107
Ph: 215/629-6175
Fax: 215/629-6480
Lewis Chapman, Adv Dir
Gilda Tasca, Asst Adv Dir
Ph: 215/629-6886
William Timmons, VP-Sls Prom
Ph: 215/629-6654
Peter Strawbridge, President
Ph: 215/629-6607
Fax: 215/629-7835

**STREAMSIDE
OUTFITTERS**
7791 Cooper Rd
Cincinnati, OH 45242
Ph: 513/891-0020
David Snell, President

STS SYSTEMS
2800 Trans Canada Highway
Pointe Claire, QB H9R 1B1
Canada
Ph: 514/426-0822
Fax: 514/426-0824
Sylvia Apostolakis, Cust Profile
Systems Spec
Derek Gaucher
Leo Rabinovitch, VP-New
Product Dev

STS SYSTEMS
1026 Madowlark Ln
Darien, IL 60559
Phillip Siewerth, Sls Rep

STS SYSTEM
32 Colin Ave
Toronto, ON H5P 2B9
Canada
Ph: 416/481-3437
Fax: 416/322-5805
Mary Pat Frey, Sls Rep

STUDIO GRAPHICS
1854 Marietta Blvd, NW
Atlanta, GA 30318
Ph: 404/355-1916
Fax: 404/355-2883
James Richards, President

STUDIO XIII
9310 W Jefferson
Culver City, CA 90232
Ph: 213/837-3114
Fax: 213/837-2846
Howard Spear, Gen Mgr

SULLIVAN GRAPHICS
10129 Wedge Court
Charlotte, NC 28226
Ph: 704/846-8177
Bryan Brazell

SULLIVAN GRAPHICS
100 Winners Circle
Brentwood, TN 37027
Ph: 615/377-0377
Fax: 615/377-0370
Jim Grigsby, Mktg Asst
Rich Lindner, Sr VP
Alan Zeigler, VP-Mktg

SULLIVAN GRAPHICS
P O Box 130
Stevensville, ON L0S 1S0
Canada
William Gross, Sr Sls Rep

SULLIVAN GRAPHICS
302 Grote St
Buffalo, NY 14207
Ph: 716/876-6410
Cory Ireland, Prod Mgr

G M SUMMERS & CO
36 King Circle
Malvern, PA 19355
Ph: 215/296-8014
Gerard Summers, President

SUN SENTINEL
200 East Las Olas Blvd
Fort Lauderdale, FL 33301
Ph: 305/356-4130
Fax: 305/356-4130
Lynn Wood Lange, Sls Mgr

**SUNCOAST MKTG
CONSULTANTS INC**
333 N Michigan Ave
Bradenton, FL 34209
Ph: 813/794-3711
George Walthius, PR/
Consultant

**SUPER 8
MOTELS INC**
1910 Eighth Ave NE
Aberdeen, SD 57401
Ph: 605/225-2272
Fax: 605/225-1140
Jon Kennedy, VP-Mktg/Adv

**SUPER MARKETING
PRODUCTIONS**
11500 W Burleigh St
Wauwatosa, WI 53222
Ph: 414/778-1373
Richard Fox, VP/Treasurer

**SUPER VALU
STORES**
101 Jefferson Ave
Hopkins, MN 55343
Ph: 612/932-4411
Fax: 612/932-4601
Gregory Dietz

**SUPER VALU
STORES**
3501 12th Ave, North
Fargo, ND 58102
Ph: 701/293-2125
Fax: 701/293-2124
Bill McCarthy, Adv Mgr

SUPER X
P O Box 1679
Fairborn, OH 45324
Ph: 513/879-5678
Bob Bacik, Creative Dir
Carl Palmiter, Adv Mgr
Ph: 513/879-5678

SYCAMORE
6075 Lakeside Blvd
Indianapolis, IN 46268-0884
Ph: 317/298-1620
Fax: 317/298-1609
Melissa Clark, Adv Dir
Janet Knorr, VP-Sls Prom/
Publicity

**THE SYRACUSE
NEWSPAPERS**
Clinton Square
Syracuse, NY 13202
Ph: 315/470-2006
Steve Hodgens, Acct Mgr

SZUBA
1434 N Astor
Chicago, IL 60610
Ph: 312/944-5999
Joseph Szuba, Consultant

TADWARE & CO
716 N First St
Minneapolis, MN 55401
Ph: 612/338-2311
Fax: 612/338-2344
Marcy Jacobs, Acct Exec

TALBOTS
175 Beal St
Higham, MA 02043
Ph: 617/749-7600
Tom Casey, Art Dir
Jennifer Gowasack-Fisher,
Creative Dir
Mary Pasciucco, VP-
Catalog Dev

**TAPPER'S
FINE JEWLERY**
26400 W 12 Mile Rd
Southfield, MI 48034
Ph: 313/357-5578
Fax: 313/357-1264
Steven Tapper, Owner

TAPSCAN INC
3000 Riverchase Galleria
#1111
Birmingham, AL 35244
Ph: 205/987-7456
Fax: 205/733-0949
Ann Foster, Exec VP

TARGET STORES
33 S 6th St, CC-18A
Minneapolis, MN 55402
Ph: 612/370-6095
Fax: 612/370-5807
Rod Eaton, Dir-Sls Prom
Nancy Fuller
Ph: 612/370-5816
Fax: 612/335-5104
Gail Heller, Mgr, Media
Ph: 612/370-6069
Chuck Herrig, Mgr/Art Dir
Ph: 612/370-8215
John Pellegrene, Sr VP-Mktg
Ph: 612/370-5816
Ken Sorenson, Dir-Creative
Services
Ph: 612/370-5816
Chuck Swenson, Copy Supv
Ph: 612/370-5983
Cleo Waldhauser, Copy Chief
Ph: 612/370-6080

**TATHAM
& ASSOCIATES**
P O Box 180129
Atlanta, GA 30318
Ph: 404/351-3114
Fax: 404/352-1392
Mike Tatham, President
Dennis Turner, VP

TAUBMAN COMPANY
200 E Long Lake Rd
Bloomfield Hills, MI 48304
Ph: 313/258-7325
Fax: 313/258-7481
Thomas Adams, VP-
Business Plng
Sheila Armstrong, Sls
Prom Mgr
Ph: 313/258-7460
Fax: 313/258-7653
Denise Anton David, Group
VP-Mktg
Ph: 313/258-6800
Fax: 313/258-7615
Patti Derderian, Regl Mktg Mgr
Ph: 313/258-7525
Fax: 313/258-7653
Susan Zuckert, Regl Mktg Mgr
Ph: 313/258-7642
Fax: 313/258-7653

TAUBMAN COMPANY
27500 Novi Rd
Novi, MI 48050
Ph: 313/348-9438
Elaine Kah, Mktg Dir

TAUBMAN COMPANY
2200 Hilltop Mall Rd
Richmond, CA 94806
Ph: 415/223-6900
Fax: 415/223-1453
Lance Lew, Mktg Dir

TAUBMAN-LAKESIDE
14000 Lakesie Circle
Sterling Heights, MI 48313
Ph: 313/247-1744
Fax: 313/247-0762
Karen MacDonald, Mktg Dir

TAUBMAN COMPANY
1 Meadwood Mall Circle
Reno, NV 89502
Ph: 702/827-8450
Fax: 702/826-0560
Lauri Nitz, Mktg Dir

**TAYLOR
MUSIC COMPANY**
1135 N. Easton Rd
Willow Grove, PA 19090
Ph: 215/659-5420
Fax: 215/659-8149
Fred Taylor, President

**TELECABLE
TARGETING**
740 Duke St
Norfolk, VA 23510
Ph: 804/624-5061
Thomas Emmi, Sls Prom Mgr

**TELECHECK
MICHIGAN**
23800 W Ten Mile Rd, Ste 150
Southfield, MI 48037-9813
Ph: 313/354-5000
Fax: 313/354-1515
Kathleen Burnie, VP

TELEGRAPH HERALD
8th & Bluff St
Dubuque, IA 52001
Ph: 319/588-5723
Fax: 319/588-5782
Jandell Herum, Adv Dir

**TELEMEDIA TSN
RDS SALES**
40 Holly St
Toronto, ON M4S 3C3
Canada
Ph: 416/482-4164
Fax: 416/482-9544
Gerry Tymon, VP-Gen Mgr

**TELEVISION
MKTG SERVICE**
288 Godfrey Rd, East
Weston, CT 06883
Ph: 203/226-5055
Fax: 203/222-1890
Donald Draeger

**TELEVISION
BUREAU CANADA**
890 Yonge St, Ste 700
Toronto, ON M4W3P4
Canada
Ph: 416/923-8813
Fax: 416/923-8739
Brian Ludgate, VP-Retail Adv

**TELEVISION BUREAU
OF ADVERTISING**
477 Madison Ave
New York, NY 10022
Ph: 212/486-1111
Lynn Fairbanks, VP-Regl
Mkt Dev

TERDOSLAVICH
275 Greenwich St #9J0
New York, NY 10007
Ph: 212/481-3421
Daniel Terdoslavich,
Creative Dir

TEXAS MONTHLY
P O Box 1569
Austin, TX 78767
Ph: 512/476-7085
Stephen Childs, President

TEXAS MONTHLY
3232 McKinney Ave, #950
Dallas, TX 75218
Ph: 214/871-7717
Fax: 214/871-7719
Jalane Garza, Adv Sls Dir
Dan Riordan, Retail Adv Mgr

TEXAS MONTHLY
420 Lexington Ave
New York, NY 10021
Ph: 212/986-7295
Fax: 212/949-4292
Sandra Jaffa, New York Mgr

THALHIMERS
615 E Broad St
Richmond, VA 23219
Ph: 804/343-2750
Fax: 804/343-2937
Betty Bauder, Sr VP-Sls Prom

THAMES
149 Tottenham Court Rd
London, W1P 9LL
England
Ph: 01-387-9494
Linda Greenhalgh, Dev Exec
Jonathon Shier, Dir-Sls/Mktg

**THIS WEEK
PUBLICATION**
425 Smith St
Farmingdale, NY 11735
Ph: 516/753-5440
Fax: 516/753-0358
Frank Gallagher, Adv Dir

**JANET THOMAS
PRODUCTIONS**
249 Henry Clay Blvd
Lexington, KY 40502
Ph: 606/269-7579
Janet Thomas, Owner

**THOMASVILLE
FURNITURE**
401 E Main St
Thomasville, NC 27360
Ph: 919/472-4000
Fax: 919/472-4071
Ann Noblin, Supv-Adv/
Prom
Sarah Soles, Asst Mgr-
Adv/Mktg
Larry Spangler, Mgr-Adv/Mktg

**J WALTER
THOMPSON**
600 Renaissance Center
Detroit, MI 48243
Ph: 313/568-3800
Fax: 313/568-3130
Bruce Phillips, Acct Supv

**THOMSON
NEWSPAPERS CORP**
65 Quenn St West
Toronto, ON M5H 2M8
Ph: 416/864-1710
Fax: 416/864-0109
Robert Hogg, Dir-Mktg

**THORNDIKE
DELAND ASSOC**
275 Madison Ave, Ste 1300
New York, NY 10016
Ph: 212/661-6200
Phyllis Tama, Principal

THREE SCORE INC
P O Box 450809
Atlanta, GA 30345-0809
Ph: 404/934-1224
Fax: 404/621-9445
B J Garrett, Sls Rep
Amy Harris, Sls Rep
John Hart, Exec VP President/
Admin
James Hernandez Jr, President
Clifford Penrose, Exec VP-
Sls/Mktg
Shelby Cochran, VP-Creative
Services
Ron Starke, Regl Sls Mgr

**THREE M/
ENCAPSULATED**
Building 223-4NW-10
St. Paul, MN 55144
Ph: 612/733-6139
Fax: 612/733-4012
Andrew Fraser, Mktg Mgr

THRIFTWAY
9280 Plainfield Rd
Cincinnati, OH 45236
Ph: 513/984-0500
John Volz, Adv Dir

THURMON
8632 W 85th St
Justice, IL 60485
Rita Thurmon
Ph: 708/563-2741

TIMES PUBLISHING
490 First Ave So
St. Petersburg, FL 33701
Ph: 813/893-8638
Fax: 813/893-8578
Alfred Corey, Jr, Adv Dir

TIMES PUBLISHING
W 12th & Sassafras St
Erie, PA 16534
Ph: 814/870-1658
Fax: 814/870-1632
Alan Haskins, Retail Adv Mgr

TV TIMES
20 York Mills Rd
Toronto, ON M2P 2C2
Canada
Ph: 416/222-8000
Fax: 416/222-3400
Phil Panneton, Mgr

TIP TOP TAILORS
637 Lakeshore Blvd
Toronto, ON M5V 1G1
Canada
Ph: 416/586-7039
Greg Crombie, Mktg Mgr

**WILLIAM J
TOMLINSON CO**
440 Union Pl
Excelsior, MN 55331
Ph: 612/474-1138
Fax: 612/474-1544
William Tomlinson, President

TOPS MARKETS INC
60 Dingens St
Buffalo, NY 14206
Ph: 716/823-3712
Tom Zarbo, Dir-Corp Comm

TORONTO SUN
333 King St East
Toronto, ON M5A 3X5
Canada
Ph: 416/947-2329
Fax: 416/947-2303
Bev Bester, Acct Exec

TORONTO GLOBE & MAIL
444 Front St
Toronto, ON M5V 2S9
Canada
Ph: 416/585-5422
Jocelyn Hird, Gen Sls Mgr

TORONTO STAR
1 Yonge St
Toronto, ON M5E 1E6
Canada
Ph: 416/869-4079
Fax: 416/869-4155
Jim McManus, Sr Sls Mgr/
Retail Merch
Bill Perkins, Acct Exec
Ph: 416/869-4086
Mark Shapiro, Asst Sls Mgr
Rob Smith, Acct Exec
Ph: 416/869-4085

TORONTO SUN
333 King St, East
Toronto, ON M5A 3X5
Canada
Ph: 416/947-2303
Fax: 416/947-3139
Gottfried Wirth, Retail Adv Mgr

TOSHACH QUALITY HOME FURNISHINGS
221 N Railway, SE
Medicine Hat, AB T1A 2Y9
Canada
Ph: 403/526-3600
Fax: 403/527-0166
Walt Sauve, Adv Chairman

TOWERS DEPT STORES
6509 Airport Rd
Mississauga, ON L4V 1S7
Canada
Ph: 416/671-8222
Fax: 416/677-5398
Diana Monaghan, Dir-
Research/Dev
Janet Robertson, Dir-Adv
Sls Prom

TOWN & COUNTRY MAGAZINE
1700 Broadway, 30th Fl
New York, NY 10019
Ph: 212/903-5321
Fax: 212/765-8308
William David, Adv Dir
Fred Jackson, Publisher
Ph: 212/903-5314

TOWN & COUNTRY MAGAZINE
4100 Weston Rd
Weston, ON M9L 2Y6
Canada
Ph: 416/741-7420
Fax: 416/741-7426
Greg Fenske, Sr VP

TOYS "R" US
461 From Rd
Paramus, NJ 07652
Ph: 201/599-7882
Fax: 201/262-7581
Susan McLaughlin, Media Mgr
Michael Minasi, Intl Adv Dir
Ph: 201/599-7819
Sue Montecallo, Dir-US Adv
Ph: 201/599-7933
Ernest Speranza, VP-Adv/Mktg
Ph: 201/599-6954
Pamela Troxel, Dir-Worldwide
Adv

TRACY-LOCKE
200 Crescent Ct
Dallas, TX 75201
Margaret Bonner, Acct Dir
Ph: 214/969-9000

TRACY-LOCKE
P O Box 50129
Dallas, TX 75250
Ph: 214/855-2062
Elwanda Edwards, VP-Acct Supv

TRANSCONTINENTAL MIAMI
678 Fairfield - Yellow Spgs Rd
Fairborn, OH 45324
Ph: 513/879-5678
Fax: 513/878-5283
Bob Bacik
Cheryle Kling

TRANSCONTINENTAL
138 East Dr
Brampton, ON L6T 4A4
Canada
Ph: 416/458-4777
Fax: 416/458-6957
Denis Longpre, Sls Mgr

TRANSCONTINENTAL
5516 Fifth St, SE
Calgary, AB T2E 1L3
Canada
Ph: 403/258-3788
Fax: 403/255-4863
Norrie Meth, VP

TRANSCONTINENTAL
393 Lebeau Blvd
St. Laurent, PQ H4N 1S2
Canada
Luc Ranger, VP-Sls
Ph: 514/337-8560
Fax: 514/339-2240

TREASURE CHEST ADVETISING
1931 Rohlwing Rd, Ste E
Rolling Meadows, IL 60008
Roger McGregor, Sls Mgr
Ph: 708/253-3633
Pete Ribaudo, VP-Natl Sls

TREASURE CHEST
511 W Citrus Edge
Glendora, CA 91740-5098
Ph: 818/914-3981
Richard Olerich, Sr VP-Sls Mktg

ALISON TRESS MARKETING
1323 Red Rambler Rd
Rydal, PA 19046
Ph: 215/887-5573
Fax: 215/887-5574
Alison Tress

TRI-STATE DISTRIBUTORS
1104 Pullman Rd
Moscow, ID 83843
Ph: 208/882-4555
Fax: 208/882-8427
Shane O'Donnell, Adv Mgr
Eddie Tout, Adv Merchan Mgr

TRIAD GRAPHIC
2 Dorchester Ave
Toronto, ON M8Z 4W3
Canada
Ph: 416/252-9331
Fax: 416/252-3043
Janko Herak, President
Don Padley, Acct Exec
Murray Pollock, VP-Sls/Mktg

THE NEW TRIBUNE
1 Hoover Way
Woodbridge, NJ 07095
Ph: 201/324-7109
Fax: 201/442-8705
Joesph Colasurdo, Acct Mgr

TRIMINGHAM BROTHERS
P O Box HM 471
Hamilton, BM HMBC
Bermuda
Ph: 809/295-1183
Fax: 809/292-2840
Judith McKirdy, Graphic Artist
Mary Van de Weg, Copywriter
Connie Weeks, Adv Mgr

TRITINY GRAPHICS
76 Ninth Ave
New York, NY 10001
Ph: 212/255-4500
Fax: 212/633-6549
Helene Ukrain, President

TROUTMAN'S EMPORIUM
P O Box 5467
Eugene, OR 97405
Ph: 503/746-9611
Fax: 503/747-7891
J. Carl Bamford, Prod Mgr
Dick Speelman, Gen Merch
Mgr
Steve Thorwald, Sls Prom Dir
Ron Troutman, Gen Merch Mgr

TRUEPENNY STUDIOS INC
1710 Guthrie Ave, Ste J
Des Moines, IA 50316
Ph: 515/262-5466
Fax: 515/266-8538
Duane Swensen, President

TRUWORTHS
93 Long Market St
Cape Town, 8001
S. Africa
Ph: 021/407-3293
Fax: 021/407-3409
Dawn Dickerson, VP-Mktg

TSC INDUSTRIES
320 Plus Park Blvd
Nashville, TN 37217
Ph: 615/366-4763
Fax: 615/366-4686
Joseph Maxwell, VP-Mktg

TKR ENTERPRISES
4045 Travis St
Dallas, TX 75204
Ph: 214/528-7382
Fax: 214/528-0153
Thomas Raney, Principal

TV BUREAU ADV
400 N Michigan, Ste 616
Chicago, IL 60611
Ph: 312/527-3373
Fax: 312/527-4539
Pam Edwards, Dir-Station
Relations

US SHOE CORP
1 Eastwood Dr
Cincinnati, OH 45227
Ph: 513/527-7532
Sue Blaney, Art Dir

US SHOE CORP/ WOMEN SPECIALTY
107 Phoenix Ave
Enfield, CT 06082
Ph: 203/741-0771
Greg Lechner, Mktg Dir

UDELL DESIGN INC
39 W 37th St
New York, NY 10018
Ph: 212/840-1140
James Udell, Sr VP

F W UHLMAN CO
126 North Main St
Bowling Green, OH 43402
Ph: 419/352-7505
Gerry Kallenbach, Adv Dir

UNION NEWS
1860 Main St
Springfield, MA 01101
Ph: 413/788-1108
Fax: 413/788-1199
Dwight Brouillard, Adv Mgr

UNITED AUDIO CENTERS
1907 Janke Dr
Northbrook, IL 60062
Ph: 708/205-1950
Fax: 708/205-1961
Shelley Miller, President

UNITED HARDWARE
5005 Nathan Ln
Plymouth, MN 55442
Ph: 612/557-2728
Fax: 612/559-5031
Rosie LaBree, Adv Mgr

UPTONS
6251 Crooked Creek Rd
Norcross, GA 30092
Ph: 404/622-2700
Fax: 404/448-9402
Neil Ashworth, Business/
Prod Mgr
Phyllis Covelli, Adv Mgr
Ph: 404/662-2500
Ruth Hines, Dir-Sls Prom
Ph: 404/662-2736
Rosa Ravelo, Creative Mgr
Ph: 404/662-2500

U S MERCHANDISE
4577 Hinckley Industrial Pkwy
Cleveland, OH 44109
Ph: 216/749-0220
Donna King, Adv Coord

U S COMMUNICATIONS
300 Clifton Ave
Minneapolis, MN 55403
Ph: 612/870-8910
Fax: 612/874-2446
Kristine Choate, Acct Exec

U S WEST MARKETING RESOURCES
10375 E Harvard Ave, Ste 201
Denver, CO 80231
Ph: 303/369-1370
Fax: 303/369-1377
Ronald Kahan, Acct Exec

USA WEEKEND MAGAZINE
444 N Michigan, #200
Chicago, IL 60611
Ph: 312/467-0510
Joe Frazer, VP-Natl Retail
Adv Dir

V I P STORES LTD
400-333-3rd Ave, N
Saskatoon, SK S7K 6R9
Canada
Ph: 306/242-7366
Bobbi Chilliak, Adv Coord

VAL-PAK
8605 Largo Lakes Dr
Largo, FL 34643
Ph: 813/393-1170
Fax: 813/391-2710
Jim Sampey, Mgr Support
Services

VAN HEUSEN
P O Box 6804
Piscataway, NJ 08855-6804
Ph: 201/885-1121
Marcella Maffei, Mktg Dir

VAN HULTEN PHOTOGRAPHY
38 Alpark Ave
Pittsburgh, PA 15216-3002
Ph: 412/381-6680
Rudolf Van Hulten, President/
Owner

VANCOUVER FURNITURE
1101 Broadway
Vancouver, WA 98660
Ph: 206/695-3391
Fax: 206/694-2071
Allan Weinstein, President

VANDERVELDE'S FURNITURE
630 Seminole
Muskegon, MI 49441
Ph: 616/733-2141
Bill Vandervelde, President

VANGUARD PUBLICATIONS
6604 W Saginaw
Lansing, MI 48917
Ph: 517/321-0406
Ralph Ward, Editor

VANITY FAIR
350 Madison Ave
New York, NY 10021
Ph: 212/888-0007
Fax: 212/888-0087
Joyce Castleberry, Sls Mgr

VANITY FAIR MAGAZINE
350 Madison Ave
New York, NY 10017
Ph: 212/880-7260
Fax: 212/880-8883
Helene Tricarico, Retail
Adv Mgr

VENDOR PLUS
350 Sevilla Ave, Ste 210
Coral Gables, FL 33134
Ph: 305/445-1909
Fax: 305/445-8646
A Clay Mitchell, Mktg Mgr

VENTURE STORES
2001 E Terra Ln
O'Fallon, MO 63366
Ph: 314/281-6650
Fax: 314/281-6907
George Bruce, VP-Sls Prom
Carmen Gallo, Div VP-
Adv Admin/Prod
Ph: 314/344-2706
Thomas Gent, VP-Adv
Ph: 314/281-5500
Jim Miller, Exec VP-Mktg
Ph: 314/281-6116
Fax: 314/281-7233

VICKERS & BENSON
1133 Yonge St
Toronto, ON M4T 3Z2
Canada
Ph: 416/925-9393
Fax: 416/925-7837
Ronald Bremner, Sr VP-Media/
Research

VICTORIA MAGAZINE
224 W 57th St
New York, NY 10019
Ph: 212/649-3717
Fax: 212/757-6109
John Thomas, Beauty/
Fashion Mgr

VIDEO TOWNE INC
6450 Poe Ave, Ste 210
Dayton, OH 45414
Ph: 513/454-7100
Fax: 513/454-0123
Kim Huemmer, Adv Mgr
Janice Zosh, Sr VP

VIEW INC
5555 Oakbrook Pky #390
Norcross, GA 30093
Ph: 404/368-0033
Fax: 404/368-0036
Susan Beighey, Dir-Sls/Oper
Tim Engle, Designer
David Mimbs, President

VIRGINIAN PILOT/ LEDGER STAR
150 W Brambleton Ave
Norfolk, VA 23501
Ph: 804/446-2534
Fax: 804/640-0419
Mike Herron, Training/Dev
Deborah Woodward, Adv
Mktg Mgr
Ph: 804/446-2110
Fax: 804/626-1375

VOGUE
350 Madison Ave
New York, NY 10017
Ph: 212/880-8408
Sarah Chubb Sauvayre, Retail
Adv Dir
Wendy Talbot, Retail Dir
Ph: 212/880-6675
Fax: 212/880-6921
Norman Waterman, Assoc
Publisher
Verne Westerberg, Publisher
Ph: 212/880-8401

VOGUE SHOPPE
500 Montreal Rd
Cornwall, ON K6H 1B9
Canada
Ph: 613/932-1312
Anne Abugov, Owner
Alex Abugov, Owner

VOGUE WRIGHT STUDIOS
423 W 55th St
New York, NY 10019
Ph: 212/977-3400
Fax: 212/974-5298
Mary Beth Alexander, Acct
Exec
Albert Dungan, President

W T QUINN INC
285 Davidson Ave
Somerset, NJ 08873
Ph: 201/563-6900
Fax: 201/563-9633
Howard Kenworthy, Sr.VP

WACCAMAW CORP
3200 Pottery Dr
Myrtle Beach, SC 29577
Ph: 803/236-4606
Marian Jenkinson, Asst
Adv Dir
Debra Trapp, Adv Dir

WAFF TV
P O Box 2116
Huntsville, AL 35804
Ph: 205/533-4848
Fax: 205/539-5556
Dorothy Fees, Local Sls Mgr

JACK WAHL AB
Box 5332, S-102 46
Stockholm, Sweden,
Ph: 08/783-0505
Fax: 08/660-8186
Jack Wahl, Dir

WAL-MART STORES INC
702 SW 8th St
Bentonville, AR 72716-8040
Ph: 501/273-4111
Fax: 501/273-1931
Paul Higham, VP/Mktg
Roger McNitt, Dir-Mktg/Sls
Ph: 501/273-4569

WALDENBOOKS
201 High Ridge Rd
Stamford, CT 06904
Ph: 203/352-2128
Fax: 203/352-2191
Sandy Long, Sr Mgr/
Adv Comm
Bonnie Predd, Exec VP
Ph: 203/352-2121

WALDOFF'S
999 Broadway Dr
Hattiesburg, MS 39401
Ph: 601/544-8511
Fax: 601/544-8529
George Baumgarn, VP/Sls
Prom Dir
Carol O'Neal, Sr VP/GMM

WALDOFF'S
5915 Hwy 49 N
Hattiesburg, MS 39401
Ph: 601/544-8511
Fax: 601/544-8529
Milton Waldoff, President/CEO

**WALDROP
FURNITURE**
201 Walnut, Box 909
Abilene, TX 79601
Ph: 915/677-5283
Fax: 915/677-5771
David Waldrop, VP

**WALSH
GUENTHER ASSOC**
1101 Broadway
Vancouver, WA 98660
Ph: 206/694-1127
Fax: 206/694-2071
Sheila Walsh Guenther,
President

WARD
427 N Sawyer
Chicago, IL 60624
Ph: 312/380-3707
Angelia Ward

S D WARREN CO
225 Franklin St
Boston, MA 02110
Ph: 617/423-7300
Fax: 617/423-5491
Daniel Craven, Ad/Mktg
Specialist
Thomas Jeffry, Mktg Mgr

WASHINGTON POST
1150 15th St, NW
Washington, DC 20071
Ph: 202/334-4320
Fax: 202/334-5672
Richard Eychner, Asst Retail
Mgr
Mark Gross, Mgr-Fashion Adv
Ph: 202/334-7609
Parks Rogers, Sls Rep
Ph: 202/334-5219
June Adkinson, Fashion
Adv Mgr
Ph: 202/334-7632
Tom Might, VP-Mktg/Prod
Ph: 202/334-7800
Fax: 202/334-6740
William Schwartz, Adv Sls Mgr
Ph: 202/334-4408

**WATS
MARKETING GROUP**
2102 N 117 Ave
Omaha, NE 68164
Ph: 402/498-7702
Fax: 402/498-7879
S. Christensen, Sls Dir

IRA A WATSON CO
200 Hayfield Rd
Knoxville, TN 37933-0900
Ph: 615/690-6000
Judy Kieffer, Asst Art Dir
Kim Tibbals, Layout Dir

**WATSON WEIS
& ASSOC**
8500 Leslie St, #310
Thornhill, ON L3T 2M8
Canada
Ph: 416/882-4191
Fax: 416/882-4193
Dennis Watson, Partner

WATT & SHAND
2 E King Street
Lancaster, PA 17603
Ph: 717/397-5221
Fax: 717/293-9486
Jane Webster, Adv/Prom Mgr

WAVM
2 Henry Adams St, #M57
San Francisco, CA 94103
Gerald Greenwood, Exec Dir
Ph: 415/431-1234
Fax: 415/431-0514

ROBERT WAXMAN
1514 Curtiss St
Denver, CO 80202
Paul Dahlstrom, Dir-
Media Mktg
Ph: 303/623-1200

WBRZ-TV
P O Box 2906
Baton Rouge, LA 70821
Ph: 504/336-2231
Fax: 504/336-2246
Fred Reno, Dir-Mkt Dev

WCBS - TV
51 W 52nd St
New York, NY 10019
Ph: 212/975-3967
Fax: 212/975-7609
Michael Caporlingua, Mgr-
Sls Mktg

WCCO TV
90 S 11th St
Minneapolis, MN 55403
Ph: 612/330-2620
Fax: 612/330-2603
William Bradley, Dir-Sls

WCDJ RADIO
68 Commercial Wharf
Boston, MA 02110
Ph: 617/523-6611
Fax: 617/720-5783
Kathryn Biddy, Co-op/
Vendor Dir

WCYB TV
101 Lee St, Box 2069
Bristol, VA 24203
Ph: 703/669-4161
Fax: 703/466-4202
Richard Torbett, Acting Gen
Sls Mgr
Lisa Kelechava, Prom Dir

WDBJ TV
P O Box 7
Roanoke, VA 24002-0007
Ph: 703/344-7000
Fax: 703/344-5097
Mel Mayfield, Dir-Research
Joan Turner, Local Sls Mgr

WDIV TV4
550 W Lafayette
Detroit, MI 48231
Ph: 313/222-0417
Fax: 313/222-0454
Amy Grambeau, Sls Mgr

WEALL & CULLEN
400 Alden Rd
Markham, ON L3R 4C1
Canada
Ph: 416/479-0220
Fax: 416/479-1421
Elizabeth Mueller, Adv Co-ord

**WEATHERVANE
STORES**
300 John Downey Dr
New Britain, CT 06051
Ph: 203/223-6045
Janis Genovese, Adv Dir

WEBB & SONS INC
P O Box 613
Sherburne, NY 13460
Ph: 607/674-5111
Anne Voelker, Adv Mgr

**WEDDING
BELLS MAGAZINE**
120 Front St E, Ste 200
Toronto, Canada M5A 4L9
Ph: 416/862-8479
Fax: 416/862-2184
Michael Grier, Retail Adv

**WEIMERS O'CONNOR
& PARTNERS**
5910 N Central Expy #1400
Dallas, TX 75206
Ph: 214/891-6611
David Smith, Sr Acct Exec

WEINER'S STORES
P O Box 2612
Houston, TX 77252
Ph: 713/688-1331
Fax: 713/688-1396
Bill Sandera, Adv Mgr
Don Stine, Dir-Adv

WEINSTEIN
5719 Coral Lake Dr
Margate, FL 33063
Ph: 305/971-8991
Linda Weinstein

WEINSTOCK'S
600 K St
Sacramento, CA 95814
Ph: 916/449-8888
Fax: 916/449-2571
Monica Lang

**WEINTRAUB
& ASSOCIATES**
10427 Old Olive, Ste 202
St. Louis, MO 63141
Ph: 314/991-5800
Fax: 314/991-3577
Rob Weintraub, President

**WEST COAST
FURNITURE**
2953 San Pablo Ave
Oakland, CA 94608
Ph: 415/444-1000
Fax: 415/444-0879
Barry Noss, President

**WEST MARINE
PRODUCTS**
500 Westridge Dr
Wattsonville, CA 95076
Ph: 408/728-2700
Fax: 408/728-2736
Geoff Eisemberg, Sr VP

**WESTCHESTER
ROCKLAND**
One Gannett Dr
White Plains, NY 10604
Ph: 914/694-5330
Fax: 914/694-5112
Kelvin Gold, Retail Adv Dir

WESTERN UNION
303 W Colfax, Ste 101
Denver, CO 80204
Ph: 303/573-7248
Fax: 303/629-1012
Liz Walker, Natl Acct Exec

**WESTLAKE
HARDWARE**
15501 W 99th St
Lenexa, KS 66219
Ph: 913/888-0808
Richard Shank, Dir-Adv

**WESTPOINT
PEPPERELL**
P O Box 609
West Point, GA 31833
Ph: 404/645-7307
Fax: 404/645-7503
Harvey Jones, Dir-Adv
Stores Div

WFAA TV
Communications Center
Dallas, TX 75202
Ph: 214/748-9631
Buff Parham, Gen Sls Mgr

**WFAA/
A H BELO CORP**
606 Young St
Dallas, TX 75202
Ph: 214/977-6228
Fax: 214/977-6460
Victor Savelli, Acct Exec

WFAN-SPORTS RAD
34-12 36th St
Astoria, NY 11106
Jody Dunowitz, Sls Mgr
Ph: 718/706-7690
Fax: 718/361-9234

WFYR RADIO
130 E Randolph #2303
Chicago, IL 60613
Ph: 312/861-8155
Launa Thompson, Retail
Sls Mgr

WGAL TV
P O Box 7127
Lancaster, PA 17604
Ph: 717/393-5851
Fax: 717/393-9484
John Feeser, Sls Mgr
Rigby Wilson, Gen Sls Mgr
Fax: 717/295-7457

WGRZ TV
259 Delaware Ave
Buffalo, NY 14202
Ph: 716/856-1414
Fax: 716/856-1506
Linda Andreozzi, Mktg
Research Dir

WHNT TV
P O Box 19
Huntsville, AL 35804
Ph: 205/539-2229
Fax: 205/533-4503
Linda Spalla, Dir-Mktg

WI-TV
P O Box 468
Washington, NC 27889
Ph: 919/946-3131
William Stanley, Owner

WICKES LUMBER
706 Deerpath Dr
Vernon Hills, IL 60061
Ph: 708/367-3574
Fax: 708/367-3580
Bobbi VanAlstine, Media Plnr
Tammy Wiard, Media Plnr
Ph: 708/367-3425

**WIL-CAR
ENTERPRISES INC**
10451 Old Gallia Pike
Wheelersburg, OH 45694
Ph: 614/574-2583
Fax: 614/574-2113
William James, Adv Mgr

WILAND SERVICES
6707 Winchester Circle
Boulder, CO 80301
Ph: 303/530-0606
Fax: 303/530-7495
Curt Blattner, Mktg Mgr
Mike Buoncristiano, Exec
VP- Sls
Andrew Eiss, Sls Exec

**M WILLIAMS
DESIGN STUDIO**
P O Box 289
Harmony, PA 16037
Ph: 412/323-1300
Margaret Williams-McGowan,
Owner

WILSON CHAPMAN
7007 College Blvd, Ste 525
Overland Park, KS 66211
Ph: 913/469-1044
Fax: 913/469-1913
Dave Wilson, Partner

**WILSONS SUEDE
& LEATHER**
7401 Boone Ave N
Brooklyn Park, MN 55428
Ph: 612/424-7360
Marny Marshall-Reed, Dir-
Adv Prom
Paul Tomlinson, VP
Ph: 612/424-7356

**WINNING
STRATEGIES**
800 Brick Mill Run #216
Westlake, OH 44145
Ph: 216/331-3755
Fax: 216/331-8557
Susan Rotman, Principal

WINONA KNITS
1200 Storr's Pond Rd
Winona, MN 55987
Ph: 507/454-1400
Fax: 507/454-7402
Bud Baechler, VP-Mktg Comm

**WINSTON-
SALEM JOURNAL**
P O Box 3159
Winston-Salem, NC 27102
Ph: 919/727-7408
Fax: 919/727-7424
James Fowler, Mktg Dir
Jeffrey Green, Adv Dir
Ph: 919/727-7335
Fax: 919/727-7485
Ken Warren, Retail Adv Mgr
Ph: 919/727-7439

WISC TV
7025 Raymond Rd
Madison, WI 53719
Ph: 608/271-4321
Fax: 608/271-1709
MaryAnn Heilprin, Retail
Dev Specialist

WISN TV
759 N 19th St
Milwaukee, WI 53233
Ph: 414/937-3313
Fax: 414/342-6844
Jackie Johnson, Mktg
Client Services

WITTKIN-GOODMAN
19 Easton Ave
White Plains, NY 10605
Ph: 914/948-5417
E Larry Goodman, Partner

WJKW TV
5800 S Marginal Rd
Cleveland, OH 44105
Ph: 216/431-8888
Fax: 216/432-4239
Spencer Koch, Gen Sls Mgr
Joanne Gowdy, Mktg Dir

WJXT TV
P O Box 5270
Jacksonville, FL 32207
Ph: 904/393-9803
Fax: 904/393-9822
Gary Corbitt, Research Dir

WJYE RADIO CORP
1700 Rand Bldg
Buffalo, NY 14203
Ph: 716/856-3550
Fax: 716/852-0537
Donna Vullo, Local Sls Mgr

FM 105 WKAZ/WKLC
100 Kanawha Terrace
St. Albans, WV 25177
Ph: 304/722-3308
David Gibson, Gen Sls Mgr

WKQX Q101
Merchandise Mart
Chicago, IL 60654
Ph: 312/245-1255
Fax: 312/527-5682
Marssie Mencotti, Dir-
Retail Dev

WKSE/WWKB RADIO
695 Delaware
Buffalo, NY 14209
Ph: 716/884-5101
Fax: 716/882-2048
Ken Casseri, VP Sls/Gen Sls Mgr

WKXT TV
P O Box 59088
Knoxville, TN 37950-9088
Ph: 615/689-8000
Fax: 615/689-9047
R Lamar Reid, Local Sls Mgr

WLS-TV
190 N State
Chicago, IL 60601
Ph: 312/750-7369
Fax: 312/750-7015
Sharon McGill, Acct Exec

WLVI TV
75 Morrissey Blvd
Boston, MA 02125
Ph: 617/265-5656
Bob McCaughey, Local Sls Mgr

WNBH WCTK
P O Box H3201
New Bedford, MA 02741
Ph: 508/996-3371
Fax: 508/990-3453
Christine Lodge

WOMC RADIO
2201 Woodward Heights
Detroit, MI 48220
Ph: 313/546-9600
Fax: 313/546-5446
Dorothe Riley-Green, Gen
Sls Mgr

WOODBURYS
679 Glen St
Queensbury, NY 12804
Ph: 518/793-2505
Fax: 518/793-1267
James Urch, Adv Dir

**WOODFIELD
SHOPPING CENTER**
5 Woodfield Mall
Schaumburg, IL 60173
Ph: 708/330-0220
Fax: 708/330-0251
Betty Bryant, Mktg Dir

219

WOODWARD
& LOTHROP
10th & "G" St, NW
Washington, DC 20013
Ph: 202/879-8376
Fax: 202/879-8159
Kai Frost, Sr VP-Mktg

WOODWARD
& LOTHROP
1025 F St, NW
Washington, DC 20013
Ph: 202/879-8701
Fax: 202/879-8725
Joel Nichols, Div VP-Adv
Mary Wilson, Creative Dir
Ph: 202/879-8702

WOOLCO/
WOOLWORTH
33 Adelaide St W
Toronto, ONT M5H 1P5
Canada
Ph: 416/332-5419
Fred Roy, President

WORLD
COLOR PRESS
8755 W Higgins Rd, #1070
Chicago, IL 60631
Ph: 312/693-0333
Fax: 312/693-0340
Suzette Eshoo, Acct Exec

WORLD
COLOR PRESS
600 Third Ave
New York, NY 10016
Ph: 212/986-2440
Fax: 212/455-9266
Henry May, VP-Mgr Comm Sls

WPGH-TV
750 Ivory Ave
Pittsburg, PA 15214
Ph: 412/931-8010
Fax: 412/931-8029
Mike Wolff, Local Sls Mgr

WPLG TV
3900 Biscayne Blvd
Miami, FL 33137
Ph: 305/325-2315
Linda Lucas, Mktg Dev Mgr

WPVI TV
4100 City Line Ave
Philadelphia, PA 19130
Ph: 215/581-4506
Fax: 215/581-4515
Valari Dobson, Mktg/
Research Mgr
Lisa Hipp, Local Sls Mgr

WRCB TV
900 Whitehall Rd
Chattanooga, TN 37405
Ph: 615/267-5412
Lisa Gann, Research Dir

G A WRIGHT INC
P O Box 44278
Denver, CO 80201
Ph: 303/295-6222
Fax: 303/292-5102
Gary Wright, President

WSB TV
1601 W Peachtree NE
Atlanta, GA 30309
Ph: 404/897-7351
Fax: 404/897-7439
Curt Bolak, Retail Mktg Dir

WSB-TV
1601 W. Peachtree St NE
Atlanta, GE 30309
Ph: 404/897-7 419
Fax: 404/897-7439
Deborah Schwartz, Co-op Mgr

WSMV-TV
5700 Knob Rd
Nashville, TN 37215
Ph: 615/749-2269
Debbie Laffey, Vendor/
Coop Dir

W S R G
100 Phoenix Ave
Enfield, CT 06082
Ph: 203/741-0771
Fax: 203/745-3904
Greg Lechner, Dir-Mktg

WSYX TV
1261 Dublin Rd
Columbus, OH 43216
Ph: 614/481-6634
Fax: 614/481-6818
Pat Cramer, Local Sls Mgr
Robert Wagley, Sls Mgr

WTAE TV
400 Ardmore Blvd
Pittsburgh, PA 15221
Ph: 412/244-4495
Fax: 412/244-4482
Linda Guiler, Sls Mgr

WTOC - TV
P O Box 8086
Savannah, GA 31412
Ph: 912/234-1111
Fax: 912/238-5133
Randall Peltier, Retail Dev Mgr

WTOL TV
730 N Summit, Box 715
Toledo, OH 43695-0715
Ph: 419/248-1136
Fax: 419/244-7104
Cathy Clark, Acct Exec
Paul Ladrow, Sls Mgr
Ph: 419/385-5689

WTVJ TV
316 N Miami Ave
Miami, FL 33128
Ph: 305/789-4104
Fax: 305/789-4168
Linda Perry, Mktg Mgr

RADIO WWEZ/WCKY
219 McFarland
Cincinnati, OH 45202
Ph: 513/721-5678
Fax: 513/723-9221
Ron Steinman

WWF NATIONAL
529 Main St
Boston, MA 02139
Ph: 914/277-8129
Glen Karoglanian, VP

WWMT TV
590 W Maple
Kalamazoo, MI 49008
Ph: 616/388-3333
Fax: 616/388-6089
Chris Cornelius, Local Sls Mgr

WXON TV20
27777 Franklin Rd, #708
Southfield, MI 48034
Ph: 313/355-2900
Fax: 313/355-0368
Sandee Henry, Sls Dev Mgr

WYFF TV
505 Rutherford St
Greenville, SC 29602
Ph: 803/242-4404
Fax: 803/240-5329
Barbara Mercers
Libby Spencer, Local Sls Mgr
Ph: 803/240-5226

XONIX
TECHNOLOGIES
P O Box 10087
Portland, OR 97266
Ph: 503/242-2981
Michael Rothery, Adv Mktg Mgr

XXCELL STUDIOS
4000 Dekalb Tech Pkwy
Atlanta, GA 30340
Ph: 404/986-9095
Fax: 404/986-9098
Stephen Best, VP/Photography
Andrew Foster Jr, President
Sherry Payor, VP/Creative Dir
Steve Turner, VP/Sls

YEILDING
554-37th St, N
Birmingham, AL 35222
Ph: 205/592-8700
Fax: 205/599-2148
Melanie Poole, Adv Sls
Prom Dir

YESNER
MARKETING INC
9384 Home Circle
Des Plaines, IL 60016
Ph: 708/297-6024
Michael Yesner, President

YOUNGS FURNITURE
P O Box 1358
Portland, ME 04104
Ph: 207/775-3747
Sylvie Montello, Buyer

YOUNKERS
7th & Walnut
Des Moines, IA 50309
Ph: 515/247-7087
Fax: 515/246-3170
Robert Ferguson, Sr VP-Mktg
Joe Matson, Div VP-Adv
Ph: 515/247-7081
Michele Sayles, Art Dir
Ph: 515/244-1112

ZCMI
2200 S 900 W
Salt Lake City, UT 84137
Ph: 801/321-6026
Fax: 801/321-6769
Nancy Mortensen, VP-Mktg
Services

ZALE CORP
901 W Walnut Hill Ln
Irving, TX 75038
Ph: 214/580-4386
Fax: 214/580-4623
Sharon Longshaw, Dir- Adv

ZAYRE CORP
770 Cochituate Rd
Framingham, MA 01701
Ph: 617/651-6178
Edward Gillooly, Asst VP-Mgr/
Print Prom
Robin Morris, Asst VP-
Creative Services

ZCMI
2200 S 900 W
Salt Lake City, UT 84137
Ph: 801/321-6242
Fax: 801/321-6769
Brent Baker, Adv Dir

ZED GRAPHIC
COMMUNICATIONS
2110 Bonin St
St. Laurent, PQ H4M 1A3
Canada
Ph: 514/331-2419
Fax: 514/331-7757
Elizabeth Kabbash, President

ZELLERS INC
5100 de Maisonneuve W
Montreal, PQ H4A 1Y6
Canada
Ph: 514/483-8229
Fax: 514/483-7780
Garnet Kinch, VP-Sls/Adv
David Middleton, Adv Dir
Terry Oliver, Prom Resource
Mgr
John Urie, Exec VP
Ph: 514/483-7991

IT'S ABOUT TIME

This first volume of "Excellence in Advertising" should be celebrated and viewed as an important milestone in RAC and RAMA history.

For the retail industry, such a publication is long overdue. Fortunately, it arrives when the industry is at a crossroads of dramatic change. This annual will help serve as a document of prevailing change, and how we as marketers responded to the challenge.

Our industry, for too long, did not treat its own creative product and sales promotion efforts with enough self confidence or respect. It is no professional secret that in-house creative departments, including retail, have usually not commanded that respect from their outside peers in advertising and design.

For years there seemed to be a self-imposed separatism that retail creatives placed upon themselves with an often common resignation that retail advertising just somehow didn't belong in the first tier of either status, or worse, importance.

In the past decade, however, influential stores and retailers helped to even the score. Many of them, interestingly enough, were not headquartered in New York, reflecting an important concurrent trend on Madison Avenue.

While New York's maturing Madison Avenue was being seriously challenged, and often surpassed at creative awards shows, by upstart competitors such as Fallon Mc Elligott, later Wieden and Kennedy, and of course Chiat-Day, several New York stores began to break new ground.

Saks' early 80's, lifestyle generic fashion commercials were copied again and again, and even today the influence can still be seen. Barney's collaboration with agencies would often become that agency's best work. In past years, retail accounts were the scourge of Madison Avenue. Now agency's are participating in creative reviews to win retail clients.

Macy's new liason with The Lintas Group, and Saks' awarding their account to Margeotes, Fertitta & Weiss, are examples of this new love affair. This new sophistication of retailers, seeking both image and long term strategic planning, will create new synergies between the creative departments of both client and agency.

For years, Bloomingdale's has enjoyed such a relationship with Grey Advertising for television.

On a personal note: Looking back at past moments, daydreaming of where the pasture might be greener, I could never think simply about another job, only about other eras. One fantasy might lead me to the creative workshop of the legendary art director, Alexey Brodovitch of *Harper's Bazaar* in the 50's, where I would rub shoulders with fellow students Irving Penn and Richard Avedon.

Anther blink of an eye would take me to the 60's. This era represents a lot of images for America. For advertising, it is considered the "Renaissance" period. I dream about being part of the start-up of America's greatest ad agencies or working next to the legendary art directors and writers at Doyle Dane Bernbach, on the Volkswagen account.

Other fantasies included apprenticeships with Walter Gropius or Man Ray.

On May 20, 1991, I was jolted back to reality when Marvin Traub announced his retirement as Chairman of Bloomingdale's. It was at that precise moment that I really appreciated the power of his influence. It was then I fully realized, I had been working with one of the great creative legends of any era.

Bloomingdale's, like retailing, with its newly found pride and self confidence shining, will never look back. The future, precisely because of its challenges, looks brighter than ever.

John C. Jay

THE LAST WORD

RAMA, the Retail Advertising and Marketing Association Intl., is 2,300 members strong. Each individual is part of the spectacular constellation called the retail business. RAMA is also the creator and producer of the Retail Advertising Conference. The only annual International conference for retail advertising and marketing executives. Now in its 40th year, its warmth attracts more than 1,200 participants to the wintry shores of Lake Michigan.

Each January, the three and one half day conference, filled to the top with inspiration and excitement, begins with a salute to excellence in creative achievement: the glittering RAC Awards Banquet. Many attend in black tie; everyone has a wonderful time.

Going back to the beginning, the RAC awards program actually begins in early fall, with a stirring call for entries, and is culminated with the glittering dinner. In between, serious-minded judges perform due diligence. They choose the winners and finalists, in all media, the current crop of which you will find in the pages of this beautiful book — "Excellence in Advertising."

The special spirit of personal and professional excellence, that has made RAC the place to be each winter in Chicago, bonds us with our members. This special book was created in that same spirit. And to celebrate the unlimited horizons of human creativity.

We hope you enjoy it.

Sincerely,

Morris Saffer
Chairman, RAMA

Douglas E. Raymond
President, CEO, RAMA

Tom Holliday
Executive VP, RAMA